*Magellan's Voyage
Around the World*

Reproduced from Melon y Ruiz de Gordejuela,
Magallanes y la primera vuelta al mundo

The Ship "Vitoria" Which
Completed the Voyage around
the World

Antonio Pigafetta
Maximilian of Transylvania
Gaspar Corrêa

Magellan's Voyage Around the World

Three Contemporary Accounts

Edited and with an introduction by
CHARLES E. NOWELL

NORTHWESTERN UNIVERSITY PRESS
Evanston—1962

64428

Contents

List of Maps

Introduction

Introduction

In the early 1500's, almost four and a half centuries before men first orbited the earth, an expedition planned and led by Ferdinand Magellan performed a feat of comparable significance for that age. Magellan, a Portuguese navigator in the service of Spain, sailed westward with a fleet of five ships from the port of Sanlúcar de Barrameda in September, 1519. Nearly three years later one ship returned, having circumnavigated the globe and traversed its largest ocean. The importance of this achievement was sufficiently appreciated so that several contemporary accounts of the expedition were soon written and published, including reports by Magellan's own men as well as accounts based on interviews with them. The three most interesting of these sixteenth-century narratives are here offered to modern readers.

The longest and by far the most important of the narratives is the one by Antonio Pigafetta. This author, though not a professional seafarer, sailed with the expedition and was one of the fortunate eighteen who returned to Spain in Juan Sebastián del Cano's "Victoria" following Magellan's death in

3

battle in the Philippines. He took copious notes during the voyage and, as soon as he was back in Spain, wrote them up under the title *Primo viaggio intorno al Mondo*. The manuscript of *Primo viaggio* considered most authentic is the one belonging to the Biblioteca Ambrosiana in Milan, and the translation now offered was made by the American scholar James Alexander Robertson and published in 1906.[1]* Robertson's translation appeared as a limited edition of only 350 copies, and these are today mostly out of reach of the general reading public. A reasonably good edition of the Ambrosiana manuscript had been published in 1894 by Andrea da Mosto in the *Raccolta Colombiana*[2] collection in honor of the fourth centenary of the discovery of America, but this too is rare. Robertson, instead of translating Da Mosto's printed version, went back to the original manuscript and found that the Italian scholar had committed several errors of transcription. We may therefore assume that the present text, although a translation, is the best available. Robertson provided 650 footnotes, many of them long, and while they are most valuable, the present editor and publisher have considered them too elaborate an apparatus of scholarship for the necessary limits of this edition. Accordingly, the original Robertson notes have been deleted and replaced by a lesser number designed to clarify only those passages by Pigafetta most in need of explanation.

* Notes for the Introduction and the Aftermath come at the end of their respective sections. Notes for the narratives of Magellan's voyage appear at the bottom of the page.

The second document in this collection is a letter by Maximilian of Transylvania, who signs himself Maximilianus Transylvanus, to his father Matthäus Lang, cardinal of Salzburg and bishop of Cartagena. Maximilian himself held the post of secretary to Emperor Charles V, who was also Charles I of Castile and Aragon. The original Latin version of the letter, called *De Molucis insulis,* was composed in October 1522, several weeks after the return of El Cano's "Victoria" to Sanlúcar de Barrameda, though there is some confusion as to the exact date that should accompany Transylvanus' signature. The first printed edition appeared at Cologne in January 1523 and was soon followed by two at Rome.

Maximilian, evidently a native of Brussels (though the "Transylvanus" part of his name would indicate Hungarian origin), was with King-Emperor Charles at Valladolid when El Cano reached Sanlúcar. Maximilian and the learned Italian priest Peter Martyr assisted the young ruler with the reception at court of El Cano and other survivors of the expedition. Besides taking part in the official interviews, he interrogated the returned mariners on his own initiative, quickly digested their accounts, and then hastened to get his letter off to the cardinal. The document is important not only for the valuable information it contains but also because it was the first account released to the European public of the great voyage just concluded. The translation used here appeared in Lord Stanley of Alderley's *First Voyage around the World by Magellan*, published by the Hakluyt Society in 1874. The translation itself is by James Baynes of the British Museum.

The third and last selection, which also appeared in Lord Stanley's *First Voyage*, is taken from *Lendas da India* by the sixteenth-century Portuguese historian Gaspar Corrêa. Although Corrêa died about 1563, his work remained unpublished until 1858–66, when it was issued by the Academy of Sciences of Lisbon. Corrêa is guilty of some inaccuracies here, as elsewhere in the *Lendas,* but the errors will be pointed out as they occur, and the account has the merit of giving a detailed version of the mutiny at San Julián Bay in Patagonia, which Pigafetta passes over very lightly. Corrêa is, furthermore, rather moderate in his judgment of Magellan —and in a century when other Portuguese historians felt antagonistic toward a man whom they considered a traitor to his country.

Among the sources other than those included here is the log of the pilot Francisco Albo, or Alvo (evidently a Greek despite his Spanish name), another of the fortunate survivors in the "Victoria." He kept a log of the voyage from the time the fleet sighted Cape Santo Agostinho in Brazil until El Cano's ship came to Rio Grande in the Cape Verde Islands a few weeks before reaching home. He even dutifully recorded the latitude of Rio Grande, though the position of the Cape Verdes had been common knowledge among seamen for more than sixty years. The Albo log, which is little more than a table of longitudes and directions in which the fleet traveled, would be of small interest to the general reader.

An unnamed Genoese pilot with the expedition, who may have been either Giovanni Battista or Leone Pancaldo, wrote an account of the voyage from Spain to the Moluccas,[3] at which point the author and his manuscript fell into Portuguese hands. The pilot is informative but uninteresting, as he tells his story in a humdrum way. António de Brito, the Portuguese official who captured this pilot together with the entire crew of the ship "Trinidad," used the narrative as the basis of his own report to King John III of Portugal, in which he also described how he had treated, and further intended to treat, the prisoners.

Besides Corrêa, four sixteenth-century Portuguese writers—Fernão Lopes de Castanheda, João de Barros, Damião de Góis, and António Galvão—included descriptions of the Magellan expedition in more general histories of their countrymen's exploits.[4] Only the last named, Galvão, is temperate in dealing with the great discoverer's desertion of Spain for Portugal; the other three display bitterness. Castanheda says Magellan "committed a great treason"; Barros writes of the "demon that in the spirit of men [in this case, of Magellan] arranges affairs for some evil act"; and Góis, though taking a more moderate tone, makes it clear that he considers Magellan a disgruntled man who planned the voyage for Castile principally to spite the Portuguese sovereign, Manuel.[5]

Following the return of El Cano to Spain, there was considerable uncertainty at court regarding the merits of Magellan and his conduct of the expedition. El Cano was obliged to appear before Alcalde Santiago Díaz de Leguizamo at Valladolid and give sworn testimony in answer to thirteen questions regarding both Magellan's behavior and his own after the leadership had passed to him.[6] The commander of the "Victoria" appears to have been an honest man and to have given answers that he considered truthful, but he had not liked Magellan and had been suspicious enough of him to take part in the San Julián mutiny. His statements were therefore detrimental to the fallen leader. They do reveal, however, the line of reasoning a conscientious Spaniard might take in justifying his opposition to the commander and planner of the expedition.

The Italian priest Peter Martyr, or Pietro Martire d'Anghiera, resided at the court of Spain at the time of El Cano's return. For years he had been compiling an event-by-event narrative of Spanish activities overseas, and this was published, partly during his lifetime and partly after his death in 1526, as *De orbe novo*. A translation of this Latin text in modern English was made by Francis A. MacNutt in 1912.[7] The Magellan voyage, to us a matter of distant Renaissance history, was to Martyr an exciting current event about which judgments and opinions differed widely. It is not surprising that the learned prelate, writing before all the existing information was available, committed several errors of fact and mistakes in judgment. He demonstrates nonetheless the state of confusion of even the best informed Europeans when they attempted to assess an event as important as the recent voyage, whose own participants gave different interpretations of various details.

Of the many twentieth-century historians of Magellan and his voyage, the best, in addition to Robertson, are probably the Belgian Jean Denucé, the Chilean José Toribio Medina, the Portuguese Viscount de Lagôa, and the latter's countryman José Maria de Queiroz Velloso. A favorable word should also be spoken for the American writer Charles McKew Parr, whose work is the most recent of all.[8]

The source narratives describe details of the Magellan voyage very well, but they neither explain the idea behind it nor make clear just what the leader thought he was doing as against what he actually accomplished. Their authors did not follow the line of geographical reasoning Magellan adopted and could not consult a modern map of the earth. An explanation not furnished by Pigafetta, Maximilian, and Corrêa is therefore required, and to this we shall now turn our attention.

TARSHISH AND OPHIR TO THE EAST

Magellan did not plan to circumnavigate the earth but instead tried to find a western route to the

Moluccas and other lands, partly real and partly imaginary, that he believed lay nearby. If he had found these places where he expected to find them, he would have tried to return to Spain by the way he had come.

To modern geographers the Moluccas make up a large part of the central East Indies, but in Magellan's time the name was given to a limited group of islands, principally Ternate, Tidore, and Halmahera, almost directly on the equator and lying between Celebes and New Guinea. On those and a few neighboring islands grew the principal supply of cloves, the most esteemed and highly priced of all spices in the European market. When the Portuguese first rounded the Cape of Good Hope and reached India under Vasco da Gama in 1498, they believed for a time that the spices grew mostly in the Indian peninsula. Subsequent exploration and information picked up from Orientals brought realization that they had not yet reached their main goal and that the real spice habitat was the great archipelago lying beyond the Malacca strait and Sumatra. Their desire to reach the source of the valuable traffic explains why, during the governorship of the Portuguese East by Afonso de Albuquerque (1509–15), they captured Malacca near modern Singapore and straightway pushed expeditions in various directions beyond the strait.

Even before the Gama expedition opened water communication between Europe and Asia, Christopher Columbus had crossed the Atlantic under the colors of Castile. He discovered the Bahamas, Cuba, and Hispaniola and returned to Spain in March 1493, believing and claiming that he had found Marco Polo's island of Cipangu (Japan) and the Asiatic mainland. Before getting back to Palos, his original point of embarcation, Columbus was forced by bad weather into the mouth of the Tagus and there had an interview with King John II (1481–95) of Portugal. John may have had his doubts about the discovery of Cipangu and Asia, but he did wish to avoid competition in Atlantic exploration from Columbus' sovereigns, Ferdinand and Isabella of Spain. By a farfetched interpretation of a treaty made years before between Portugal and Castile,[9] he claimed that the lands discovered by Columbus across the ocean rightly belonged to him.

Ferdinand and Isabella, warned by their voyager that the king of Portugal meant to give trouble, quickly appealed for confirmation of their transatlantic claims to Pope Alexander VI, who had been born Rodrigo de Borja y Doms in the kingdom of Aragon. The pope issued a series of bulls during the year 1493, the most important of which was second *Inter caetera,* which drew an imaginary line from pole to pole a hundred leagues west and south of "any" of the Azores and Cape Verde Islands.[10] Spain should own all lands beyond this line and ships of other nations were forbidden to cross it. Since Portugal was not mentioned in the bull, there is no basis for the frequent assertion that the pope divided the non-Christian part of the earth between

11

the two Iberian kingdoms. Alexander intended no division; he meant only to serve Spain. In another bull, *Dudum siquidem,* in September 1493, he went further than in *Inter caetera* and practically awarded the Eastern Hemisphere, as well as the Western, to Castile.

John II had no intention of being crowded off the earth by any papal decision in favor of his powerful neighbors. Without wasting time in futile appeals to Alexander, he pressed the matter diplomatically with Spain. Ferdinand and Isabella soon realized that the pope's award (which was really theirs, as they and Columbus had practically dictated the wording of the bulls) was beyond all reason and must be considerably modified. Abating their claims, they consented to sign the Treaty of Tordesillas with Portugal on June 7, 1494.[11] Its principal clause, called "Agreement for the partition of the ocean sea," established a line from pole to pole passing 370 leagues west of the Cape Verde Islands. It stipulated a free hand for Castile west of the line and for Portugal east of it. Any assumption that the Tordesillas treaty divided the earth between Castile and Portugal is somewhat too pretentious for the conditions of the year 1494 when so little had yet been discovered. Evidently the Iberian countries thought then only in terms of separate spheres in the Atlantic. Within a generation, however, the two had pushed their explorations so far that they had progressed to global thinking. The question of where the Tordesillas line bisected the other side of the earth then became the real point at issue.

This very problem of precisely fixing the other half of the Tordesillas line became intertwined with that of the ownership of the Moluccas. The line must be drawn exactly 180° east and west of the original line, which ran 370 leagues west of the Cape Verdes. That, however, was hard to do. No one knew the circumference of the still uncircumnavigated earth, about which conflicting theories existed, and in consequence the exact length of a degree of longitude at the equator could not be determined to everyone's satisfaction. The Portuguese, when they took Malacca in 1511, came within striking distance of the Moluccas but were not sure how far east of the original Tordesillas meridian Malacca lay. They feared, just as Magellan came to believe, that the treasured Moluccas were beyond the oriental half of the Tordesillas line and hence in the part of the globe reserved to Spain. Until Magellan crossed the Pacific and revealed its tremendous extent, such a belief could not be lightly dismissed, no matter how much the Portuguese wished to do so. Vasco Núñez de Balboa crossed the Isthmus of Darien for Spain in 1513 and reached the Pacific, but for all he knew, the *Mar del Sur,* as he called it, might be only a little body of water. For a few years the general impression among Spaniards was that Balboa's *Mar* and the sea east of Malacca were one and the same body. The opinion prevailed that the Moluccas could be reached by a short voyage west from the American continent, which, in spite of Amerigo Vespucci's theory of a "New World," was still thought by many—and perhaps most—to be merely the easternmost peninsula of Asia.

The Portuguese had not physically occupied the Moluccas at the time of Magellan's voyage across the Pacific, and the furthest outpost in their outright possession remained Malacca. However, when Afonso de Albuquerque captured this city on the Malay Peninsula in 1511, he straightway arranged for tapping and exploring the resources of the islands farther east. To the best of our knowledge, no European had visited the Moluccas up to this time. Lodovico di Varthema, a Bolognese Italian free-lance traveler in the East, had been close enough to the islands in 1504 to furnish some description of their clove trees and also of the nutmeg that grew in the Banda Islands farther south.[12] The published narrative of his travels had been printed at Rome late in 1510, too late certainly for Albuquerque and his Portuguese to have read it, though some of them may have talked with Varthema himself during his stay in the Orient.

For the discovery of the Moluccas, Albuquerque selected António de Abreu and gave him three ships, with which he departed from Malacca in December 1511. Some historians have believed that Ferdinand Magellan, who had certainly taken part in the conquest of Malacca, sailed toward the Moluccas with Abreu. The weight of evidence, however, suggests that he did not go, and even if he did he certainly did not reach these clove-bearing islands that were to be the goal of his last and most famous voyage. Abreu sailed through the Strait of Malacca and along the coasts of Sumatra and Java, engaging the services of several Javanese pilots. The small Portuguese fleet coasted Bali, Sumbava, and various other islands of the Sunda group and then turned northward to Buru, Amboina, and Ceram just above the little Banda archipelago.[13] From there the Portuguese dropped down to the Bandas and took aboard a valuable load of nutmeg and mace, because Abreu considered the season too far advanced to continue his voyage to the Moluccas and wished to return to Malacca with his cargo. Since leaving the Sundas, he had been in the Pacific, and as this was the year 1512 and Balboa did not sight the Pacific from his "peak in Darien" until September 25, 1513,[14] we seem justified in calling Abreu the European discoverer of the great ocean.[15]

Although António de Abreu did not reach the Moluccas, a member of his expedition, Francisco Serrão, soon did. Serrão had started the voyage in command of one of the three ships, but while the fleet was moving eastward between Bali and Kangean his vessel went down in a heavy wind.[16] At Banda, Abreu bought a junk for Serrão to command and in the port of Lutatan loaded it with a cargo of nutmeg and cloves. With this, Serrão started to accompany his commander back to Malacca, but another storm dispersed the Portuguese ships and the

junk was blown off course and wrecked on the Luco-
pino Isles, southwest of Banda. From here, after a
series of adventures, Serrão and six companions
reached Ternate, where the leader made friends
with the ruler, Boleyse. This kinglet was a Moslem,
although the religion was comparatively new in the
island, having been the dominant one for only a
generation.[17] The Moluccans were too far from Europe and perhaps too lukewarm in their faith to
share the western Moslem prejudice against Christians. Boleyse welcomed Serrão and rejoiced in ob-
taining the services of a Portuguese, whose countrymen's prowess he had learned about from Chinese
and Malay traders. Serrão became the most trusted
and influential counselor of the ruler of Ternate,
married an attractive group of native women, and
settled down to spend the rest of his life on the island.[18]

He did not altogether lose touch with his fellow Portuguese. In 1513 Governor Ruy de Brito
Patalim of Malacca sent a trading expedition to the
Moluccas. It brought back all the Portuguese except
Serrão, who showed no desire to leave. Nevertheless he wrote a letter to King Manuel, preening himself on the discovery of the Moluccas and professing
an allegiance to the monarch that he probably did
not feel. More important, he wrote to Ferdinand
Magellan, who had been his friend ever since the
two men had gone from Portugal to India in the expedition of 1505 commanded by Viceroy Francisco
de Almeida.[19] The text of Serrão's letter to Magellan

is not preserved, but according to Barros the voluntary exile on Ternate exaggerated the wealth of the Moluccas. Furthermore he doubled the true distance between Malacca and the islands, thus leading his friend to believe for a while that they were much farther east than they really are.[20]

By this time Magellan had left the East to return to Portugal, but he eventually received the letter, pondered it deeply, and made it an important factor in the formulation of his plan. He wrote Serrão a reply, saying (still according to Barros) that "if it should be pleasing to God, he would soon be with him, if not by way of Portugal, then by way of Castile, for matters were now pointing that way; therefore he should await him where he was." [21] After both men were dead, the letter was found among Serrão's papers by António de Brito, the Portuguese commander who went to the Moluccas to establish the sovereignty of his king.[22]

During the later years of Serrão's stay on Ternate, he fell under suspicion at the court of Portugal. Some report of his correspondence with Magellan had leaked out. When it became known that Magellan had obtained a Castilian fleet and departed for the Moluccas by a westward route, the court naturally feared that if the expedition reached the islands, Serrão would influence the natives in behalf of Magellan. According to one report, Jorge de Albuquerque, governor of Malacca, enticed him back to that city, but he perceived the governor's malevolent intentions in time and

17

made a hasty escape in a junk bound for Banda and the Moluccas.[23] Later Albuquerque sent a fleet to Ternate with orders to seize Serrão and bring him again to Malacca. By one means or another the stout adventurer managed to avoid capture, but the commander of the Portuguese expedition, Tristão de Meneses, evidently arranged with a native woman to poison him. The lady kept her promise, and Serrão died a few weeks after the departure of Meneses' fleet, at about the time of Magellan's death on Mactan in the Philippines.[24]

Magellan, then, expected to reach the Moluccas by sailing westward, to claim them for Castile, and to have the support of his friend Serrão in establishing the claim. Nevertheless we cannot overlook the possibility that he had additional plans and intentions involving other lands or islands. He knew, through his Portuguese associations and no doubt particularly from Serrão, that the Moluccas lie directly athwart the equator. Yet when he approached the Marianas after nearly completing his voyage across the Pacific, he was sailing at a latitude that Albo gives as 13° N. and the Genoese pilot as 12° N.[25] Pigafetta agrees with the latter (page 128). This shows that the chroniclers of the expedition, however uncertain they might be as to their longitude, were substantially accurate as to latitude, since the correct figure for the probable island in question, Guam, is 13° N. The expedition, therefore, temporarily abandoned the search for the Moluccas to seek something else. Pigafetta says:

After we had passed the equinoctial line we sailed west northwest, and west by north, and then for two hundred leguas toward the west, changing our course to west by south until we reached thirteen degrees toward the Arctic Pole in order that we might approach nearer to the land of cape Gaticara. That cape (with the pardon of geographers, for they have not seen it), is not found where it is imagined to be, but to the north in twelve degrees or thereabouts [p. 128].

Pigafetta mentions as the immediate objective not the Moluccas but Cattigara, a name that comes from Ptolemy in the second century and applies to a part of the Asiatic mainland. (See the version of Ptolemy's map, p. 37.)

The Genoese pilot explains Magellan's deviation from the route to the Moluccas as follows: "They had information that in the Moluccas there was no food; so he [Magellan] said that he wished to go in the direction of the north as much as ten or twelve degrees." [26] Admittedly the expedition at the end of the Pacific crossing was near its last gasp from hunger, thirst, fever, and scurvy, but why should Magellan believe that starvation awaited his fleet in the Moluccas? He knew the islands to be inhabited; he also knew that Portuguese had lived there and that his friend Serrão had resided comfortably on Ternate for years. Something else was on his agenda of discovery, and he thought he knew where to find it.

That something was the island cluster composed of Formosa and the Ryukyus, the latter known to the Portuguese, who had not yet visited them, as Lequios. Duarte Barbosa, who wrote a geographical account of the countries bordering on the Indian Ocean and those within range of the ocean, has this to say of the Ryukyu inhabitants:

From Malaca they take the same goods as the Chins [Chinese] take. These islands are called Lequios [in one version 'Liquii']. The Malaca people say that they are better men, and richer and more eminent merchants than the Chins. Of these folk we as yet know but little, as they have not yet come to Malaca since it has been under the King our Lord.[27]

The Duarte Barbosa who wrote this book has been identified by some with the Portuguese of the same name who became Magellan's cousin by marriage and accompanied him on his great voyage. Medina has shown that this was probably not the same man, but it makes little difference.[28] The Barbosa book was finished by 1516 and was available in manuscript to Magellan as he studied to complete his plan in Portugal before transferring allegiance to Spain. Magellan digested Barbosa's work and with his own hand rewrote one passage, which consisted of a list of places between the Cape of Good Hope and the Lequios that were known but not yet occupied by the Portuguese. Magellan's version substitutes for Barbosa's "Lequios" the words "Tarsis" and "Ofir." [29]

These are, of course, the biblical Tarshish and Ophir associated with Solomon and his trading partner, Hiram of Tyre. In I Kings 10:11 the statement is: "And the navy also of Hiram, that brought gold from Ophir, brought in from Ophir great plenty of almug trees, and precious stones." II Chronicles 9:21 says: "For the king's ships went to Tarshish with the servants of Huram: every three years once came the ships of Tarshish bringing gold, and silver, ivory, and apes, and peacocks." Elsewhere these Old Testament books agree in saying that Solomon received more than four hundred talents of gold from Ophir.

We shall not enter into the centuries-old debate as to what and where these lands actually were. The writer of I Kings certainly meant that the journey to Ophir began by way of the Red Sea, because in connection with Ophir (9:26) he says: "And the king Solomon made a navy of ships in Eziongeber, which is beside Eloth, on the shore of the Red Sea, in the land of Edom." Later Christian writers for centuries associated the gold of Ophir with East Africa, but at the time of the Portuguese discoveries Ophir was thought of as the Aurea Chersonnesus (Golden Peninsula) of Ptolemy, in which that Greek geographer also placed Cattigara, mentioned by Pigafetta as the immediate transpacific goal of Magellan. But Magellan connected Solomon's treasure with something else he had read in Barbosa:

Facing this great land of China there are many islands in the sea, beyond which [on the other side of the sea] there is a very large land which they say is mainland, from which there come to Malacca every year three or four ships, like those of the Chins, belonging to white men who are said to

21

be great and rich merchants: they bring much gold, and silver in bars, silk, rich cloth, and much very good wheat, beautiful porcelains, and many other merchandises.[30]

Barbosa, in mentioning this great land across the water from China, might have been referring to Japan. More likely, though, he meant the island of Taiwan, or Formosa, separated by the Gulf of Fukien from mainland China. At the time Barbosa wrote, the Portuguese can scarcely have had information about Japan. They had some regarding Formosa and the Ryukyus, whose exact latitudinal position they did not know but correctly placed northward of Malacca and the Moluccas and hence north of the equator. These are obviously what Magellan took to be Tarshish and Ophir.

If further proof is needed that he sought these places in addition to the Moluccas, we have it in the agreement between the Spanish crown and Sebastian Cabot. On April 4, 1525, less than six years after Magellan sailed, Cabot, now pilot major of Spain, signed a contract to make much the same voyage, though with objectives more concisely stated. He offered to go with three ships through the Strait of Magellan to reach the Moluccas "and other islands and lands of Tarshish and Ophir and eastern Cathay and Cipangu." [31] The Spanish government had preferred to leave the names Tarshish and Ophir out of the earlier Magellan contract, but now that the western route to the Orient had been discovered, security regulations could be relaxed to the extent of openly mentioning the biblical lands.

22

We now see what Magellan's aim in the Far East was: He expected to claim for Spain the Moluccas and the lands known to Solomon and Hiram of Tyre. It remains to be shown how he expected to reach those lands, and for this we must understand his mental image of the New World across the Atlantic.

THE NEW WORLD TO THE WEST

By the time Magellan left Sanlúcar on September 20, 1519, to sail westward in quest of the East Indies, a long stretch of the Atlantic, Caribbean, and Gulf coasts of the Americas had been explored. Columbus, besides discovering the largest West Indian islands, had struck the mainland of Venezuela on his third voyage and on the fourth had traversed the east side of Central America from Guanaja in the Gulf of Honduras to the coast of Colombia. Even before this last Columbus expedition, Alonso de Hojeda, Amerigo Vespucci, Vicente Yáñez Pinzón, Pero Alonso Niño, Cristóbal Guerra, Juan de la Cosa, Diego de Lepe, and Rodrigo de Bastidas had among them explored all the coast from a point south of Cape Santo Agostinho in Brazil to the Isthmus of Panama. In 1501–2 a Portuguese expedition accompanied by Amerigo Vespucci of Florence traced the South American contour from above Cape São Roque at the shoulder of Brazil to a point in Patagonia now reliably estimated to have been 47° S.[32] Vespucci, who did not command at the start, was placed in complete charge as the voyage progressed.[33] He certainly deserves credit for discovering the Río de la Plata, which, if not clearly described in his written narrative, does appear convincingly on maps made as a result of his discovery. He started in hopes of doing very much what Magellan later planned—that is, of finding a strait through the western land mass and of traversing it to reach the Orient. He did come close to Magellan's strait, but he turned back because of the cold and on reaching Europe described the South American continent as a New World.[34]

Vespucci's failure to find a strait did not keep others from taking up the search. The Portuguese crown could legitimately lay claim to most of the coast of Santa Cruz, or Brazil, by the Treaty of Tordesillas but, after making preliminary surveys of that country, turned the exploitation of its natural resources over to private initiative. We know of several visits to Brazil early in the sixteenth century to exploit the trade opportunities there. One was the expedition planned and financed by Cristóbal de Haro, who later paid part of the expense of the Magellan enterprise. The house of Haro, an opulent trading firm with a particular interest in oriental pepper, had originated in Burgos but had its main offices in Lisbon with Cristóbal as family agent there. Haro now anticipated Magellan in seeking a western route to the Moluccas, which the Abreu expedition from Malacca had almost reached. His two Portuguese ships went south of the Río de la Plata, turned northward, and explored that great estuary before sailing home.[35] Haro's seamen, on returning to Portugal in 1514, believed they had been in a strait leading to Malacca, which they thought lay only six hundred leagues from their farthest point of penetration.[36] The geographer Johann Schöner at once made a globe that seems to incorporate some of their discovery data. The Río de la Plata appears on it as a strait leading to a western ocean, and south of this strait is an Antarctic land of continental size labeled *Brazile Regio*.[37]

Balboa's crossing of the isthmus and discovery of the *Mar del Sur* in 1513 had of course stimulated interest in finding a waterway to this sea. Juan Díaz de Solís, a seaman of Portuguese birth and Spanish ancestry, succeeded Amerigo Vespucci as pilot major of Spain on Vespucci's death in 1512. Aging King Ferdinand, who now acted as regent of Castile for his mentally unstable daughter Juana, gave Solís instructions for a new expedition on November 24, 1514.[38] The royal orders told the pilot to sail to the "shoulders" of Castilla del Oro and beyond. Castilla del Oro was the Spanish name for the isthmian region, now governed by Balboa's successor Pedrarias Dávila. By "shoulders" the king meant the Pacific, or rear, side of narrow Central America. The assumption existed, on the basis of very slight exploration, that from Castilla del Oro the Pacific coast bent in a westerly direction and connected with the mainland of eastern Asia, with which the Portuguese already had some acquaintance. Solís should follow that shore westward for seventeen hundred leagues if possible, being careful not to touch any of the king of Portugal's possessions as defined by the Treaty of Tordesillas. Should Castilla del Oro prove to be an island around which a message could be sent by water to Cuba, Solís should communicate with Cuba at once.

Despite some attempts at sabotage by the Portuguese,[39] who knew the goal of Solís to be the Far East, the expedition set sail in October 1515. As the Spaniards had thoroughly explored the coasts of northern South America, the pilot major thought his best chance of getting to the shoulders of Castilla de Oro was to seek a water passage to the south. He coasted South America to the Río de la Plata, called Río Jordán by Vespucci and now named Río Dulce by the pilot, after whom it was to be known as Río de Solís for some years to come. Although the Plata had already been explored at least twice, the voyagers took it for a strait leading to Balboa's sea and Castilla del Oro. So promising did it seem that Solís went ahead of the fleet in a small caravel to the island of Martín Garcia. Near there he ventured ashore and was seized and presumably eaten by savage Indians, probably Charruas.[40]

With their leader gone, the others hastened back to Spain, reaching Seville in September 1516. Instead of the riches they had hoped to bring, they bore only some Brazilian dyewood, a few sealskins, and a small Indian girl.[41] Had Solís lived he would have learned that the Plata estuary was not the passageway he sought and, weather permitting, might have continued southward to Magellan's strait itself. As matters stood, the great water opening still figured as a possible strait in men's minds. Magellan explored it again only four years later, but even his demonstration that no strait existed there failed to convince others. Still later Sebastian Cabot sought the route to Tarshish, Ophir, Cathay, and Cipangu by ascending the Plata's principal tributary, the Paraná.[42]

Between the failure of Solís in 1516 and the Magellan voyage other explorations increased the likelihood that the strait, if it existed at all, must be sought in the south. In 1517 a party of Spaniards from Cuba, led by Francisco Hernández de Córdoba, explored the mainland from the northeast corner of Yucatan to Champotón on the Bay of Campeche.[43] The next year another Cuban expedition under Juan de Grijalva retraced Córdoba's route around Yucatan and coasted the Gulf of Mexico northward to Tampico.[44] The main importance of these reconnaissances was that they informed Governor Diego Velásquez of Cuba about the wealth of Aztec Mexico and caused him to prepare the Cortés expedition.[45] Their significance is that they added hundreds of additional miles to the explored part of the American coast without revealing any sign of a strait. Meanwhile Ponce de León had investigated Florida, and John and Sebastian Cabot had explored for England long stretches of the North American coast, Sebastian having probably penetrated as far north as the entrance to Hudson's Bay in 1509.[46]

Portuguese voyagers, notably Gaspar and Miguel Côrte-Real and João Fernandes Lavrador, had visited parts of North America, although specific information concerning what they accomplished is sparse.[47]

Even as Magellan sailed from Sanlúcar, Alonso Alvarez de Pineda, too late to influence him, was exploring the last unknown stretch of the Gulf of Mexico by order of Governor Francisco de Garay of Jamaica.[48] Pineda, looking for a strait, sailed from Florida to the part of Mexico already known to the Cortés expedition, but though he found a very large river, probably the Mississippi, he naturally could not discover a strait that did not exist. Magellan, through his daily contact with the *Casa de Contratación* at Seville, must have known of all these Spanish failures, except Pineda's, by the time he sailed.

Besides these explorations that almost eliminated a possible strait into Balboa's sea from every region except the extreme south, Magellan had other information that he considered his own secret. Pigafetta, in writing of that part of the great voyage in which the explorers had just discovered the Cape of Eleven Thousand Virgins[49] at the entrance to the strait, says: "But the captain-general . . . knew where to find a well-hidden strait, which he saw depicted on a map in the treasury of the King of Portugal, which was made by that excellent man, Martin de Boemia [Martin Behaim]" (p. 114). Las Casas much later repeated Pigafetta's statement and added on his own initiative that

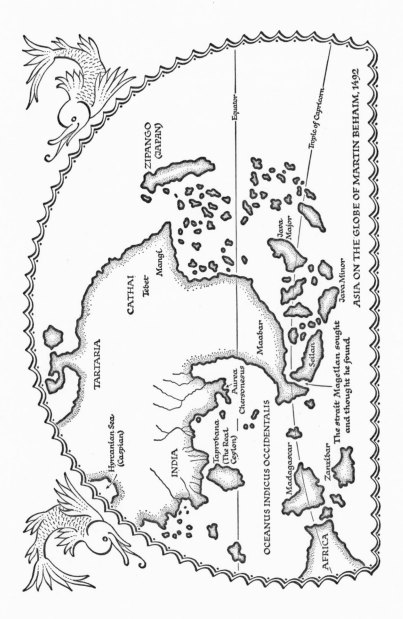

ASIA ON THE GLOBE OF MARTIN BEHAIM, 1492

Equator

Tropic of Capricorn

ZIPANGO
(JAPAN)

TARTARIA

CATHAI

Tebet

Mangi

Java
Major

Java Minor

Seilan

Maabar

Aurea
Chersonesus

OCEANUS INDICUS OCCIDENTALIS

The strait Magellan sought
and thought he found

Hyrcanian Sea
(Caspian)

INDIA

Taprobana
(The Real
Ceylon)

Madagascar

Zanzibar

AFRICA

Magellan had observed the Behaim strait to lie within the limits assigned to Spain at Tordesillas.[50]

Martin Behaim (1459–1506) was a German merchant who for commercial reasons had lived some years in Portugal and the Azores.[51] He does not seem to have taken part in any explorations but evidently followed the discoveries of the Portuguese with interest. In 1492, on the eve of Columbus' first voyage, he completed at his Nuremberg birthplace a globe that fairly well depicted ideas of world geography at the time. Behaim gathered his data from such ancient writers as Strabo, Pliny, and Ptolemy, from the book of Marco Polo, and from recent results of Portuguese explorations down the African coast and in the Atlantic. He gives indications, too, of having seen the letter, and perhaps the map, sent by the Florentine scholar Paolo dal Pozzo Toscanelli in 1474 to Canon Fernão Martins in Lisbon,[52] illustrating the practicability of reaching Japan by a voyage westward in the Atlantic. Behaim mixed this material in the construction of his *Erdapfel* (globe), which showed the three continents of Europe, Africa, and Asia, the Indian Ocean, and an Atlantic that occupied the area between western Europe and eastern Asia.

Magellan had probably never seen the Behaim globe; as far as we know, it remained in Nuremberg, where it is still preserved. But Behaim could have drawn a map along similar lines in Portugal, and there are others so much like his globe in their depiction of the continents that they could have been taken for his work. One such possibility is the planisphere constructed by another German, Henricus Martellus (Heinrich Hammer), about 1489.[53] Though drawn on a flat surface, this has continents so nearly resembling those of the globe that Behaim could largely have copied Martellus or else both men could have taken some earlier cartographer, such as Toscanelli, as a model.

Of greatest interest to Magellan on a Behaim-type map would have been the long peninsula extending from eastern Asia well down into the southern hemisphere. To him that peninsula was South America, and his conviction was strengthened by the fact that explorers had observed a westward bending of the continent as they went south from the shoulder of Brazil. By a coincidence the Behaim peninsula had the same westward slant. Near the end of it Behaim had drawn an out-of-place version of the island of Ceylon.[54] The strait Magellan had in mind, as reported by Pigafetta and Las Casas, was the water passage on the globe between this island and the peninsula. When the great discoverer finally traversed the strait between Tierra del Fuego and the mainland of South America, he believed himself in the imaginary waterway of the Behaim globe. Once past the strait and in the Pacific, Magellan took this ocean for the *Magnus Sinus*, the sea appearing as the eastern part of the Indian Ocean on the Ptolemy map and on that of Martellus, who appropriated the *Sinus* from Ptolemy.

The idea of the long peninsula appended to

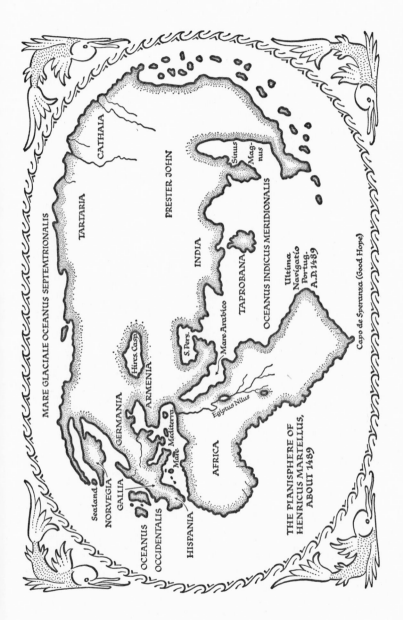

THE PLANISPHERE OF
HENRICUS MARTELLUS,
ABOUT 1489

MARE GLACIALE OCEANUS SEPTEMTRIONALIS

CATHAIA

TARTARIA

PRESTER JOHN

Sinus
Mag-
nus

INDIA

TAPROBANA

OCEANUS INDICUS MERIDIONALIS

Ultima
Navigatio
Portug.
A.D. 1489

Hircs. Casp.

ARMENIA

S. Pers.

Mare Arabico

GERMANIA

Egiptus Nilus

Mare Mediterr.

Scotland

NORVEGIA

GALLIA

OCEANUS
OCCIDENTALIS

HISPANIA

AFRICA

Capo de Speranza (Good Hope)

Asia came originally from Ptolemy. That Alexandrian Greek geographer of the second century showed on his world map, at the extreme east of Asia, a shore line extending to the far south. But instead of being a peninsula, as it became with Behaim and Martellus, this shore was connected with another labeled *Terra Incognita,* which formed a southern coast of the Indian Ocean and extended eastward from a point south of the equator in Africa. Together, these closed the ocean to the east and south and made it an inland sea. But during the Middle Ages, Arab shippers sailed to the East Indies and China, and late in the thirteenth century the Polos traveled from Chinese Zaiton around Malaya to India. Obviously the Ptolemy concept of a closed sea had to be modified, so European mapmakers opened the Indian Ocean at its eastern end. Some of them retained most of Ptolemy's southward-extending land bridge, however, and modified it into the very long peninsula seen by Magellan on a Behaim map or something similar.

Ptolemy, in drawing the southward-dropping shore line at the east of the Indian Ocean, had been displaying the Malay Peninsula to the best of his inadequate knowledge. When Magellan, accompanied Albuquerque to Malacca, he had of course been to that peninsula, but he did not correctly identify it as the one Behaim and others had drawn in their modification of Ptolemy. The real Malaya, as Magellan knew, does not extend quite to the equator, whereas the Behaim peninsula crossed the

Tropic of Capricorn. Magellan therefore thought, as did others at the time, that Behaim's peninsula lay farther east and was the mainland the Spaniards had somewhat explored by water and were beginning to penetrate in places by land. Amerigo Vespucci had called the southern part of this a New World, but by no means everyone accepted his opinion. Magellan certainly did not agree with Amerigo. Instead he thought of Asia as bending to the northeast beyond Malacca around the *Sinus* and then bending southeast to become the Behaim peninsula that the geographer Martin Waldseemüller had already labeled "America." [55] Thus what we call the Pacific Ocean Magellan took to be Ptolemy's and Martellus' *Magnus Sinus,* a partially enclosed sea at the eastern end of the Indian Ocean. In this sea, on the equator east of Malacca, would lie the clove-growing Moluccas. North of them would be found Solomon's Tarshish and Ophir, or, in correct geographical terms, Formosa and the Ryukyus. East of them all was the great peninsula already crossed by the Spaniards at Darien, at whose southern tip a strait must exist.

How far would Magellan need to sail west of the strait and the peninsula to reach the Moluccas and the Ryukyus? In his opinion the trip would not be long because the *Sinus,* as shown by Ptolemy and Martellus, was not large. With no conception of the width of the Pacific, he thought of Spanish Panama and Portuguese Malacca as close together. This geographical distortion placed the Moluccas

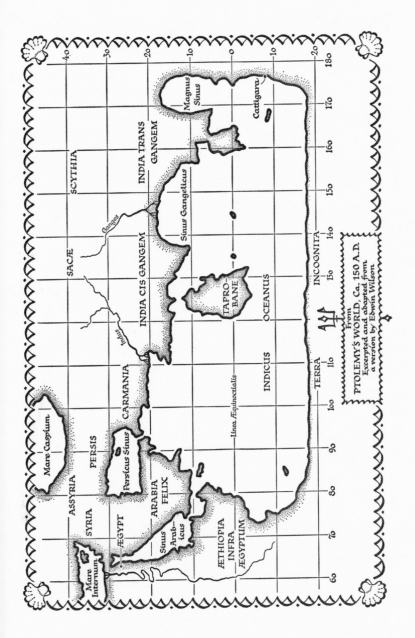

From
PTOLEMY'S WORLD, Ca. 150 A.D.
Excerpted and adapted from
a version by Edwin Wilson.

easily within the Spanish zone according to the Tordesillas agreement. The navigational task, as Magellan saw it, was to sail to the end of the Behaim peninsula, meaning South America, pass through the strait that must be there, go northward to the known latitude of the Moluccas or the supposed one of the Ryukyus, and by a short sail westward attain whichever goal he preferred to reach first. His plan resembled the assignment given Solís earlier, except that Solís had been ordered to chart the northern coast of the *Magnus Sinus*—or the land bending northwest of Panama—and Magellan meant to cut out all unnecessary exploration and go straight across.

Who was this Magellan? How had he spent his early life? Why had he left Portuguese for Spanish service, and how did he manage, in such short negotiations, to persuade the Spanish government to give him backing?

FERDINAND MAGELLAN

The discoverer's name was Fernão de Magalhães e Sousa. He was born about 1480 in the province of Entre-Douro-e-Minho in the extreme north of Portugal.[56] His paternal line, though not noble, had pretensions to gentility, and his mother's people, the Sousas, evidently outranked the Magalhães family.[57] The young Ferdinand Magellan, whose anglicized name will be more convenient to use, was twelve when he went to Lisbon to become a page to Queen Leonor, wife of King John II. He had learned to read and write at home, and at court he completed his education, consisting of riding, swordsmanship, dancing, the acquisition of polite manners, and a little study of Latin.

Magellan had reached his late teens when Vasco da Gama returned from India with a cargo of spice and the news that the seaway to the East lay open. The quest for oriental fame and riches immediately became the major interest of well-born young Portuguese, and Magellan was fascinated by the prospect. In 1505 he embarked for India in the fleet commanded by Viceroy Francisco de Almeida, who bore orders to tighten Portuguese control of the Indian Ocean by the acquisition of strongholds on land.[58] Francisco Serrão, whose career would henceforth be closely woven with that of Magellan, also sailed in the fleet.[59]

On the outward voyage Magellan took part in the capture of Kilwa and Mombasa on the eastern African coast under the orders of Almeida. We cannot follow his career in detail after he reached India, but he appears to have returned to eastern Africa in 1506 with an expedition commanded by Nuno Vaz Pereira. He was back in India by the beginning of 1509, however, because on February 2 and 3 of that year he fought in the great battle of the Rumes off Diu, where Almeida defeated an Egyptian fleet allied with several Indian contingents and consolidated Portuguese hegemony in the waters of Hindustan.[60]

A dispute then arose between the viceroy and

his appointed successor Afonso de Albuquerque, as Almeida did not wish to surrender the power he had held for four years.[61] Portuguese officers took sides in the wrangle, and Magellan and Serrão appear to have been among those backing Albuquerque. This may have been the reason why Almeida got them out of the way by attaching them to a ship ordered to join the squandron of Diogo Lopes de Sequeira who had just come out from Lisbon with orders to visit Malacca, the great commercial center at the eastern end of the Indian Ocean.[62]

After passing Ceylon, Sequeira's fleet proceeded eastward through waters still unknown to Europeans, with the Portuguese navigators probably trying to read native sea charts and relying somewhat on the aid of Indian or Javanese pilots. Sequeira touched northwestern Sumatra and passed along the northern shore of the great island until he dropped anchor in Malacca harbor on September 11, 1509.[63] At first all seemed to go well. The king of the city and his *bendara,* or uncle, the chief magistrate, spoke fair words and promised eternal peace and a commercial arrangement with Portugal. Danger lurked, however, in the shape of Moslem merchants from India who had been virtually ousted by the Portuguese there and feared that the same would happen in Malaya. They so worked upon the feelings of king and *bendara* that these two gave their consent to a plan to attack the white men without warning, massacre them, and seize their four ships.

The opportunity seemed to come a few days later when Sequeira sent most of his men ashore to trade and crowds of Malays were allowed to clamber upon the almost deserted decks. One of the captains, Garcia de Sousa, suddenly grew suspicious. Collecting what men he had, he chased the Malays from his ship and sent Magellan in a small boat to warn Sequeira. The commander sat playing chess in his cabin, while eight Malays stood behind him, awaiting a signal that the slaughter had commenced on shore before attacking him with their knives. At Magellan's low-voiced warning, which the natives could not understand, Sequeira ordered the boatswain's mate to climb a mast and observe what was going on in the town. As the sailor looked, he gave cries of warning. Sequeira leaped to his feet, upset the chessboard, energetically swept the natives from the deck, and escaped unhurt. Meanwhile attackers in the city had killed some Portuguese and driven others, including Serrão, down to the shore. There they would all have perished if Magellan and a friend had not gone to their rescue in a small boat and brought them aboard. The Portuguese in the ships quickly pulled away from Malacca, leaving some of their comrades dead and others prisoners in Malay hands.[64]

During the return voyage to India, Magellan saved Serrão's life a second time in a battle with a Malayan junk and a little later rescued twenty-nine Portuguese shipmates when a boat towed from the flagship, in which they were riding, was scuttled by native prisoners.[65] Such deeds of bravery must have given Sequeira a good opinion of Magellan, but this commander, under whom he might have risen to fortune, soon departed for Portugal. Albuquerque, who had by now taken charge in India, planned to send two more ships loaded with cargo from Cochin to follow Sequeira to Lisbon, and Magellan prepared to go home in one of these. The commanders navigated carelessly and ran the vessels aground on Padua Reef about a hundred miles from Cananor. The crews had just time to put their cargoes and part of the provisions ashore on a small neighboring island before the ships sank. Maritime etiquette being then just the reverse of what it is today, the officers and men of high birth prepared to go to Cananor in the ship's boats, leaving the common sailors on the island to wait for a rescue party. Magellan was entitled to go, but he thought someone of rank should stay to keep up the morale of the ignorant seamen and volunteered to remain if a ship would be sent to pick them up. For days he waited with the men until the Portuguese governor of Cananor sent a relief caravel. He discharged his responsibility so well that no one laid a hand on any of the valuables left in his care.[66]

It is not certain that Magellan took part in the capture of Goa in November 1510, but just before that he had a serious falling out with Albuquerque that may have ruined forever his prospects in Portuguese service. The governor wished to augment his fleet by taking several trading ships from Cochin to Goa in order to utilize them and their crews in the assault. To give his proposal an air of democracy, he asked the opinions of several officers and ship captains. As Albuquerque later reported:

Ferdinand Magellan said that it seemed to him that the Lord Captain should not take the cargo ships to Goa because if they went they could not sail this year to Portugal, it being now the twelfth of October, and if they went straight there [to Goa] without touching at Cananor or at any other port they could still not arrive before the eighth of November, the winds being unfavorable for that purpose, and as for the men aboard that His Excellency thought should go, it seemed to [Magellan] that they should not be taken, because there would not be time for them to make the necessary use of their money or to do other things needful for their [homeward] voyage.[67]

Magellan's analysis of the sailing conditions of the Indian Ocean was correct, but Albuquerque nonetheless took the ships and retained an unfavorable opinion of his subordinate. He did not complain of him to the king in any dispatch known to us, but there is every reason to think that he let Manuel know of his dissatisfaction and that this counted against Magellan at court.

Albuquerque's next major move was against Malacca, to avenge the defeat Sequeira had suffered there. Magellan paid his second visit to the Malayan city with this expedition, as did Serrão. The Portuguese fleet, numbering nineteen ships, made its appearance before Malacca on July 1, 1511, and after several hard fights and a siege lasting six weeks, resistance collapsed.[68] This was probably Albuquerque's crowning achievement, for possession of the city and its strait gave Portugal the real key to the trade in spices, drugs, gold, and all the other precious products of the Far East.

The next step, as we have already seen, was the dispatch of António de Abreu east of the strait to attempt to reach the Moluccas. Serrão went on this expedition; Magellan's participation in it is doubtful. Abreu did not return to Malacca until January, 1513,[69] and by that time Magellan appears to have left for India. He may in the meantime, however, have made a voyage, independent of Abreu's, as far north as the China Sea and as far east as New Guinea.[70] It was probably not until after his return to Portugal that he received Serrão's letter praising the Molucca Islands and exaggerating their distance east of Malacca.

During the last part of his stay in the East, Magellan was chiefly concerned with private business affairs. He is known to have lent the sum of two hundred cruzados at Cochin to a Jewish merchant named Pedro Anes Abraldez, payable in Portugal at a heavy rate of interest, though the contract had to be drawn in a somewhat complicated manner to cope with the Portuguese laws against usury.[71] He was also in touch with agents of business firms, among them Giovanni da Empoli, who represented the Florentine house of Gualtierotti and Frescobaldi in the East.[72] He appears to have been

45

unsuccessful in his mercantile endeavors, since all
evidence indicates that he possessed no means when
he returned to Europe.

Magellan was back in Portugal by 1513, though
we cannot say just when he arrived. He was then
about thirty-three. If he had a plan of voyaging to
the Moluccas by a western route, he lacked the
means for doing so and furthermore required time
for the studies and calculations that must precede
such a voyage. He must meanwhile earn a living,
and the need for employment caused him to enlist
immediately in the Portuguese expedition commanded by Jaime, Duke of Bragança, against Azemmour in Morocco. The city fell without serious resistance, but Magellan's stay in Africa proved extremely unfortunate. In a skirmish he lost a horse,
for which the army authorities refused compensa-
tion, and received a leg wound that caused him to
limp the rest of his days.[73] He was then unjustly
accused of selling for his own profit four hundred
head of stock that had been taken from the enemy
and entrusted to his care. Charges were evidently
not pressed against him, but so much unfavorable
talk circulated in the army that he took the unwise
step of returning to Portugal without leave to demand justice of King Manuel.

When he saw the monarch, Magellan chose
that inopportune time to ask for a raise in his meager stipend, which amounted to one thousand two
hundred and fifty reis a month and a bushel of bar-
ley a day.[74] The importance of the increase, in his

eyes, would lie not so much in the paltry amount involved as in the mark of royal esteem it would represent. Manuel, already prejudiced against Magellan by Albuquerque's reports from India, and now irritated by his leaving the army without permission, curtly refused his request and ordered him to return to Azemmour to face whatever accusations awaited him. Magellan therefore went back, to find that the cattle matter had blown over and that his name had been cleared.

Now that he could return to Portugal as a properly discharged soldier, he felt he had further business with the king. At either the end of 1515 or the beginning of 1516 he obtained what was to be his final audience with Manuel. He made the monarch some proposal; all that we can say for certain is that he requested to be sent on a voyage to the Moluccas. But how, and by what route? Knowing that pilots and geographers believed these islands rightly belonged to Spain, the king would certainly have rejected any plan of opening a westward water passage to them through the Castilian zone. Magellan surely had sense enough to realize this, and the main thing he wanted was to join his friend Serrão on Ternate. The most reasonable assumption, therefore, is that he merely asked Manuel for a ship in which to go to the Moluccas by the familiar Portuguese route around the Cape of Good Hope. His nomination of himself for such a command could have been justified by the fact that he knew the waters from Africa to the seas beyond Malacca as few others did and hence could expect to make the voyage in record time. Whatever he asked, Magellan pleased the king no more on this occasion than on earlier ones. Manuel coldly rejected the proposal and furthermore offered him no hope of future employment. When Magellan then asked permission to leave Portugal for the service of some other ruler, he was told that he might go where he pleased. The historian Corrêa adds a final touch that seems a bit too dramatic, for he says that when Magellan stooped to kiss the royal hand in departure the hand was brusquely drawn away.[75]

Yet Magellan did not leave Portugal immediately. He must first study and increase his geographical learning, and the best place to do so was his own country, for Portugal at that time led the world in cartography and navigational attainments. He needed also to collect the cruzados owed him since his Indian days by Abraldez, who had meanwhile died and whose heirs showed no concern about honoring the debt. Damião de Góis, in his biography of King Manuel, makes a peculiar statement which can be taken to mean that Magellan, before going to Spain, went through a legal process of denaturalizing himself and renouncing all Portuguese allegiance.[76] Most historians have drawn this conclusion from Góis' words, but Queiroz Velloso has recently shown that such an action would have been not only illegal but stupid, as Magellan intended to remain a while longer in Portugal.[77] Góis probably referred to the later contract with

48

Charles of Spain, by which Magellan was accepted as a subject of Castile.

There now enters on the scene an odd character, Ruy Faleiro. This eccentric person held a bachelor's degree and purportedly possessed a great amount of learning, particularly about that vexing question of the time, determination of longitudes. Castanheda, who always wrote most contemptuously of the Magellan enterprise, declared that Faleiro "made himself out to be a great astrologer, but really knew nothing and all he feigned to know came from a familiar demon he had, as was later learned." [78] Demon or not, Faleiro considered himself slighted and his merits overlooked by the king of Portugal, perhaps because Manuel had no intention of giving him the chair of astronomy at the University of Lisbon (later Coimbra) and preferred the court physician, Master Philip, for the post.[79] The disgruntled Faleiro now joined forces with Magellan and because of his learning was at first looked upon as the more important of the two partners.[80] He was a man of exceedingly nervous temperament—irritable, vain, and hypochondriacal. As time passed, his tendency toward mental instability became so pronounced that he finally proved unable to sail with the expedition.

At the beginning of 1516 Magellan left Lisbon, where the king's disfavor and reports of his own planned defection to Spain made life uncomfortable, and went to Oporto near his birthplace. In the northern city he at last received his cruzados from

João Abraldez, father and heir of the deceased Pedro Anes,[81] and this made his financial circumstances easier. At Oporto he presumably continued his studies, unhampered by the hostility of the Lisbon atmosphere, and pondered the scientific information he had gained from Faleiro.

Late in the year 1517 Magellan felt ready to try his fortunes in Spain and arrived in Seville on October 20. He was accompanied by his page, Cristovão Rebelo, who may have been his natural son, and by a young slave, baptized with the Christian name Henry, whom he had brought from Malacca. At Seville he was received into the home of Diogo Barbosa, a wealthy Portuguese who had once commanded a ship to India and had since become a resident of the Spanish city. Barbosa had two daughters, Beatriz and Guiomar, a son, Jaime, and a nephew, Duarte—probably not the same Duarte Barbosa as the author of the travel manuscript from which Magellan had derived his inspiration concerning Tarshish and Ophir.

Diogo had influence in the city and put Magellan in touch with officials of the *Casa de Contratación,* or *Antillas,* an organization founded by the late Ferdinand and Isabella that, among other powers, had the authority to license ships putting out for Spanish America and to determine their destination. Most of these officers showed little interest in Magellan, but the factor of the *Casa,* Juan de Aranda, smelling profits, resolved to look further into the matter. He secretly wrote to two merchants in Portugal, Diego Cobarrubias and Diego de Haro, asking their opinions of Magellan and Faleiro. The replies were favorable, and Aranda decided to support the proposal of the two Portuguese.[82]

The political situation in Spain at that time was as follows: Ferdinand of Aragon, widowed husband of the late Isabella, had governed Castile for some years as regent for his insane daughter Juana until his death in January 1516. With him the House of Trastamara came to an end, for Juana could not govern. The thrones of Castile and Aragon passed to her son Charles of Hapsburg, whose father Philip had died years earlier. When his grandfather's death made him king young Charles was just sixteen and was in Belgium completing his education. The aged Cardinal Francisco Jiménez de Cisneros governed Castile as regent until the young ruler arrived in September 1517, barely a month before Magellan reached Seville. Charles entered the country unable to speak Castilian and surrounded by a group of Flemish favorites who looked upon Spain as a conquered country ripe for plunder. They planned to divide the most profitable offices of church and state among themselves and to keep the king isolated from the Spanish bishops and noblemen. Charles I of Castile, Aragon, and Navarre, who did not yet have the Holy Roman crown that made him Charles V, thus began his reign as an unpopular foreigner, distrusted by Spaniards and with small apparent interest in their affairs, either domestic or colonial. He did not, however, prove as foolish as his youth and bad advisers might give reason to suppose. He made the Dutch Cardinal Adrian of Utrecht president of the Council of the Indies, appointed the Fleming Jean Sauvage chancellor, and made the Frenchman Guillaume de Croy, Seigneur de Chièvres, his chief adviser.[83] Juan Rodríguez Fonseca, bishop of Burgos, he kept as vice-president of the Council of the Indies and effective head of that organization.[84] No more greedy or less spiritual churchman than Fonseca ever lived, but he had intelligence, some learning in cosmographical matters, and a genuine attachment to the interests of Spain as he understood them. Though he had been consistently hostile to Christopher Columbus, he did not prove altogether so to Magellan and Faleiro, to whom for a time he was reasonably friendly.

Soon after Magellan arrived in Seville he found time for matrimony. About the end of the year 1517 he married Beatriz Barbosa, daughter of his host.[85] Magellan would have been about thirty-seven, but of the bride's age we have no knowledge beyond the fact that she was evidently older than her sister, Guiomar. She brought her husband a dowry of six hundred thousand maravedís, accompanied him on his journey to court, bore him a son, Rodrigo, and another child that was stillborn. She died in March 1522, before news came of her husband's death in battle in the Philippines. That is all we can say of Lady Beatriz, whose marriage to Magellan was evidently one of convenience to him. Her family was influential, and this fact certainly increased his importance in the eyes of the Spanish government he wished so much to impress. The dowry also proved very useful, though we know Magellan was reduced to borrowing money of Cristóbal de Haro before he finally sailed.

Faleiro, with his wife Eva Afonso and his brother Francisco, arrived in Seville in December 1517. The bachelor of arts exploded with anger when he learned that Magellan had revealed the essence of their plan to Aranda and other officials of the *Casa*. When reminded that the Castilians could hardly be expected to pay for a sea adventure without receiving some explanation of it, he calmed and consented to accompany Magellan and Aranda to Valladolid, where the king then resided. The three traveled to court with Beatriz early in 1518, the journey enlivened by a noisy argument between the partners and Aranda, who took this early occasion to demand a fifth of their profits provided he could persuade the king to pay for the expedition. Faleiro again staged a tantrum, and Magellan, who was chiefly interested in getting the voyage started, proposed a compromise of an eighth for Aranda.[86] This suggestion was first spurned by the factor, but at last they made him consent and drew up a legal agreement to that effect on reaching Valladolid.[87]

Aranda introduced his Portuguese friends first to Chancellor Sauvage and then to Bishop Fonseca, whose reaction to their proposal would determine whether it should be carried to the king himself.

Magellan and Faleiro talked fluently with the bishop and gave the appearance of being men who knew what they were about. Fonseca, very favorably impressed, advised them to write their plan in the form of a memoir, and in the meantime introduced them to Chièvres, who arranged for an audience with Charles. They soon saw the king, probably conversing through an interpreter, and showed him their memoir outlining the voyage they planned. The young monarch was greatly taken with their idea, especially as they displayed either a map or a globe to illustrate Magellan's arguments in support of his thesis that the Moluccas lay 2° 30′ across the oriental part of the line of demarcation in the Spanish zone.[88] Faleiro definitely had his part in this conversation, for he could talk the language of learning in a way that Magellan perhaps could not. Those who heard him invariably accepted his opinions on longitude, which was the crux of the whole plan. Regarding the strait which the voyagers must find in order to sail from the Atlantic into Balboa's recently discovered sea, there must have been considerable questioning by Charles and his advisers. We do not know exactly what Magellan and Faleiro said. Perhaps the map they displayed was a copy of the Behaim one, with its long peninsula stretching southward from Asia with a strait at the end.

Bartolomé de las Casas, the famous missionary and historian of the Indies, was in Valladolid at this time and saw both the Portuguese adventurers. He had a poor opinion of Faleiro, accepting the view that his bachelor's degree was faked and apparently agreeing with Castanheda that he owed his supposed learning to the familiar demon. Of Magellan, who had become a historical character of some fame by the time Las Casas wrote forty years later, the priest had a higher opinion. He recollected that

Magellan brought a well-painted globe, which showed all the earth, and there he pointed out the route to be followed, except that he left the strait purposely blank in order that no one might steal a march on him; and I found myself that day and hour in the grand chancellor's room when the bishop brought it in and showed the chancellor the voyage that was to take place. And, speaking with Magellan, I asked him what route he intended to follow, and he replied that he was going by way of Cape Santa Maria, which we now call the Río de la Plata, and that from there, following the coast, he thought he would run into the strait. Then I asked, "What if you do not find the strait through which you must pass to the other sea?" He replied that if he did not find it he would go by the route that the Portuguese followed.[89]

In other words, Magellan would round the Cape of Good Hope. If he talked thus freely to a comparative stranger like Las Casas, it is likely that he mentioned the same alternative to Bishop Fonseca and the other royal advisers. No one appears to have been shocked at this possible violation of the Treaty of Tordesillas.

FITTING OUT

The royal backing that Columbus had needed so many years to obtain came quickly and easily to Magellan and Faleiro. On March 22, 1518,

Charles issued a *Capitulación,* or contract, "to the Bachelor Rui Falero and Fernando de Magallanes, gentlemen, natives of the kingdom of Portugal." [90] He authorized an exploration to discover "that which until now has not been found within our demarcation." The king promised them a twentieth of the profits that might accrue and conceded them permission to take the titles of *adelantados* and governors of the lands discovered, with the right to pass these titles on to their heirs. He also undertook to fit out for them five ships—two of 130 tons, two of 90, and one of 60—with provisions for two years, a proper amount of artillery, and a total complement of 234 men. Orders to start preparations were immediately sent to the *Casa de Contratación* in Seville. At about the same time Charles issued supplementary warrants, defining the powers Faleiro and Magellan should have while in command of their fleet and guaranteeing each an annual salary of 50,-000 maravedís.[91]

When they saw these orders the members of the *Casa,* except for Aranda, protested that they had been bypassed and that this voyage, which fell under their legitimate jurisdiction, had been arranged for by the crown without consulting them.[92] The inexperienced Charles had probably acted in ignorance of the customary Spanish red tape. Now, to placate the touchy bureaucrats, he apologetically replied that the affair had seemed of such urgency as to require speed and that the bishop of Burgos would furnish any further details they required.[93]

The original schedule called for a sailing date of August 25, 1518, but when Magellan and Faleiro reached Seville they found nothing approaching readiness. The ships, which it was Aranda's duty to buy, were not even there, and the *Casa* members soon wrote the king that a departure in August was out of the question. Charles accordingly postponed the sailing until December and instructed the *Casa* to make the required expenditures with that month in mind.[94] The officials replied that, with all the good will in the world, they could do nothing without the necessary funds, a matter that appears to have been overlooked during the hasty drawing up of the *Capitulaciones* at Valladolid. Charles then began to scrape for cash and authorized the *Casa* to use six thousand ducats from a gold cargo that had just arrived from the island of Fernandina (Cuba).[95] This sum proving insufficient, the king issued a series of additional decrees, each one empowering the *Casa* to levy additional sums on bullion shipments coming from the Antilles.[96] Even so, Charles had forgotten a very important item—that of cargoes for trading purposes at the oriental destination of Magellan and Faleiro. When reminded of this, the Spanish monarch ceased relying on his own funds to equip the expedition and turned to private capital.

Men of wealth stood ready and eager to invest. One such was Cristóbal de Haro, who had financed the expedition to the Río de la Plata in 1514. Another was Alonso Gutiérrez of Madrid, and there appears to have been some investment by the house of Fugger in Augsburg, then headed by the Jacob Fugger who lent Charles of Spain the enormous sum he needed to bribe the electors of the Holy Roman Empire and gain the imperial crown.

The Haro family, Spanish in origin but with interests hitherto centered in Lisbon because of Portugal's lucrative oriental trade, now showed a willingness to transfer its main activities back to Spain. Cristóbal took the Castilian claim to the Moluccas quite seriously and was probably interested in Magellan's theory regarding the location of Tarshish and Ophir. He knew how Portuguese expeditions for the East were equipped, and he practically took charge of outfitting the Magellan fleet.[97] The total cost has been estimated at 8,334,335 maravedís, or 24,018 ducats, of which Cristóbal de Haro contributed 5,418 ducats.[98] Some of the Haro contribution went for urgently needed last-minute expenses without which the fleet could not sail. A great deal more went for merchandise which Portuguese experience proved could be profitably traded in the East: bars of copper, flasks of quicksilver, bolts of cheap cloth, bales of brilliantly dyed cotton cloth, and choice pieces of fabric for trade with the wealthier and more discriminating customers. Trinkets included 20,000 little bells, 10,000 fishhooks, 1,000 large and small looking glasses, an abundance of cheap German knives, and numerous brass and copper bracelets.[99]

Alonso Gutiérrez invested 420 ducats, and the

Fugger interests secretly advanced a sum unknown to us.[100] The Fugger share was made an off-the-record transaction because the family had important interests in Portugal and did not want to offend its government. These German capitalists later had trouble collecting the amount owed them, since no clear record seems to have been kept of the transaction. Several Spaniards appear to have put small amounts of cash into the enterprise. All investors except Haro were eventually bilked of the profits they hoped to win, because when El Cano's "Victoria" returned to Sanlúcar the king-emperor divided its cargo of spices with Cristóbal and with no one else.

Juan de Aranda finally acquired the five ships stipulated and had them brought to Seville for fitting out. King Manuel's agent in the city, Sebastião Alvares, scornfully wrote his master that they were very old and so worn out that he would not dare embark aboard them for the Canary Islands. "Their joints are made of soft wood," he added.[101] Obviously he exaggerated the deficiencies of these ships in view of the fact that one proved able to sail around the world, and two sailed most of the way around. The royal instructions regarding size had been obeyed almost to the letter. The "San Antonio" displaced 120 *toneles*; the "Trinidad," 110; the "Concepción," 90; the "Victoria," 85; and the "Santiago," 75.[102] As the Spanish word *tonel* referred to a weight somewhat heavier than our ton, the displacement of the "San Antonio" should be reckoned at 143 in modern terms and that of the other ships increased in the same proportion.

Much of the voyage would take place in waters which were unknown to the Spaniards but of which the Portuguese had some information. The carto-graphical bureau of the *Casa* could be of no help to Magellan and Faleiro, so they did some of the map work themselves, leaning heavily upon three Portu-guese, Pedro and Jorge Reinel and Diogo Ribeiro.[103] The Reinels were father and son, the elder, Pedro, being accounted the foremost map-maker of his time.[104] The son followed his father's profession and in 1519, dissatisfied (as so many were) with the service of King Manuel, he came to Seville and worked on a globe and planisphere for Magellan's use. The senior Reinel followed him there for a brief stay and evidently put on the finishing touches. There is no evidence that Pedro renounced Portugal; he was back there and at work within a few years, and he may even have done his map-drawing in Seville more in accordance with what Magellan wished than with what he himself be-lieved.

A planisphere in the Bayerische Armeebibli-othek at Munich is believed to be the work of Jorge Reinel in Seville in 1519.[105] It shows the Molucca Islands on the equator and almost due west of the Isthmus of Panama, which is placed too far to the south. The Moluccas, furthermore, are in the Span-ish zone according to the Treaty of Tordesillas, and they are not decorated with a flag bearing the

Portuguese coat of arms as are the other Portuguese possessions and discoveries, including some East Indian islands beyond Malacca. The South American coast comes to an end at Cape Santa Maria at the entrance to the Río de la Plata. It is hard to see how this planisphere could have been of much help to Magellan, for it showed pretty much what he already knew or chose to believe.

Magellan, with whatever help Faleiro could give, labored hard to prepare the ships for sea. But progress was slow, and the sailing date had to be postponed again and yet again. Alvaro da Costa, Portuguese ambassador at the court of Spain, then at Zaragoza, tried to dissuade Charles from using the services of Magellan and Faleiro, whom he described as a couple of malcontents. Failing to accomplish this, he suggested to Manuel that Magellan might be enticed back to Portugal. "It seems to me, Sire," he wrote, "that Your Highness should persuade Ferdinand Magellan to return, which would be a great blow to them here; as regards the bachelor no store should be set by him; he sleeps badly and has almost lost his mind." [106] Manuel, who had once thought of Magellan as a nobody, had changed his opinion when he saw him entrusted with a fleet for discovery. Impressed by Costa's idea, he summoned at Sintra a council composed of several grandees of his realm and asked their advice. The most extreme proposal came from the bishop of Lamego, who suggested that Magellan be coaxed back and then put to death.[107] The king decided not to ruin his own reputation by such open villainy, but he did instruct Alvares in Seville to use any means, fair or foul, to prevent the expedition from sailing.

Poor Magellan meanwhile had troubles enough of his own. While having the "Trinidad" careened for calking on the bank of the Guadalquivir, he had placed banners bearing his own coat of arms on the capstans that drew the ship ashore. This was correct and established maritime custom, but the watching crowd, thinking he was using the Portuguese flag, grew turbulent. A prudent Spanish official persuaded Magellan to remove his emblems in the interest of harmony. The shouters had grown quiet when another officer dashed up and demanded that the offending banners be handed over to him. As Magellan refused to comply, the hot-tempered official tried to arrest him, and a scuffle took place in which the pilot Juan Rodríguez de Mafra was wounded by water-front ruffians. Calm handling by the first officer finally dispersed the crowd before any damage was done to the ship.[108]

Alvares did his best to carry out the wishes of Manuel. Magellan had enlisted many Portuguese seamen because he considered them the best in the world, but Alvares spread a rumor that he meant to use them in an act of treason against Spain. When this malicious report reached the court, Charles was alarmed into ordering Magellan to reduce his Portuguese contingent.[109] Alvares next paid Magellan a secret call at his home, stressed the dangers of the impending voyage, and tried to coax him to return

to what he described as the safe and profitable service of the Portuguese ruler.[110] In a letter to Manuel
—in which Alvares may have lied just as he ad-
mitted lying to Magellan—he reported that Magellan, deeply moved, had said he would never do anything contrary to the interests of his former sovereign. But he saw no reason to leave King Charles,
who had shown him so many favors, and would do
so only if what had been promised him in the *Capitulaciones* should be withdrawn.

Alvares next tried his luck with Ruy Faleiro,
but reported that the bachelor merely reiterated
Magellan's refusal to abandon the ruler of Spain.
"He seems to me," reflected Alvares, "to be a man
troubled in spirit; that familiar demon of his appears to have deprived him of all wisdom, if he had
any before. I believe that if Ferdinand Magellan can
be moved, he will follow Magellan's lead." [111] But
the Portuguese agent knew he was beaten and could
only tell Manuel that he prayed God to give the two
partners "a voyage like that of the Côrte-Reals,[112] so
that Your Highness may remain unworried and the
envy of all princes, as is now the case."

Faleiro had deteriorated in physical and mental health since his first meeting with Magellan in
Portugal. When Costa and Alvares insisted that his
mind was giving way, they were exaggerating but
not altogether falsifying. Faleiro proved almost useless in the arduous work of preparing the ships for
the voyage and showed no talent for command or
leadership. He constantly nagged Magellan and

grew so touchy about each imagined slight to his authority that he objected to every small decision made without consulting him., Bishop Fonseca wished to get him out of the way, either because he feared Faleiro would ruin any ship committed to his charge or because he had grown uneasy about the strongly Portuguese character of this expedition under the Spanish flag. With the vessels almost ready for sea, a royal *cédula* of July 26, 1519, ordered that Faleiro should not sail with the fleet and that his place should be taken by the Spaniard Juan de Cartagena.[113] Andrés de San Martín took over the portion of his duties that involved piloting. As the original *Capitulación* had been issued as much to Faleiro as to Magellan, the king created busy work for the astronomer by saying that he should superintend preparations for the next Spanish expedition to the Moluccas. The bachelor made no recorded protest at being left behind, and some authorities have suggested that as the departure date approached he grew afraid. Castanheda says, with what sounds like sarcasm but probably is not, "This astrologer [Andrés de San Martín] went with Magellan because at the time of departure Ruy Faleiro begged off from going: it seems he learned from his familiar how badly that voyage would turn out for those making it."[114]

Whatever other considerations may have been involved, Faleiro was shelved principally because the Spanish authorities did not consider him up to the task ahead. He fell seriously ill just after the fleet sailed and was abandoned by both his wife and his father as a result of a family quarrel. On his return to Portugal the king had him seized and imprisoned, presumably for treason. His brother Francisco remained faithful, perhaps because Ruy still had claims against the Spanish crown. When released from his Portuguese prison, the bachelor returned to Castile. He spent the rest of his life, which lasted until at least 1544, appealing either in person or through Francisco for the salary promised him in the original *Capitulacion*.[115]

Juan de Cartagena, who now received the appointment as conjoint person (*conjunta persona*) [116] in authority, is the villain of the Magellan epic to most historians. He considered himself co-commander of the fleet, and though it is not certain that Charles had quite that idea in mind,[117] Bishop Fonseca evidently had. Cartagena believed it his first duty to look out for Spanish interests and keep a tight rein on the untrustworthy Portuguese who held so many responsible positions aboard. Owing to Charles's recent arrival with his greedy throng of alien favorites, Spaniards regarded foreigners very sourly just then. Cartagena disliked Magellan from the start. Magellan refused to treat him as an equal. He gave Cartagena no share, beyond routine duties, in the direction of the expedition. Above all, he refused to explain how he expected to reach the Spice Islands, an attitude that exasperated the *conjunta* and other Spanish officers. In history Magellan rightly appears as a great hero, but his officials were not thinking of history as they tried to pry information from him during their southward voyage through the Atlantic and down the South American coast. They could make no sense of the expedition, and Magellan, when questioned, would only issue blunt orders and let them know it was not theirs to reason why. The mutiny of San Julián started to brew almost as the fleet left Spain, and we do not have to place the sole blame, as some writers do, on the malevolent influence of Bishop Fonseca upon the Spanish officers. The leader helped bring it about by his stubborn aloofness, and could likely have prevented it by a more frank and cooperative attitude. Could Juan de Cartagena have escaped from the Patagonian wasteland where Magellan marooned him and returned to Spain, he might have had a great deal to say that would have sounded reasonable. His remarks would have been much like those El Cano actually made before Alcalde Leguizamo at Valladolid, and they were not the remarks of a jealous mutineer.[118]

The *cédula* ousting Faleiro in favor of Cartagena also ordered Magellan to dismiss nearly all the Portuguese in the fleet. (The previous order, issued a month earlier, had reduced the number to no more than eight or ten.)[119] "At the time they were accepted," said the order, "it was because of the shortage of men; but now there are plenty of seamen available: I order you to see to it that these [Portuguese] do not go in this fleet."[120] When the *Casa* made this decree known to Magellan, he pro-

tested that his original *Capitulación* had imposed
no such limitation and pointed out many bad results
that would come of last-minute changes in person-
nel. The king weakened somewhat and allowed him
to take ten or twelve Portuguese, but in reality more
than thirty finally embarked.[121]

As nearly as can be determined, Magellan
sailed with 241 men.[122] Besides Spaniards and Portuguese, they included Italians, Frenchmen, Germans,
Flemings, Greeks, an Englishman, and two Malay-
ans, including the leader's slave Henry. Several
monks went to act as chaplains during the voyage
and as missionaries to the heathen later on. Magellan took various blood relatives and relatives by
marriage, including his wife's cousin Duarte.
Though Duarte had no post of command at first and
behaved so badly with the Indians in Rio de Janeiro
Bay that he was placed in irons, he redeemed himself in the San Julián mutiny and received command of the "Victoria." The most important pas-
senger the fleet carried was Antonio Pigafetta, future historian of the expedition, who appears on
the rolls as Antonio Lombardo.

Magellan commanded the "Trinidad" in person. Juan de Cartagena had charge of the "San Antonio," with the new astronomer Andrés de San
Martín as pilot. Gaspar de Quesada had the "Concepción," in which Juan Sebastián del Cano sailed
as mate; Luís de Mendoza commanded the "Victoria"; and Juan Rodríguez Serrano, often mistakenly considered a Portuguese and taken for the

brother of Francisco Serrão of Ternate, had the "Santiago." [123] This arrangement underwent frequent alterations during the voyage, owing to the mutiny and deaths among the commanding officers.

In the eyes of the Spanish government the Magellan enterprise was not an isolated effort but part of a double undertaking. Even as Magellan put the finishing touches to his preparations, Gil González Dávila and Andrés Niño departed from Sanlúcar to undertake a piece of exploration that was regarded as equally important. The starting point would be the Panama isthmus, from which they would explore the shores of Balboa's sea with the purpose of locating the Spice Islands. The king instructed González and Niño to follow the coast beyond Panama by sea or land for one thousand leagues, which should be far enough to familiarize them with the *Magnus Sinus*, in which the Moluccas were presumably located.[124] They should also look for a channel between the *Sinus,* or Balboa's *Mar del Sur,* and the Atlantic. Recent Spanish explorations in search of a strait, though discouraging, had not altogether killed the prospect.

González and Niño reached the isthmus and quarreled with Pedrarias Dávila, the governor who had recently executed Balboa. The partners brought a royal order obliging him to hand over the ships constructed by Balboa on the Pacific side of the isthmus. Pedrarias refused to do so, and as they had no means of coercing him, they built their own vessels, which required two years.[125] In January

1522 they embarked from Pearl Island, near Panama City, and explored the coast westward, turning north as Central America bent in that direction. Their principal discovery was Nicaragua and the inland lake of that name, originally called Cocibolca and rechristened by them in honor of the nearby Indian cacique, Nicoraguamia, or Nicarao.[126] They coasted as far as Fonseca Gulf, which they named for the Bishop of Burgos and took to be the entrance to a strait leading to the Atlantic. The deteriorating condition of their ships compelled them to return to Panama by the Pacific, confident that the water passage they thought they had found more than compensated for their failure to explore the *Sinus* farther.

Magellan meanwhile had gone through the official ceremony of departure at Seville. The church of Santa Maria de la Victoria in the Triana suburb was filled with crew members and interested onlookers. The king, now Charles V of the Holy Roman Empire, sent the leader a standard that was presented by the corregidor of Seville, Sancho Martínez de Leiva, as Magellan knelt before an image of the Virgin Mary.[127] He swore fidelity to Charles, and the other officers bound themselves to follow and obey Magellan. The fleet left the Seville moorings on August 10, 1519, and dropped down the Guadalquivir to Sanlúcar de Barrameda on the Atlantic. Here the ships remained for more than a month, and Magellan several times visited his family in Seville. On one of these last-minute visits he made his final will and testament, bequeathing most of what he had to his six-months-old son Rodrigo and making alternate arrangements in case Rodrigo should die in childhood.[128] Finally, on September 20, 1519, the fleet weighed anchor for the Canaries, and the great voyage began.

At this point Pigafetta takes up the story. In general he tells it well, and we shall interrupt him only when his remarks or omissions require elucidation.

Notes

1. *Magellan's Voyage around the World by Antonio Pigafetta,* 3 vols., Cleveland, 1906. Hereinafter cited as *Magellan's
Voyage.*
   2. *Raccolta di documenti e studi pubblicati dalla R. Com-
missione Colombiana,* Rome, 1894. Part V., Vol. III, 51–131.
Hereinafter cited as *Raccolta Colombiana.*
   3. *Il primo viaggio intorno al mondo,* ed. Camillo Manfroni,
Milan, 1956. Hereinafter cited as *Primo viaggio.*
   4. Fernão Lopes de Castanheda, *Historia do descobrimento e
conquista da India pelos portugueses,* 8 vols., Lisbon, 1833; hereinafter cited as Castanheda; first published 1551; João de Barros,
Asia, ed. Hernani Cidade and Manuel Múrias, 4 vols., Lisbon
1945–46; hereinafter cited as Barros; first published 1552–63.
Damião de Goís, *Crónica do felicissimo rei D. Manuel,* 4 vols.,
Coimbra, 1926; hereinafter cited as Góis; first published 1556.
António Galvão, *Tratado dos descobrimentos,* Oporto, 1944; first
published 1563.
   5. Castanheda, VI, 8; Barros, III, 282–83; Góis, IV, 83–84.
   6. Martín Fernández de Navarrete, *Colección de los viages
y descubrimientos que hicieron por mar los españoles desde fines
del siglo xv,* 2d. ed., 5 vols., Buenos Aires, 1946, IV, 259–64.
Hereinafter cited as Navarrete, *Colección.*
   7. *De orbe novo. The Eight Books of Peter Martyr d'Anghera,*
transl. and ed. Francis Augustus MacNutt, 2 vols., New York and
London, 1912.
   8. Jean Denucé, *Magellan: La question des Moluques et la
première circumnavigation du globe,* Brussels, 1911; hereinafter
cited as Denucé, *Magellan. José Toribio Medina, El descubrimiento del Océano Pacífico,* 4 vols., Santiago de Chile, 1914–20;
hereinafter cited as Medina. Viscount de Lagôa, *Fernão de Magalhães (a sua vida e a sua viagem),* 2 vols., Lisbon, 1938; hereinafter cited as Lagôa; Portuguese translation of Pigafetta, II, 11–215.

71

Introduction

José Maria de Queiroz Velloso, "Fernão de Magalhães: sa vie et son voyage," *Revue d'histoire moderne*, XIV, 1939, 417–515; hereinafter cited as Queiroz Velloso. Charles McKew Parr, *So Noble a Captain: The Life and Times of Ferdinand Magellan*, New York, 1953.

9. Charles E. Nowell, "The Treaty of Tordesillas and the Diplomatic Background of American History," *Greater America: Essays in Honor of Herbert Eugene Bolton*, Berkeley and Los Angeles, 1945, p. 2.

10. Manuel Giménez Fernández, *Las bulas alejandrinas de 1493 referentes a las Indias*, Seville, 1944, pp. 182–83. The line the pope drew was a geographical impossibility, as the Azores lie west of the Cape Verdes.

11. Spanish text in Giménez Fernández, pp. 214–31. Also Navarrete, *Colección*, II, 156–71.

12. *The Travels of Ludovico di Varthema in Egypt, Syria, Arabia Deserta and Arabia Felix, in Persia, India and Ethiopia* A.D. *1503 to 1508*, transl. John Winter Jones, ed. George Percy Badger, London, Hakluyt Society, 1868, pp. 243–46. This version had Varthema writing of the Moluccas and Bandas as an eyewitness, but it is now believed that he visited neither group.

13. Galvão, *Tratado*, pp. 369–70.

14. Amando Melón y Ruiz de Gordejuela, *Los primeros tiempos de la colonización; Cuba y las Antillas: Magallanes y la primera vuelta al mundo*, Barcelona, Madrid, Buenos Aires, Mexico, Rio de Janeiro, 1952, p. 324. Hereinafter cited as Melón.

15. Nowell, "The Discovery of the Pacific: A Suggested Change of Approach," *Pacific Historical Review*, XVI, 1947, 6–7.

16. Galvão, *Tratado*, p. 171, footnote 4.

17. A ruler, Marham, who died in 1486, seems to have partially embraced Islam before the end of his reign. His successor, Zainalabdan, became a full-fledged Moslem. John Crawfurd, *History of the Indian Archipelago*, 3 vols., Edinburgh, 1820, II, 487–88.

18. Denucé, *Magellan*, p. 124.

19. A. Braancamp Freire, "Ementa da Casa da India," *Boletim da Sociedade de Geografia de Lisboa*, XXV, 1907, 236–38.

20. Barros, III, 272. Magellan, however, evidently came to distrust Serrão's statements with respect to the Moluccas. In a final letter to the king of Spain, just before beginning his great voyage, he considerably lessened their distance from Malacca. Navarrete, *Colección*, IV, 173–74; Lagôa, I, 76.

21. Barros, III, 282.

22. Queiroz Velloso, p. 433.

23. Denucé, *Magellan*, p. 126.

24. *Ibid.*, p. 127.

25. Navarrete, *Colección*, IV, 201; *Primo viaggio*, p. 197.

Magellan's Voyage Around the World

26. *Primo viaggio,* p. 197.

27. *The Book of Duarte Barbosa,* transl. and ed. Mansel Longworth Dames, London, Hakluyt Society, 1921, II, 216.

28. Medina, III, cccl–liii.

29. Denucé, "Les Îles Lequois (Formose et Riu-Kiu) et Ophir," *Bulletin de la Société Royale Belge de Géographie,* XXXI, 1907, 438.

30. "Livro de Duarte Barbosa," *Collecção de noticias para a historia e geografia das nações ultramarinas que vivem nos dominios portuguezes,* II, Lisbon, 1867, 375.

31. Medina, *El veneciano Sebastián Caboto al servicio de España,* 2 vols., Santiago de Chile, 1908, I, 421. There are frequent references to Tarshish and Ophir in the Cabot documents.

32. Roberto Levillier, *América la bien llamada,* 2 vols., Buenos Aires, 1948, II, 333.

33. Américo Vespucio. *El nuevo mundo: cartas relativas a sus viajes y descubrimientos,* ed. Roberto Levillier, Buenos Aires, 1951, p. 333.

34. *Ibid.,* p. 299.

35. Konrad Haebler, "Die 'Neuwe Zeitung aus Presilig-Land' im Fürstlich Fugger'schen Archiv," *Zeitschrift der Gesellschaft für Erdkunde zu Berlin,* XXX, 1895, 352–68; Denucé, *Magellan,* p. 75.

36. *Ibid.*

37. A sketch of the South American part of the Schöner globe is shown in Medina, III, lxii.

38. Navarrete, *Colección,* III, 147–48.

39. Denucé, *Magellan,* p. 80.

40. Medina, III, lxiv.

41. Medina, *Juan Díaz de Solís, estudio histórico,* 2 vols., Santiago de Chile, 1897, I, ccxciv.

42. Roberto Almagià, *I primi esploratori dell' America,* Rome, 1937, pp. 328 ff.

43. Bernal Díaz del Castillo, *The Discovery and Conquest of Mexico, 1517–1521,* transl. and ed. A. P. Maudslay, introduction Irving A. Leonard, New York, 1956, pp. 4–16. First published 1632.

44. *Ibid.,* pp. 17–28.

45. *Ibid.,* pp. 31–32.

46. Almagià, *Primi esploratori,* p. 306.

47. Samuel Eliot Morison, *Portuguese Voyages to America in the Fifteenth Century,* Cambridge, Mass., 1940, pp. 68–72, 51–68.

48. Navarrete, *Colección,* III, 160.

49. The story of the eleven thousand virgins is connected with the career of St. Ursula of Cologne, whose legend probably dates from the third century. Details of the story will be found in holy writings devoted to her.

50. *Historia de las Indias*, ed. Agustín Millares Carlo, 3 vols., Mexico, Buenos Aires, 1951, III, 175. First published 1875.

51. The leading work on Behaim is Ernest G. Ravenstein, *Martin Behaim, His Life and His Globe*, London, 1908.

52. Probably not to Columbus, as some have thought. Almagià, *Primi esploratori*, p. 64.

53. A planisphere was a world map, in contrast to the portolanic, or harbor-finding, charts that closely mapped limited stretches of coast, especially in the Mediterranean. See illustration, page 33.

54. Ravenstein, *Behaim*, p. 86.

55. Waldseemüller did this on a map made in 1507 at St. Dié in Lorraine. For a more extensive description of the Magellan plan, see George Emra Nunn, *The Columbus and Magellan Concepts of South American Geography*, Glenside, 1932, pp. 43–58. Also Nunn, *Origin of the Strait of Anian Concept*, Philadelphia, 1929, pp. 10–13.

56. Queiroz Velloso, pp. 419, 424.

57. *Ibid.*, pp. 417–18.

58. Barros, I, 309.

59. See note 19.

60. Barros, II, 131 ff; Queiroz Velloso, p. 426; Frederick Charles Danvers, *The Portuguese in India*, 2 vols., London, 1894, I, 141. The name Rumes was given in India to a certain caste of Turks sent by the sultan of Egypt to battle the Portuguese.

61. Denucé, *Magellan*, p. 104.

62. *Ibid.*, p. 105.

63. Castanheda, II, 358.

64. Lagôa, I, 131.

65. Castanheda, II, 370.

66. Denucé, *Magellan*, p. 108–9.

67. *Ibid.*, p. 110, footnote 5; Lagôa, I, 140; Medina III, xxiii, footnote 14.

68. Barros, II, 260–81.

69. Queiroz Velloso, p. 432.

70. Denucé, *Magellan*, p. 119; E. T. Hamy, "L'Oeuvre géographique des Reinel et la découverte des Moluques," *Bulletin de Géographie Historique et Descriptive*, VI, 1892, 141.

71. Parr, *So Noble a Captain*, p. 114.

72. Denucé, *Magellan*, p. 113.

73. Queiroz Velloso, p. 434. Magellan eventually received payment for the horse.

74. *Ibid.*, p. 435.

75. Parr, *So Noble a Captain*, p. 146.

76. Góis, IV, 84.

77. Queiroz Velloso, pp. 440–41. Lagôa (I, 215) prints an un-

dated document issued by King Manuel ordering that all property of pilots deserting their country be confiscated and that they be exiled to the island of St. Helena. If Corrêa is correct in saying the king gave Magellan permission to enter foreign service, Manuel must have spoken in a fit of temper.

78. Castanheda, VI, 9.
79. Denucé, *Magellan*, p. 141.
80. For instance, in the royal Spanish award making both men captains of the fleet, Faleiro's name appears first. Navarrete, *Colección*, IV, 113.
81. Parr, *So Noble a Captain*, pp. 148–49.
82. Melón, p. 510.
83. *Ibid.*, p. 516; Roger Bigelow Merriman, *The Rise of the Spanish Empire in the Old World and the New*, 4 vols., New York, 1918–1934, III, 33; *ibid.*, p. 12.
84. Melón, p. 516.
85. Medina, III, c.
86. Melón, p. 512.
87. Navarrete, *Colección*, IV, 103–6. Aranda had been guilty of an illegal act in forcing this agreement from Faleiro and Magellan. When the Council of the Indies learned of the transaction, it was abrogated.
88. The memoir in question is evidently the one dated March (no day given) 1518, and printed by Navarrete, *Colección*, IV, 106–8.
89. *Historia de las Indias*, III, 175.
90. Navarrete, *Colección*, IV, 109–13. Faleiro's name appears first, and both names are altered from the Portuguese to the Spanish form.
91. *Ibid.*, IV, 113–14: *Denucé*, Magellan, p. 188.
92. Queiroz Velloso, p. 446.
93. *Ibid.*
94. *Ibid.*
95. Navarrete, *Colección*, IV, 114–15.
96. Queiroz Velloso, p. 446.
97. Denucé, *Magellan*, pp. 209–19.
98. *Ibid.*, p. 215.
99. Parr, *So Noble a Captain*, p. 252.
100. Denucé, *Magellan*, pp. 216–17. We also know that Gutiérrez' part of the cargo consisted of quicksilver and vermilion. Medina, IV, 56.
101. *Alguns documentos do Archivo Nacional da Tôrre do Tombo ácerca das navegações e conquistas portuguezas*, ed. José Ramos-Coelho, Lisbon, 1892, p. 433. Hereinafter cited as *Alguns Documentos*.
102. Medina, III, cxli.

Introduction

103. *Alguns documentos,* p. 434; Armando Cortesão, *Cartografia e cartógrafos portugueses dos séculos xv e xvi,* 2 vols., Lisbon, 1935, I, 251–59.

104. *Ibid.,* 249.

105. *Ibid.,* II, estampa V.

106. Navarrete, *Colección,* IV, 115.

107. Góis, IV, 84.

108. Queiroz Velloso, pp. 448–49. Antonio de Herrera y Tordesillas, *Historia general de los hechos de los castellanos en las islas, y tierra firme de el mar océano,* 17 vols., Asunción, 1944, III, 77; hereinafter cited as Herrera; first published 1601–15.

109. Queiroz Velloso, p. 454.

110. *Alguns documentos,* p. 431.

111. *Ibid.,* p. 435.

112. Meaning he hoped they would disappear in the ocean as had the Côrte-Reals. See Morison, *Portuguese Voyages,* p. 71.

113. Navarrete, *Colección,* IV, 144–49.

114. Castanheda, VI, 9.

115. Denucé, *Magellan,* pp. 234–36.

116. Navarrete, *Colección,* IV, 144.

117. For example, the other leaders of the expedition, apparently by royal order, took an oath to follow Magellan wherever he might lead. Herrera, III, 78.

118. Navarrete, *Colección,* IV, 259–64.

119. *Ibid.,* p. 148.

120. *Ibid.*

121. Denucé, *Magellan,* p. 143. Lagôa (I, 266–67) says there were more than forty, but his claims of Portuguese nationality for some seamen are doubtful.

122. Queiroz Velloso, p. 464.

123. This Juan Serrano is still taken by many writers for a Portuguese, but Medina shows (III, ccccxli), on the testimony of Castanheda (VI, 10), that he was a Spaniard. Pigafetta also calls him Spanish.

124. Pablo Alvarez Rubiano, *Pedrarias Dávila,* Madrid, 1944, p. 322; Herrera, III, 52.

125. Alvarez Rubiano, *Pedrarias,* p. 321; Herrera, IV, 199.

126. Alvarez Rubiano, *Pedrarias,* p. 323.

127. Queiroz Velloso, p. 463.

128. Denucé, *Magellan,* pp. 253–54.

Three Accounts
of the Voyage

Antonio Pigafetta

This firsthand chronicler of the Magellan expedition has been much investigated, but except for what we know of him during the voyage few details of his life survive.[1] He was born at Vicenza, in the territory of Venice, of a family that had moved there from Florence in the eleventh century. The name was properly Plegafeta, which Antonio himself modified to Pagafetta, later changing the spelling to the familiar Pigafetta.[2] The family was noble and possessed a coat of arms consisting of a silver band across a black field, with three golden roses, one on the band and two on the field. At the end of the nineteenth century the Pigafetta family still possessed a house in Vicenza, a three-story dwelling that had certainly been there in Antonio's time. On the façade was carved the familiar motto *"Il nest rose sans espine"* ("There is no rose without thorns"). Some have said that Antonio the voyager had the motto inscribed there in allusion to the glory of his trip around the world and the hardships that accompanied it. On the other hand, it may refer only to the roses on the family escutcheon.

The date of Pigafetta's birth is not recorded in any document now known, and conjectures range between 1480 and 1491. Our reason for preferring the latter date is that, from various evidences, he appears to have been rather young when he sailed with Magellan, and an age of about

[1] Except when otherwise noted, the facts here presented about Pigafetta are taken from Andrea da Mosto, "Vita di Antonio Pigafetta," *Raccolta Colombiana*, V, III, 13–47.
[2] Medina, III, ccccxxi.

thirty seems more suitable for him than one of around forty.[3]

The parents of this chronicler are hard to identify, and he does not fit well into the genealogical pattern of the family. This could mean that he was born out of wedlock, but he became a member of the Knights of Rhodes (later Malta), and it would have been almost impossible for him to join that order without a legitimate family tree. A plausible father for him might be Antonio Alessandro Pigafetta, or Plegafetta, who died in 1509 leaving a son Giovanni Antonio, a minor. If these are the people we seek, the birth date 1491 becomes still more likely.

There is a story, possibly true, that at an early age Pigafetta went roving and sailed the Mediterranean in the galleys of the Knights of Rhodes. It seems to be based on the fact that he later became a member of the order, though no one can say whether he joined it before or after the voyage around the world. What we do know, from his own statement, is that he was at the court of Spain in 1519 as gentleman in waiting to Monsignor Francesco Chieregati, "then apostolic protonotary and nuncio of Pope Leo X." How long he had been in the service of this prelate we cannot say, very likely since the previous year when Chieregati had returned to Italy from a trip to England. The Spanish court remained at Zaragoza for two months and then moved to Barcelona, the protonotary and Pigafetta moving with it. Antonio now learned, if he had not heard before, of the great voyage Magellan was preparing to undertake. Having read books on the subject of overseas exploration and wishing "to experience and go to see these things for myself," he obtained permission from King Charles and Chieregati to join the expedition. He went from Barcelona to Malaga by ship and from there by land to Seville. We do not know how Magellan felt when this green young Italian presented himself with a royal order to be taken along, but

[3] For instance, he says he was never sick a day during the voyage. Furthermore, the nature of his employment by Monsignor Chieregati suggests he was young.

he of course accepted him and later came to esteem him highly. As to Pigafetta's exact place in the expedition, we know that under the name "Antonio Lombardo" he was enrolled among the *criados del capitán y sobresalientes* ("servants of the captain and supernumeraries"), which seems to mean that he was without specific duties other than to be at Magellan's disposal for such purposes as fighting and boarding.

During the voyage Pigafetta carefully noted, or thought he was noting, everything of interest that occurred. He was not much of a navigator and is of little help in informing us where the expedition was in times when it sailed the open seas. A treatise that he wrote on the subject of navigation is of small value and would have been a laughing matter to such men as El Cano or Francisco Albo. But like Marco Polo before him he possessed the gift of careful and accurate observation and a great interest in human beings of all races. His vocabularies of the Patagonian and Malayan languages are still of some interest to scholars, and he evidently gained enough speaking knowledge of basic Malayan to be of use as an interpreter after the expedition lost Magellan's slave Henry. His total lack of prudery makes him sound crude when describing some of the ways and antics of various natives, but in the interest of accuracy we would not wish him otherwise. Regarding things he had not seen and places he had not visited, he could swallow tall tales of the Sindbad variety, but he shared this gullibility with many travelers of his time.

He came to idolize Magellan, and his words "so noble a captain," in homage to the fallen hero, have been made the title of a recent book dealing with the voyage. His aversion to El Cano is hard to understand in full, especially since Magellan's archenemy Juan de Cartagena almost escapes his notice. The fact that Juan Sebastián took part in the San Julián mutiny hardly seems cause enough, for scores of others took part without incurring Pigafetta's undying hostility. There must have been bad blood between the two men for reasons that do not appear in any of the narratives or documents. Perhaps Magellan, himself a foreigner and aware that many of the Spaniards in the fleet disliked him, favored the foreign element in his company and made a special protégé of Pigafetta. With the ascendancy of gruff and severe El Cano, the Spanish element in the expedition finally took control. The new leader probably regarded the more cultured Italian as a toady of the deceased Magellan, and during the long homeward voyage in the "Victoria" he must have had many opportunities to let Pigafetta know how he felt.

Once back in Spain, when El Cano chose Albo and Bustamante to accompany him to Valladolid for the audience with the king-emperor, Pigafetta made haste to go there on his own initiative. He had, as he says, neither gold nor silver to give to the monarch but something more valuable, his day-to-day account of the voyage. We must not consider this the narrative that has come to us but rather the notes he had made, since we know he wrote up the full account later. When he writes of giving his manuscript to the king he must be speaking figuratively, for he could hardly have kept the notes in duplicate and would need them later on in the preparation of his book. In all probability he offered Charles and other listeners who were there a verbal account of the most interesting highlights. If he had had time to write anything in proper style since the "Victoria's" return, he may have lent or given this manuscript to Peter Martyr to be used in the preparation of the priest's own work.

From the court of Charles, Pigafetta proceeded to Lisbon to tell King John III, who had succeeded Manuel on the throne in 1521, the story of the expedition. He must have interested his royal hearer, but it would be strange if he met with a very cordial reception after having taken part in a voyage that was apparently so detrimental to Portuguese interests. John's court may have been encouraged, however, to learn about the length and difficulty of the voyage to the Moluccas by way of Magellan's strait.

After a brief return to Spain, Pigafetta went to France to see Maria Luisa of Savoy, mother of Francis I and a noted patron of learning. She listened with interest to his story, which he must have been rather used to reciting by now, and he presented her with "a few things from the other hemisphere." That he gave her a copy of his manuscript, as some have thought, cannot be true, for he had traveled at a great rate ever since arriving at Sanlúcar and could not have had time to make, or have made, all the copies accredited to him.

In January 1523 Pigafetta was back in his native Italy, telling his story first at the court of Mantua and then to the doge and council of Venice. Apparently he promised the Marquis of Mantua, Federico II, to put the *Relazione* into finished form and was engaged in this task at his home in Vicenza when a letter came from the newly elected pope, Clement VII, asking him to come to Rome. Although Pigafetta had not finished his work, he went. On the way he met the grand master of the Knights of Rhodes, Philippe Villiers l'Ile-Adam, of whose order he may have become a member before embarking with Magellan. He talked with the grand master about the account of the voyage, received encouragement, and ultimately dedicated the work to him. About the interview with the pope we know nothing except that it took place and that he said "many things marvelous to contemporaries and worthy of being known to posterity." Pigafetta entered the service of Clement VII but did not remain in it long, because the pay was meager and the pope seemed to lose interest in his original agreement to publish the book. He thought of now offering his services to the Marquis of Mantua, and the bearer of his letter of inquiry to that nobleman was the famous Baldassare Castiglione, author of *Il Cortegiano*. Pigafetta did not take employment with Federico, but the two remained friendly, and the marquis, through his ambassador Giovanni Malatesta, recommended to Doge Andrea Gritti of Venice the publication of the book in that city. Malatesta served Pigafetta well and secured for him a copyright of twenty years' duration. He also found a Venetian printer willing to undertake the work and to share expenses at fifteen ducats apiece with the understanding that the profits would be equally divided.

Antonio Pigafetta

At this point we lose all trace of the transaction and can only say that it fell through, because no publication was forthcoming. The first printed edition of Pigafetta was a French translation appearing in Paris about 1525 with the title *Le voyage et nauigation, faict par les Espaignolz es Isles Mollucques,* and this is only a summary. As it does not bear the name of the author, we are safe in saying that Pigafetta had nothing to do with it. The first Italian version appeared in 1536, by which time the author may well have been dead. Dead or alive, he would have disdained any connection with this publication, which is nothing but the earlier Paris edition translated back into Italian.

Pigafetta was a Knight of Rhodes by 1523, when a document refers to him as such, though this does not exclude the possibility that he may have been one before the Magellan voyage. But as the knights at this time did not have to go through a novitiate and as Grand Master Ile-Adam straightway showed great interest in him, the slender evidence points to his initiation after the great expedition.

Here his career stops, as far as reliable history is concerned. Assertions are made that he fought in several campaigns against the Turks; others, that he took part in only one, in the year 1536, and then returned to end his days in Vicenza. Still another conjecture, again without evidence, is that he died on the island of Malta, which several years after the conquest of Rhodes by the Turks became the stronghold of his order. The only agreement we can find between history and tradition is that Pigafetta, for all his health and vigor during the voyage, did not live a long life.

First Voyage
Around the World

Antonio Pigafeta, patrician of Venezia and knight of Rhodi, to the most illustrious and excellent Lord, Philipo de Villers Lisleadam, renowned grand master of Rhoddi, his most honored lord.[4]

Inasmuch as, most illustrious and excellent Lord, there are many curious persons who not only take pleasure in knowing and hearing the great and wonderful things which God has permitted me to see and suffer during my long and dangerous voyage, hereto appended, but who also wish to know the means and manners and paths that I have taken in making that voyage; and who do not lend that entire faith to the end unless they have a perfect assurance of the beginning: therefore, your most illustrious Lordship must know that, finding myself, in the year of the nativity of our Savior MCCCCCXIX in Spagnia, in the court of the most serene king of the Romans, with the reverend Monsignor, Francesco

[4] The grand master was Philippe Villiers l'Ile-Adam (1464–34). After the expulsion of his knightly order from Rhodes in 1523 and before its relocation in Malta in 1530, Villiers maintained temporary headquarters in Italy.

85

Chieregato, then apostolic protonotary and nuncio of Pope Leo X of holy memory (and who has since become bishop of Aprutino and prince of Teramo), and having learned many things from many books that I had read, as well as from various persons, who discussed the great and marvelous things of the Ocean Sea with his Lordship, I determined, by the good favor of his Caesarean Majesty, and of his Lordship abovesaid, to experience and to go to see those things for myself, so that I might be able thereby to satisfy myself somewhat, and so that I might be able to gain some renown for later posterity. Having heard that a fleet composed of five vessels had been fitted out in the city of Siviglia for the purpose of going to discover the spicery in the islands of Maluco, under command of Captain-general Fernando de Magaglianes, a Portuguese gentleman, comendador of the [Order of] Santo Jacobo de la Spada, [who] had many times traversed the Ocean Sea in various directions, whence he had acquired great praise, I set out from the city of Barsalonna, where his Majesty was then residing, bearing many letters in my favor. I went by ship as far as Malega, where, taking the highroad, I went overland to Siviglia. Having been there about three full months, waiting for the said fleet to be set in order for the departure, finally, as your most excellent Lordship will learn below, we commenced our voyage under most happy auspices. And inasmuch as when I was in Ytalia and going to see his Holiness, Pope Clement, you by your grace showed yourself very kind and good to

86

me at Monteroso, and told me that you would be greatly pleased if I would write down for you all those things which I had seen and suffered during my voyage; and although I have had little opportunity, yet I have tried to satisfy your desire according to my poor ability; therefore, I offer you, in this little book of mine, all my vigils, hardships, and wanderings, begging you, although you are busied with continual Rhodian cares, to deign to skim through it, by which I shall be enabled to receive a not slight remuneration from your most illustrious Lordship, to whose good favor I consign and commend myself.

The captain-general having resolved to make so long a voyage through the Ocean Sea, where furious winds and great storms are always reigning, but not desiring to make known to any of his men the voyage that he was about to make, so that they might not be cast down at the thought of doing so great and extraordinary a deed, as he did accomplish with the aid of God (the captains who accompanied him, hated him exceedingly, I know not why, unless because he was a Portuguese, and they Spaniards), with the desire to conclude what he promised under oath to the emperor, Don Carlo, king of Spagnia, prescribed the following orders and gave them to all the pilots and masters of his ships, so that the ships might not become separated from one another during the storms and night. These were [to the effect] that he would always precede the other ships at night, and they were to follow his ship which would have a large

torch of wood, which they call *farol*. He always carried that *farol* set at the poop of his ship as a signal
so that they might always follow him. Another light
was made by means of a lantern or by means of a
piece of wicking made from a rush and called *sparto*
rope which is well beaten in the water, and then
dried in the sun or in the smoke—a most excellent
material for such use. They were to answer him so
that he might know by that signal whether all of the
ships were coming together. If he showed two lights
besides that of the *farol*, they were to veer or take
another tack, [doing this] when the wind was not
favorable or suitable for us to continue on our way,
or when he wished to sail slowly. If he showed three
lights, they were to lower away the bonnet-sail,
which is a part of the sail that is fastened below the
mainsail, when the weather is suitable for making
better time. It is lowered so that it may be easier to
furl the mainsail when it is struck hastily during a
sudden squall. If he showed four lights, they were to
strike all the sails; after which he showed a signal by
one light, [which meant] that he was standing still.
If he showed a greater number of lights, or fired a
mortar, it was a signal of land or of shoals. Then he
showed four lights when he wished to have the sails
set full, so that they might always sail in his wake by
the torch on the poop. When he desired to set the
bonnet-sail, he showed three lights. When he desired to alter his course, he showed two; and then if
he wished to ascertain whether all the ships were
following and whether they were coming together,

he showed one light, so that each one of the ships might do the same and reply to him. Three watches were set nightly: the first at the beginning of the night; the second, which is called the midnight, and the third at the end [of the night]. All of the men in the ships were divided into three parts: the first was the division of the captain or boatswain, those two alternating nightly; the second, of either the pilot or boatswain's mate; and the third, of the master. Thus did the captain-general order that all the ships observe the above signals and watches, so that their voyage might be more propitious.

On Monday morning, August X, St. Lawrence's day, in the year abovesaid, the fleet, having been supplied with all the things necessary for the sea [and counting those of every nationality, we were two hundred and thirty-seven men], made ready to leave the harbor of Siviglia. Discharging many pieces of artillery, the ships held their forestaysails to the wind, and descended the river Betis, at present called Gadalcavir, passing by a village called Gioan dal Farax, once a large Moorish settlement. In the midst of it was once a bridge that crossed the said river, and led to Siviglia. Two columns of that bridge have remained even to this day at the bottom of the water, and when ships sail by there, they need men who know the location of the columns thoroughly, so that the ships may not strike against them. They must also be passed when the river is highest with the tide; as must also many other villages along the river, which has not sufficient depth (of itself) for ships that are laden and which are not very large to pass. Then the ships reached another village called Coria, and passed by many other villages along the river, until they came to a castle of the duke of Medina Cidonia, called San Lucar, which is a port by which to enter the Ocean Sea. It is in an east and west direction with the cape of Sanct Vincent, which lies in 37 degrees of latitude, and X leguas from the said port.[5] From Siviglia to this point [San Lucar], it is 17 or 20 leguas by river. Some days after, the captain-general, with his other captains, descended the river in the small boats belonging to their ships. We remained there for a considerable number of days in order to finish [providing] the fleet with some things that it needed. Every day we went ashore to hear mass in a village called Nostra Dona de Baremeda, near San Lucar. Before the departure, the captain-general wished all the men to confess, and would not allow any woman to sail in the fleet for the best of considerations.

We left that village, by name San Luchar, on Tuesday, September XX of the same year, and took a southwest course. On the 26th of the said month, we reached an island of the Great Canaria, called Teneriphe, which lies in a latitude of 28 degrees, [landing there] in order to get flesh, water, and wood. We stayed there for three and one-half days in order to furnish the fleet with the said supplies. Then we went to a port of the same island called

[5] There is some slip here. The distance between Sanlúcar and Cape St. Vincent is more than one hundred miles.

Monte Rosso to get pitch, staying [there] two days. Your most illustrious Lordship must know that there is a particular one of the islands of the Great Canaria, where one can not find a single drop of water which gushes up [from a spring]; but that at noontide a cloud descends from the sky and encircles a large tree which grows in the said island, the leaves and branches of which distil a quantity of water. At the foot of the said tree runs a trench which resembles a spring, where all the water falls, and from which the people living there, and the animals, both domestic and wild, fully satisfy themselves daily with this water and no other.

At midnight of Monday, October three, the sails were trimmed toward the south, and we took to the open Ocean Sea, passing between Cape Verde and its islands in 14 and one-half degrees. Thus for many days did we sail along the coast of Ghinea, or Ethiopia, where there is a mountain called Siera Leona, which lies in 8 degrees of latitude, with contrary winds, calms, and rains without wind, until we reached the equinoctial line, having sixty days of continual rain. Contrary to the opinion of the ancients, before we reached the line many furious squalls of wind, and currents of water struck us head on in 14 degrees. As we could not advance, and in order that the ships might not be wrecked, all the sails were struck; and in this manner did we wander hither and yon on the sea, waiting for the tempest to cease, for it was very furious. When it rained there was no wind. When the sun shone, it was calm. Cer-

tain large fishes called *tiburoni* [sharks] came to
the side of the ships. They have terrible teeth, and
whenever they find men in the sea they devour
them. We caught many of them with iron hooks,
although they are not good to eat unless they are
small, and even then they are not very good. During
those storms the holy body, that is to say St. Elmo,
appeared to us many times, in light—among other
times on an exceedingly dark night, with the brightness of a blazing torch, on the maintop, where he
stayed for about two hours or more, to our consola-
tion, for we were weeping. When that blessed light
was about to leave us, so dazzling was the brightness
that it cast into our eyes, that we all remained for
more than an eighth of an hour blinded and calling
for mercy.[6] And truly when we thought that we were
dead men, the sea suddenly grew calm.

Pigafetta does not mention the first serious altercation
between Magellan and Juan de Cartagena, which occurred after the fleet had left the Canaries. Magellan, instead of going in the direction of Brazil, sailed on a south-
erly course and took the ships along the African coast as
far as Sierra Leone. He did so without explanation or consulting his officers, and the captains, who favored getting
across the Atlantic at once, became worried. Magellan
seems to have been right in this case, but he would have
been wiser to satisfy his subordinates by giving them an
explanation.[7] Cartagena approached the flagship in the

[6] St. Elmo's fire is electricity in the atmosphere that appears in
star-shaped form near the masthead of a ship. Other names for it
are St. Peter, St. Nicholas, Santa Clara, and Castor and Pollux.

[7] The *roteiros,* or route guides of the experienced Portuguese
pilots, which presumably Magellan knew and his subordinates did
not, counseled sailing for some days southeast of the Cape Verdes.
Lagôa, II, 18.

"San Antonio" and protested that it was dangerous to stay so close to Africa. The captains and pilots, he said, should be consulted. Magellan replied that problems of navigation were no concern of Cartagena's; he should merely follow the flagship "Trinidad" and be guided by its signals, a banner in the daytime and a lantern at night.[8]

Magellan sailed by the Cape Verde Islands in good weather and then ran into a spell of calms followed by heavy rains and adverse winds that continued past the equator and slowed the fleet.[9] Cartagena naturally took this as proof that he had been right about the course and was meanwhile angry that his standing as conjoint commander was being ignored. Article III of the royal instructions for governing the voyage had prescribed that each night, at angelus hour, the ship captains should hail Magellan with a formal greeting in set words. Cartagena, on one occasion, had an officer call the flagship using the wrong words so as to make the greeting apply to the "Trinidad's" entire crew instead of to the captain-general alone. Magellan promptly complained and asked Cartagena not to address him in this manner in the future. He received the sarcastic reply that the best seaman in the "San Antonio" had called the greeting but that from now on a page would do the hailing. For days afterward Cartagena sent no salute at all, but Magellan did nothing about this until a suitable opportunity offered.[10] Then Antonio Salamon, an officer of the "Victoria," was caught with a seaman in an act of sodomy, which according to Spanish naval regulations was punishable by death. Such an offense against nature being rather frequent aboard ship, those guilty of it often escaped with a flogging. Magellan, however, thought discipline had grown lax and determined to make an example of the culprits. He accordingly summoned all his captains and pilots for a full-dress trial, and the court sentenced both men to death. They were in fact executed after the

[8] Herrera, III, 80.
[9] Queiroz Velloso, p. 468.
[10] Navarrete, *Colección*, IV, 186.

fleet reached Brazil.[11] After the hearing Cartagena spoke up, again questioning the course that was being followed. Magellan merely asked in return why he had omitted the salutation prescribed by the royal orders. Cartagena grew excited and evidently attempted to stand on his rights as conjoint commander of the expedition. Magellan put his hand upon the *conjunta*'s chest and declared him under arrest, ordering the constable to seize him and put him in irons. Cartagena appealed for help to the other commanders, but although they felt much as he did about Magellan, their courage failed and they allowed the arrest to take place.

Antonio de Coca, the fleet's *contador*, or purser, received command of the "San Antonio." Cartagena, who was spared being placed in stocks, was put under the personal guard of Captain Luís de Mendoza of the "Victoria." Magellan wished to maroon the unruly *conjunta* on the Brazilian coast but was dissuaded from the idea by his captains.[12] There matters still stood when the fleet reached San Julián on the eve of Palm Sunday, 1520.

I saw many kinds of birds, among them one that had no anus; and another, [which] when the female wishes to lay its eggs, it does so on the back of the male and there they are hatched.[13] The latter bird has no feet, and always lives in the sea. [There is] another kind which live on the ordure of the other birds, and in no other manner; for I often saw this bird, which is called Cagassela, fly behind the other birds, until they are constrained to drop their ordure, which the former seizes immediately and abandons the latter bird.[14] I also saw many flying

[11] *Ibid.;* Medina, III, ccccxlviii.
[12] Navarrete, *Colección,* IV, 261.
[13] The stormy petrel.
[14] Robertson identifies the pursuing bird as *Stercorarius para-*

fish, and many others collected together, so that they resembled an island.

After we had passed the equinoctial line going south, we lost the north star, and hence we sailed south south-west until [we reached] a land called the land of Verzin [Brazil] which lies in 23½ degrees of the Antarctic Pole [south latitude]. It is the land extending from the cape of Santo Augustino, which lies in 8 degrees of the same pole. There we got a plentiful refreshment of fowls, potatoes, many sweet pine-apples—in truth the most delicious fruit that can be found—the flesh of the *anta* [tapir], which resembles beef, sugarcane, and innumerable other things, which I shall not mention in order not to be prolix. For one fishhook or one knife, those people gave 5 or 6 chickens; for one comb, a brace of geese; for one mirror or one pair of scissors, as many fish as would be sufficient for X men; for a bell or one leather lace, one basketful of potatoes. These potatoes resemble chestnuts in taste, and are as long as turnips. For a king of diamonds which is a playing card, they gave me 6 fowls and thought that they had even cheated me. We entered that port on St. Lucy's day, and on that day had the sun on the zenith; and we were subjected to greater heat on that day and on the other days when we had the sun on the zenith, than when we were under the equinoctial line.

That land of Verzin is wealthier and larger than

---

siticus. The real purpose of the chase is to compel the other bird to disgorge the fish it has swallowed.

Spagnia, Fransa, and Italia, put together, and belongs to the king of Portugalo. The people of that
land are not Christians, and have no manner of worship. They live according to the dictates of nature,
and reach an age of one hundred and twenty-five and
one hundred and forty years.[15] They go naked, both
men and women. They live in certain long houses
which they call *boii,* and sleep in cotton hammocks
called *amache,* which are fastened in those houses by
each end to large beams. A fire is built on the
ground under those hammocks. In each one of those
boii, there are one hundred men with their wives
and children, and they make a great racket. They
have boats called canoes made of one single huge
tree, hollowed out by the use of stone hatchets.
Those people employ stones as we do iron, as they
have no iron. Thirty or forty men occupy one of
those boats. They paddle with blades like the shov-
els of a furnace, and thus, black, naked, and shaven,
they resemble, when paddling, the inhabitants of
the Stygian marsh. Men and women are as well proportioned as we. They eat the human flesh of their
enemies, not because it is good, but because it is a
certain established custom. That custom, which is
mutual, was begun by an old woman, who had but
one son who was killed by his enemies. In return
some days later, that old woman's friends captured
one of the company who had killed her son, and

[15] Lagôa (II, 22) says that this exaggeration of longevity
ascribed by Pigafetta to the Brazilian natives is probably owing to
their inaccurate measurement of time.

brought him to the place of her abode. She seeing him, and remembering her son, ran upon him like an infuriated bitch, and bit him on one shoulder. Shortly afterward he escaped to his own people, whom he told that they had tried to eat him, showing them [in proof] the marks on his shoulder. Whomever the latter captured afterward at any time from the former they ate, and the former did the same to the latter, so that such a custom has sprung up in this way. They do not eat the bodies all at once, but every one cuts off a piece, and carries it to his house, where he smokes it. Then every week, he cuts off a small bit, which he eats thus smoked with his other food to remind him of his enemies. The above was told me by the pilot, Johane Carnagio, who came with us, and who had lived in that land for four years.[16] Those people paint the whole body and the face in a wonderful manner with fire in various fashions, as do the women also. The men are smooth shaven and have no beard, for they pull it out. They cloth themselves in a dress made of parrot feathers, with large round arrangements at their buttocks made from the largest feathers, and it is a ridiculous sight. Almost all the people, except the women and children, have three holes pierced in the lower lip, where they carry round stones, one finger or thereabouts in length and hanging down outside. Those people are not entirely black, but of a dark brown color. They keep the privies uncovered, and the

[16] João Carvalho; see page 261. The account of the origin of cannibalism among the Brazilians is of course nonsense.

body is without hair, while both men and women always go naked. Their king is called *cacich*. They have an infinite number of parrots, and gave us 8 or 10 for one mirror; and little monkeys that look like lions, only [they are] yellow, and very beautiful. They make round white [loaves of] bread from the marrowy substance of trees, which is not very good, and is found between the wood and the bark and resembles buttermilk curds. They have swine which have their navels on their backs, and large birds with beaks like spoons and no tongues. The men gave us one or two of their young daughters as slaves for one hatchet or one large knife, but they would not give us their wives in exchange for anything at all. The women will not shame their husbands under any considerations whatever, and as was told us, refuse to consent to their husbands by day, but only by night. The women cultivate the fields, and carry all their food from the mountains in panniers or baskets on the head or fastened to the head. But they are always accompanied by their husbands, who are armed only with a bow of brazil-wood or of black palm-wood, and a bundle of cane arrows, doing this because they are jealous [of their wives]. The women carry their children hanging [in] a cotton net from their necks. I omit other particulars, in order not to be tedious. Mass was said twice on shore, during which those people remained on their knees with so great contrition and with clasped hands raised aloft, that it was an exceeding great pleasure to behold them. They built us a house as they thought that we were going to stay with them for some time, and at our departure they cut a great quantity of brazilwood to give us.[17] It had been about two months since it had rained in that land, and when we reached that port, it happened to rain, whereupon they said that we came from the sky and that we had brought the rain with us. Those people could be converted easily to the faith of Jesus Christ.

At first those people thought that the small boats were the children of the ships, and that the latter gave birth to them when they were lowered into the sea from the ships, and when they were lying so alongside the ships (as is the custom), they believed that the ships were nursing them. One day a beautiful young woman came to the flagship, where I was, for no other purpose than to seek what chance might offer. While there and waiting, she cast her eyes upon the master's room, and saw a nail longer than one's finger. Picking it up very delightedly and neatly, she trust it through the lips of her vagina, and bending down low immediately departed, the captain-general and I having seen that action.[18]

Some words of those people of Verzin

For Millet	maiz
for Flour	hui
for Fishhook	p^inda

[17] Wood whose pulp yielded a rich, red dye.

[18] Lord Stanley (*First Voyage*, p. 47), with Victorian reserve, has the girl hide the nail in her hair. Lagôa (II, 27) relegates the passage to a footnote and gives it in Pigafetta's antiquated Italian.

for Knife	tacse
for Comb	chigap
for Scissors	pirame
for Bell	itanmaraca
Good, better	tum maragathum

We remained in that land for 13 days. Then proceeding on our way, we went as far as 34 and one-third degrees toward the Antarctic Pole, where we found people at a freshwater river, called Canibali, who eat human flesh. One of them, in stature almost a giant, came to the flagship in order to assure [the safety of] the others his friends. He had a voice like a bull. While he was in the ship, the others carried away their possessions from the place where they were living into the interior, for fear of us. Seeing that, we landed one hundred men in order to have speech and converse with them, or to capture one of them by force. They fled, and in fleeing they took so large a step that we although running could not gain on their steps. There are seven islands in that river, in the largest of which precious gems are found. That place is called the cape of Santa Maria, and it was formerly thought that one passed thence to the sea of Sur, that is to say the South Sea, but nothing further was ever discovered. Now the name is not [given to] a cape, but [to] a river, with a mouth 17 leguas in width. A Spanish captain, called Johan de Solis and sixty men, who were going to discover lands like us, were formerly eaten at that river by those cannibals because of too great confidence.

100

Then proceeding on the same course toward the Antarctic Pole, coasting along the land, we came to anchor at two islands full of geese and seawolves. Truly, the great number of those geese cannot be reckoned; in one hour we loaded the five ships [with them]. Those geese are black and have all their feathers alike both on body and wings. They do not fly, and live on fish. They were so fat that it was not necessary to pluck them but to skin them. Their beak is like that of a crow. Those seawolves are of various colors, and as large as a calf, with a head like that of a calf, ears small and round, and large teeth. They have no legs but only feet with small nails attached to the body, which resemble our hands, and between their fingers the same kind of skin as the geese. They would be very fierce if they could run. They swim, and live on fish. At that place the ships suffered a very great storm, during which the three holy bodies appeared to us many times, that is to say, St. Elmo, St. Nicholas, and St. Clara, whereupon the storm quickly ceased.

Leaving that place, we finally reached 49 and one-half degrees toward the Antarctic Pole. As it was winter, the ships entered a safe port to winter. We passed two months in that place without seeing anyone. One day we suddenly saw a naked man of giant stature on the shore of the port, dancing, singing, and throwing dust on his head.[19] The captain-general sent one of our men to the giant so that he

[19] Measurements of the modern Patagonians do not show them to be of exceptional size.

might perform the same actions as a sign of peace. Having done that, the man led the giant to an islet into the presence of the captain-general. When the giant was in the captain-general's and our presence, he marveled greatly, and made signs with one finger raised upward, believing that we had come from the sky. He was so tall that we reached only to his waist, and he was well proportioned. His face was large and painted red all over, while about his eyes he was painted yellow; and he had two hearts painted on the middle of his cheeks. His scanty hair was painted white. He was dressed in the skins of animals skilfully sewn together. That animal has a head and ears as large as those of a mule, a neck and body like those of a camel, the legs of a deer, and the tail of a horse, like which it neighs, and that land has very many of them. His feet were shod with the same kind of skins which covered his feet in the manner of shoes. In his hand he carried a short, heavy bow, with a cord somewhat thicker than those of the lute, and made from the intestines of the same animal, and a bundle of rather short cane arrows feathered like ours, and with points of white and black flint stones in the manner of Turkish arrows, instead of iron. Those points were fashioned by means of another stone. The captain-general had the giant given something to eat and drink, and among other things which were shown to him was a large steel mirror. When he saw his face, he was greatly terrified, and jumped back throwing three or four of our men to the ground. After that he was given some bells, a mirrow, a comb, and certain Pater Nosters. The captain-general sent him ashore with 4 armed men. When one of his companions, who would never come to the ships, saw him coming with our men, he ran to the place where the others were, who came [down to the shore] all naked one after the other. When our men reached them, they began to dance and to sing, lifting one finger to the sky. They showed our men some white powder made from the roots of an herb, which they kept in earthen pots, and which they ate because they had nothing else. Our men made signs inviting them to the ships, and that they would help them carry their possessions. Thereupon, those men quickly took only their bows, while their women laden like asses carried everything. The latter are not so tall as the men but are very much fatter. When we saw them we were greatly surprised. Their breasts are one-half braza long, and they are painted and clothed like their husbands, except that before their privies they have a small skin which covers them. They led four of those young animals, fastened with thongs like a halter. When those people wish to catch some of those animals, they tie one of these young ones to a thornbush. Thereupon, the large ones come to play with the little ones; and those people kill them with their arrows from their place of concealment. Our men led eighteen of those people, counting men and women, to the ships, and they were distributed on the two sides of the port so that they might catch some of the said animals.

Six days after the above, a giant painted and clothed in the same manner was seen by some [of our men] who were cutting wood. When our men approached him, he first touched his head, face, and body, and then did the same to our men, afterward lifting his hands toward the sky. When the captain-general was informed of it, he ordered him to be brought in the small boat. He was taken to that island in the port where our men had built a house for the smiths and for the storage of some things from the ships. That man was even taller and better built than the others and as tractable and amiable. Jumping up and down, he danced, and when he danced, at every leap, his feet sank a palmo into the earth. He remained with us for a considerable number of days, so long that we baptized him, calling him Johanni. He uttered [the words] *Jesu, Pater Noster, Ave Maria* and *Jovani* as distinctly as we, but with an exceedingly loud voice. Then the captain-general gave him a shirt, a woolen jerkin, cloth breeches, a cap, a mirror, a comb, bells, and other things, and sent him away like his companions. He left us very joyous and happy. The following day he brought one of those large animals to the captain-general, in return for which many things were given to him, so that he might bring some more to us; but we did not see him again. We thought that his companions had killed him because he had conversed with us.

A fortnight later we saw four of those giants

104

without their arms for they had hidden them in certain bushes as the two whom we captured showed us. Each one was painted differently. The captain-general kept two of them—the youngest and best proportioned—by means of a very cunning trick, in order to take them to Spagnia. Had he used any other means [than those he employed], they could easily have killed some of us. The trick that he employed in keeping them was as follows. He gave them many knives, scissors, mirrors, bells, and glass beads; and those two having their hands filled with the said articles, the captain-general had two pairs of iron manacles brought, such as are fastened on the feet. He made motions that he would give them to the giants, whereat they were very pleased, since those manacles were of iron, but they did not know how to carry them. They were grieved at leaving them behind, but they had no place to put those gifts; for they had to hold the skin wrapped about them with their hands. The other two giants wished to help them, but the captain refused. Seeing that they were loth to leave those manacles behind, the captain made them a sign that he would put them on their feet, and that they could carry them away. They nodded assent with the head. Immediately, the captain had the manacles put on both of them at the same time. When our men were driving home the cross bolt, the giants began to suspect something, but the captain assuring them, however, they stood still. When they saw later that they were tricked, they raged like bulls, calling loudly for *Setebos* to aid them.[20] With difficulty could we bind the hands of the other two, whom we sent ashore with nine of our men, in order that the giants might guide them to the place where the wife of one of the two whom we had captured was; for the latter expressed his great grief at leaving her by signs so that we understood [that he meant] her. While they were on their way, one of the giants freed his hands, and took to his heels with such swiftness that our men lost sight of him. He went to the place where his associates were, but he did not find [there] one of his companions, who had remained behind with the women, and who had gone hunting. He immediately went in search of the latter, and told him all that had happened. The other giant endeavored so hard to free himself from his bonds, that our men struck him, wounding him slightly on the head, whereat he raging led them to where the women were. Gioan Cavagio, the pilot and commander of those men, refused to bring back the woman that night, but determined to sleep there, for night was approaching. The other two giants came, and seeing their companion wounded, hesitated, but said nothing then. But with the dawn, they spoke to the women, [whereupon] they immediately ran away (and the smaller ones ran faster than the taller), leaving all their possessions behind them. Two of them turned aside to shoot their arrows at our men.

[20] In *The Tempest* Shakespeare borrowed the name of this Patagonian god for Caliban to invoke.

The other was leading away those small animals of theirs in order to hunt. Thus fighting, one of them pierced the thigh of one of our men with an arrow, and the latter died immediately. When the giants saw that, they ran away quickly. Our men had muskets and crossbows, but they could never hit any of the giants, [for] when the latter fought, they never stood still, but leaped hither and thither. Our men buried their dead companion, and burned all the possessions left behind by the giants. Of a truth those giants run swifter than horses and are exceedingly jealous of their wives.

When those people feel sick at the stomach, instead of purging themselves, they thrust an arrow down their throat for two palmos or more and vomit [substance of a] green color mixed with blood, for they eat a certain kind of thistle. When they have a headache, they cut themselves across the forehead; and they do the same on the arms or on the legs and in any part of the body, letting a quantity of blood. One of those whom we had captured, and whom we kept in our ship, said that the blood refused to stay there [in the place of the pain], and consequently causes them suffering. They wear their hair cut with the tonsure, like friars, but it is left longer; and they have a cotton cord wrapped about the head, to which they fasten their arrows when they go hunting. They bind their privies close to their bodies because of the exceeding great cold. When one of those people die, X or twelve demons all painted appear to them and dance very joyfully about the corpse. They notice that one of those demons is much taller than the others, and he cries out and rejoices more. They paint themselves exactly in the same manner as the demon appears to them painted. They call the larger demon *Setebos,* and the others *Cheleulle.* That giant also told us by signs that he had seen the demons with two horns on their heads, and long hair which hung to the feet belching forth fire from mouth and buttocks. The captain-general called those people Patagoni. They all clothe themselves in the skins of that animal above mentioned; and they have no houses except those made from the skin of the same animal, and they wander hither and thither with those houses just as the Cingani [gypsies] do. They live on raw flesh and on a sweet root which they call *chapae.* Each of the two whom we captured ate a basketful of biscuit, and drank one-half pailful of water at a gulp. They also ate rats without skinning them.

In that port which we called the port of Santo Julianno, we remained about five months. Many things happened there. In order that your most illustrious Lordship may know some of them, it happened that as soon as we had entered the port, the captains of the other four ships plotted treason in order that they might kill the captain-general. Those conspirators consisted of the overseer of the fleet, one Johan de Cartagena, the treasurer, Alouise de Mendosa, the accountant, Anthonio Cocha, and Gaspar de Cazada. The overseer of the men having been quartered, the treasurer was killed by dagger blows, for the treason was discovered. Some days after that, Gaspar de Cazada, was banished with a priest in that land of Patagonia. The captain-general did not wish to have him killed, because the emperor, Don Carlo, had appointed him captain.[21] A ship called "Sancto Jacobo" was wrecked in an expedition made to explore the coast. All the men were saved as by a miracle, not even getting wet. Two of them came to the ships after suffering great hardships, and reported the whole occurrence to us. Consequently, the captain-general sent some men with bags full of biscuits [sufficient to last] for two months. It was necessary for us to carry them the food, for daily pieces of the ship [that was wrecked] were found. The way thither was long, [being] 24 leguas, or one hundred millas, and the path was very rough and full of thorns. The men were 4 days on the road, sleeping at night in the bushes. They found no drinking water, but only ice, which caused them the greatest hardship. There were very many long shellfish which are called *missiglioni* in that port [of Santo Julianno]. They have pearls, although small ones in the middle, but could not be eaten. Incense, ostriches, foxes, sparrows, and rabbits much smaller than ours were also found. We erected a cross on the top of the highest summit there, as a sign in that land that it belonged to the king of Spagnia; and we called that summit Monte de Christo.

[21] Pigafetta's inaccuracies here may be seen by referring to the Introduction, page 112.

Pigafetta says very little about the San Julián mutiny that took place, and the few lines he does provide are inaccurate. No doubt he failed to take his accustomed notes at the time, and later events obscured his memory of the facts.[22]

He mentions the mutiny at the end of his account of the winter's stay in San Julián, as if belatedly recalling it. Though Maximilian of Transylvania says rather more and seems to have the gist of the affair, it would be impossible from his account to reconstruct the events precisely as they occurred. He relied for information on El Cano and a few other survivors whom he met at Valladolid, but by then the sequence of happenings was somewhat obscured in their minds. Gaspar Corrêa gives the best account, but even his is confused in places, as when he says Magellan had Juan de Cartagena quartered.[23]

Cartagena, since his deposition as commander of the "San Antonio," had had many opportunities to propagandize against Magellan and had evidently taken advantage of them. He had more than his personal hatred of the captain-general to use as argument, for Magellan behaved arbitrarily and highhandedly. He consistently favored the Portuguese in his fleet over the Spaniards, seeming to feel that his contract with King Charles, himself a foreigner, entitled him to treat them as day laborers. The Spanish captains who headed the mutiny could have argued, at least to their own satisfaction, that they were looking out for the interests of their country.

Events moved very fast after the fleet entered San Julián. When Magellan invited the captains to a mass and Palm Sunday breakfast aboard the "Trinidad," they all ignored the invitation except Alvaro de Mesquita, a Portu-

[22] Pigafetta says the captains of the other four ships planned to murder Magellan, whereas Juan Rodríguez Serrano of the "Santiago" took no part in the mutiny. The rest of the brief account is confused.

[23] Corrêa says the quartered and executed men were spitted on poles ashore, but there is no evidence in other accounts to support this statement.

guese who had succeeded Coca in command of the "San Antonio." That night Antonio de Coca and Captain Gaspar de Quesada, accompanied by Cartagena, whom Magellan had transferred to the "Concepción," rowed from that ship to the "San Antonio," accompanied by thirty armed men. They climbed on deck, seized Mesquita, and wounded the mate, Juan de Eloriaga, so severely that he ultimately died. They then took possession of the ship, the largest in the squadron, and placed Juan Sebastián del Cano in command.[24] The "Victoria," under the command of Luís de Mendoza, had already passed to the mutineers.

On Monday morning Magellan found that he commanded only his own "Trinidad" and the tiny "Santiago," whose captain, Serrano, though Spanish, remained loyal. He received by small boat a letter from Quesada, now clearly established as ringleader of the mutineers, saying that the insurrection had been caused by Magellan's lack of consideration for them but that if he changed his conduct they stood ready to return to obedience.[25] This message has usually been taken as a ruse to throw Magellan off guard, but Quesada, whose message did not sound at all belligerent, may have meant what he said. However, the captain-general did not trust his mutinous subordinates and, to gain time, proposed a conference aboard the flagship to discuss the grievances. The mutineers felt no more inclined than Magellan to be at their opponents' mercy and countered by suggesting the "San Antonio" as the meeting place.

While this palaver went on, Magellan prepared a ship's boat and loaded it with his constable Gonzalo Gómez de Espinosa and six men, all bearing concealed arms. They rowed to the "Victoria," where Luís de Mendoza showed no alarm at such a small party, and were allowed on deck. Espinosa handed Mendoza a letter from Magellan and the captain started to read it with a half-humorous gesture, as if to say he could not be deceived by any of the captain-general's tricks. Espinosa suddenly drew his dagger and

[24] Medina, III, ccxvi.
[25] *Ibid.*, ccxvii.

111

struck Mendoza in the throat, just as another sailor dealt him a mortal blow in the head. At that moment, Duarte Barbosa, who had been quietly sent over by Magellan, appeared on deck with another boat crew of armed men. Within a minute they had control of the "Victoria," and Barbosa took *pro tempore* command. He ordered the anchor raised and brought the ship alongside Magellan's "Trinidad" and "Santiago," so as to block exit from the harbor.[26]

The back of the mutiny had been broken, but during the night the "San Antonio" tried to slip past the blockading ships and escape. When Magellan opened fire and boarded, the crew members, never easy in their minds about this mutiny, surrendered tamely. Quesada and Coca gave up without further resistance. There now remained only the "Concepción," with Cartagena in command. The *conjunta* too had had enough, and when Espinosa rowed toward his ship, he meekly submitted and allowed himself to be seized.[27]

To judge and punish the mutineers, Magellan set up a court presided over by Alvaro de Mesquita. Everything was conducted with proper window dressing; accusers and witnesses appeared and gave their testimony.[28] By a verdict announced on April 7, forty men received the death sentence, but this could not be carried out in more than a token way. Since the loss of so many men would weaken the expedition and seriously lessen its chances, Magellan commuted all sentences except that of Quesada, who had mortally wounded Eloriaga. Quesada's servant, Luís de Molina, who had helped strike Eloriaga down, was given the choice of beheading his master or dying in his company. Molina chose the lesser of two evils and Quesada, after decapitation, underwent quartering, as did the fallen Luís de Mendoza. Cartagena and an accomplice, the French priest Bernard Calmette, were condemned to be marooned.

[26] *Ibid.*, ccxviii.
[27] *Ibid.*, ccxix.
[28] Navarrete, *Colección,* IV, 174–91.

This sentence was carried out, not immediately but just before the fleet left San Julián. The men were placed on a lonely island with several sacks of biscuit and several bottles of wine, and nothing is known of their fate. El Cano later said that Magellan would not have meted out so heartless a punishment if Cartagena had not made a new attempt to incite mutiny.[29] As for El Cano himself, he was of course among those condemned to die and pardoned. As the voyage continued and he gave a good account of himself, Magellan appeared to forget or forgive his offense.

Leaving that place, we found, in 51 degrees less one-third degree, toward the Antarctic Pole, a river of fresh water. There the ships almost perished because of the furious winds; but God and the holy bodies aided them. We stayed about two months in that river in order to supply the ships with water, wood, and fish, [the latter being] one braccio in length and more, and covered with scales. They were very good although small. Before leaving that river, the captain-general and all of us confessed and received communion as true Christians.

Then going to fifty-two degrees toward the same pole, we found a strait on the day of the [Feast of the] Eleven Thousand Virgins [October 21], whose head is called Capo de le Undici Millia Vergine because of that very great miracle. That strait is one hundred and ten leguas or 440 miles long, and it is one-half legua broad, more or less. It leads to another sea called the Pacific Sea, and is surrounded by very lofty mountains laden with snow. There it was impossible to find bottom [for anchoring], but

[29] *Ibid.*, p. 262.

[it was necessary to fasten] the moorings on land 25 or 30 brazas away. Had it not been for the captain-general, we would not have found that strait, for we all thought and said that it was closed on all sides. But the captain-general who knew where to sail to find a well-hidden strait, which he saw depicted on a map in the treasury of the king of Portugal, which was made by that excellent man, Martin de Boemia, sent two ships, the "Santo Anthonio" and the "Conceptione" (for thus they were called), to discover what was inside the cape de la Baia. We with the other two ships, the flagship, called "Trinitade," and the other the "Victoria," stayed inside the bay to await them. A great storm struck us that night, which lasted until the middle of next day, which necessitated our lifting anchor, and letting ourselves drift hither and thither about the bay. The other two ships suffered a headwind and could not double a cape formed by the bay almost at its end, as they were trying to return to join us; so that they thought that they would have to run aground. But on approaching the end of the bay, and thinking that they were lost, they saw a small opening which did not appear to be an opening, but a sharp turn. Like desperate men they hauled into it, and thus they discovered the strait by chance. Seeing that it was not a sharp turn, but a strait with land, they proceeded farther, and found a bay. And then farther on they found another strait and another bay larger than the first two. Very joyful they immediately turned back to inform the captain-general. We thought that they had been wrecked, first, by reason of the violent storm, and second, because two days had passed and they had not appeared, and also because of certain [signals with] smoke made by two of their men who had been sent ashore to advise us. And so, while in suspense, we saw the two ships with sails full and banners flying to the wind, coming toward us. When they neared us in this manner, they suddenly discharged a number of mortars, and burst into cheers. Then all together thanking God and the Virgin Mary, we went to seek [the strait] farther on.

After entering that strait, we found two openings, one to the southeast, and the other to the southwest. The captain-general sent the ship "Sancto Anthonio" together with the "Conceptione" to ascertain whether that opening which was toward the southeast had an exit into the Pacific Sea. The ship "Sancto Anthonio" would not await the "Conceptione," because it intended to flee and return to Spagnia—which it did. The pilot of that ship was one Stefan Gomes, and he hated the captain-general exceedingly, because before that fleet was fitted out, the emperor had ordered that he be given some caravels with which to discover lands, but his Majesty did not give them to him because of the coming of the captain-general. On that account he conspired with certain Spaniards, and next night they captured the captain of their ship, a cousin of the captain-general, one Alvaro de Meschita, whom they wounded and put in irons, and in this condition took to Spagnia. The other giant whom we had captured was in that ship, but he died when the heat came on. The "Conceptione," as it could not follow that ship, waited for it, sailing about hither and thither. The "Sancto Anthonio" turned back at night and fled along the same strait.

The "Santiago" was wrecked before the expedition reached the Strait of Magellan; the "San Antonio" deserted during the exploration of the strait. Pigafetta says the deserting ship was piloted by Stefan (Estevão) Gomes, who hated Magellan because, previous to the latter's arrival in Spain, Gomes had been promised command of an expedition to make discoveries on his own. Maximilian of Transylvania believes the idea of deserting came to the crew without premeditation and not until they found themselves at some distance from the rest of the ships. Corrêa says only that Alvaro de Mesquita's ship ran away and that an astrologer had to inform those left with Magellan what had happened to it and its commander.

Mesquita did, of course, command the "San Antonio," with Gomes as his chief pilot. The desertion appears to have been an after result of the San Julián mutiny and Magellan's punishments, for certainly many officers and crewmen remained dissatisfied with the commander in chief. Pigafetta's statement that Gomes had been earlier promised an expedition of his own is evidently incorrect, but the pilot was indeed ambitious and later did conduct a Spanish exploration of the coast of North America.[30] He certainly led the mutiny in the strait and took the "San Antonio" out of Mesquita's hands. He evidently felt, as did the malcontents he led, that with the discovery of this waterway the main purpose of the expedition had been achieved. The best course now would be to return to Spain and begin anew with a fresh fleet.[31] The mutineers gave

[30] Örjan Olsen, *La conquête de la terre,* transl. from the Norwegian by E. Guerre, 6 vols., Paris, 1935–55, IV, 19.
[31] Melón, p. 612.

Magellan the slip and sailed with all possible speed to a Spanish port, arriving there on May 6, 1521.[32] They handed Mesquita over to the authorities and made grave accusations against him, also saying many derogatory things about Magellan and his leadership. The puzzled officials, hardly knowing what to make of the case, suspended final judgment until the El Cano's "Victoria" arrived the following year with a more reliable report.[33]

We had gone to explore the other opening toward the southwest. Finding, however, the same strait continuously, we came upon a river which we called the river of Sardine, because there were many sardines near it. So we stayed there for four days in order to await the two ships. During that period we sent a well-equipped boat to explore the cape of the other sea. The men returned within three days, and reported that they had seen the cape and the open sea. The captain-general wept for joy, and called that cape, Cape Dezeado, for we had been desiring it for a long time.[34] We turned back to look for the two ships, but we found only the "Conceptione." Upon asking them where the other one was, Johan Seranno, who was captain and pilot of the former ship (and also of that ship that had been wrecked) replied that he did not know, and that he had never seen it after it had entered the opening. We sought it in all parts of the strait, as far as that opening

[32] Navarrete, *Colección,* IV, 185.
[33] *Ibid.,* p. 189 ff.
[34] It will be noted that Pigafetta makes no reference to human beings along the strait itself. Maximilian of Transylvania, however, mentions fires seen on the left side that were guessed to be made by natives.

whence it had fled, and the captain-general sent the ship "Victoria" back to the entrance of the strait to ascertain whether the ship was there. Orders were given them, if they did not find it, to plant a banner on the summit of some small hill with a letter in an earthen pot buried in the earth near the banner, so that if the banner were seen the letter might be found, and the ship might learn the course that we were sailing. For this was the arrangement made between us in case that we went astray one from the other. Two banners were planted with their letters—one on a little eminence in the first bay, and the other in an islet in the third bay where there were many sea-wolves and large birds. The captain-general waited for the ship with his other ship near the river of Isleo, and he had a cross set up in an islet near that river, which flowed between high mountains covered with snow and emptied into the sea near the river of Sardine. Had we not discovered that strait, the captain-general had determined to go as far as seventy-five degrees toward the Antarctic Pole. There in that latitude, during the summer season, there is no night, or if there is any night it is but short, and so in the winter with the day. In order that your most illustrious Lordship may believe it, when we were in that strait, the nights were only three hours long, and it was then the month of October. The land on the left-hand side of that strait turned toward the southeast and was low. We called that strait the strait of Patagonia. One finds the safest of ports every half legua in it, water, the finest of wood [but not of cedar], fish, sardines, and *missiglioni,* while smallage, a sweet herb [although there is also some that is bitter] grows around the springs. We ate of it for many days as we had nothing else. I believe that there is not a more beautiful or better strait in the world than that one. In that Ocean Sea one sees a very amusing fish hunt. The fish [that hunt] are of three sorts, and are one braza and more in length, and are called *dorado, albicore,* and *bonito.* Those fish follow the flying fish called *colondrini,* which are one palmo and more in length and very good to eat. When the above three kinds [of fish] find any of those flying fish, the latter immediately leap from the water and fly as long as their wings are wet—more than a crossbow's flight. While they are flying, the others run along back of them under the water following the shadow of the flying fish. The latter have no sooner fallen into the water than the others immediately seize and eat them. It is in fine a very amusing thing to watch.

Words of the Patagonian giants

for Head	her
for Eye	other
for Nose	or
for Eyebrows	occhechel
for Eyelids	sechechiel
for Nostrils	oresche
for Mouth	xiam
for Lips	schiahame
for Teeth	phor
for Tongue	schial
for Chin	sechen

for Hair	archiz
for Face	cogechel
for Throat	ohumez
for Occiput	schialeschin
for Shoulders	pelles
for Elbow	cotel
for Hand	chene
for Palm of the hand	caimeghin
for Finger	cori
for Ears	sane
Armpit	salischin
for Teat	othen
for Bosom	ochij
for Body	gechel
for Penis	sachet
for Testicles	sacancas
for Vagina	isse
for Communication with women	jo hoi
for Thighs	chiane
for Knee	tepin
for Rump	schiaguen
for Buttocks	hoij
for Arm	maz
for Pulse	holion
for Legs	coss
for Foot	thee
for Heel	tere
for Ankle	perchi
for Sole of the foot	caotscheni
for Fingernails	colim
for Heart	thol
for to Scratch	gechare
for Cross-eyed man	calischen
for Young man	calemi
for Water	holi
for Fire	ghialeme
for Smoke	giaiche
for No	ehen

for Yes	rey
for Gold	pelpeli
for Lapis lazuli	secheg
for Sun	calexcheni
for Stars	settere
for Sea	aro
for Wind	oni
for Storm	ohone
for Fish	hoi
for to Eat	mechiere
for Bowl	elo
for Pot	aschanie
for to Ask	ghelhe
Come here	hai si
for to Look	chonne
for to Walk	rey
for to Fight	oamaghce
for Arrows	sethe
for Dog	holl
for Wolf	ani
for to Go a long distance	schien
for Guide	anti
for Snow	theu
for to Cover	hiani
for Ostrich, a bird	hoihoi
for its Eggs	jani
for the Powder of the herb which they eat	capac
for to Smell	os
for Parrot	cheche
for Birdcage	cleo
for Misiglioni	siameni
for Red Cloth	terechae
for Cap	aichel
for Black	ainel
for Red	taiche
for Yellow	peperi
for to Cook	yrocoles
for Belt	catechin

for Goose	cache
for their big Devil	Setebos
for their small Devils	Cheleule

All the above words are pronounced in the throat, for such is their method of pronunciation.

That giant whom we had in our ship told me those words; for when he, upon asking me for *capac,* that is to say, bread, as they call that root which they use as bread, and *oli,* that is to say, water, saw me write those words quickly, and afterward when I, with pen in hand, asked him for other words, he understood me. Once I made the sign of the cross, and, showing it to him, kissed it. He immediately cried out "Setebos," and made me a sign that if I made the sign of the cross again, Setebos would enter into my body and cause it to burst. When that giant was sick, he asked for the cross, and embracing it and kissing it many times, desired to become a Christian before his death. We called him Paulo. When those people wish to make a fire, they rub a sharpened piece of wood against another piece until the fire catches in the pith of a certain tree, which is placed between those two sticks.

Wednesday, November 28, 1520, we debouched from that strait, engulfing ourselves in the Pacific Sea. We were three months and twenty days without getting any kind of fresh food. We ate biscuit, which was no longer biscuit, but powder of biscuits swarming with worms, for they had eaten the good. It stank strongly of the urine of rats. We drank yellow water that had been putrid for many days. We also ate some ox hides that covered the top of the mainyard to prevent the yard from chafing the shrouds, and which had become exceedingly hard because of the sun, rain, and wind. We left them in the sea for four or five days, and then placed them for a few moments on top of the embers, and so ate them; and often we ate sawdust from boards. Rats were sold for one-half ducado apiece, and even we could not get them. But above all the other misfortunes the following was the worst. The gums of both the lower and upper teeth of some of our men swelled, so that they could not eat under any circumstances and therefore died.[35] Nineteen men died from that sickness, and the giant together with an Indian from the country of Verzin. Twenty-five or thirty men fell sick [during that time], in the arms, legs, or in another place, so that but few remained well. However, I by the grace of God, suffered no sickness. We sailed about four thousand leguas during those three months and twenty days through an open stretch in that Pacific Sea. In truth it is very pacific, for during that time we did not suffer any storm. We saw no land except two desert islets, where we found nothing but birds and trees, for which we called them the Ysolle Infortunate.[36] They are two hundred leguas apart. We found no anchorage, [but] near them saw many sharks. The first islet lies in fifteen degrees of south latitude, and the

[35] These are well-known results of scurvy, called *escorbuto* in Spanish and Portuguese and *scorbuto* in Italian.

[36] For a conjecture as to what these islands were, see the Introduction, page 124.

other in nine. Daily we made runs of fifty, sixty, or seventy leguas at the catena or at the stern.[37] Had not God and His blessed mother given us so good weather we would all have died of hunger in that exceeding vast sea. Of a verity I believe no such voyage will ever be made [again].

After Magellan had emerged from the strait with his three remaining ships and entered the Pacific, he felt sure he had surmounted his major obstacle, Behaim's peninsula, and was now in the *Magnus Sinus*. Proof of this belief lies in the fact that he immediately turned northward. How far he continued to sail in that direction before shifting to a westerly course is not altogether certain, but it now seems that he kept fairly close to the American coast until almost 20° N.[38] The two islands sighted between the strait and the Marianas Pigafetta calls the Unfortunate Isles; others with the expedition call them San Pablo and Tiburones. These have been reasonably identified as Clipperton (10° 17' N.) and Clarion (18° N.), both near the American mainland.[39] To be sure, the latitudes given in the Francisco Albo log plot another course for Magellan. They have him turning westward near the Juan Fernández group, sailing for a long distance in the South Pacific, and crossing the equator about 154° W. Yet if Magellan followed such a route he would almost surely have encountered many islands, whereas all testimonies agree in saying

[37] Some copyist has probably substituted *catena* (chain) for *antena* (mizzenyard). The *antena* bore a lateen sail that swung when the wind changed. Alberto Magnaghi, "Di una nuova interpretazione della frase 'a la catena ho a popa' nella relazione di Antonio Pigafetta," *Bollettino della Reale Società Geografica Italiana,* ser. 6, IV, 1927, 458–75. The general meaning is that the distance covered daily varied from fifty to seventy leagues depending on whether the wind came from an angle or from directly astern.

[38] Nunn, "Magellan's Route in the Pacific," *Geographical Review,* XXIV, 1935, 615–33.

[39] *Ibid.,* p. 633.

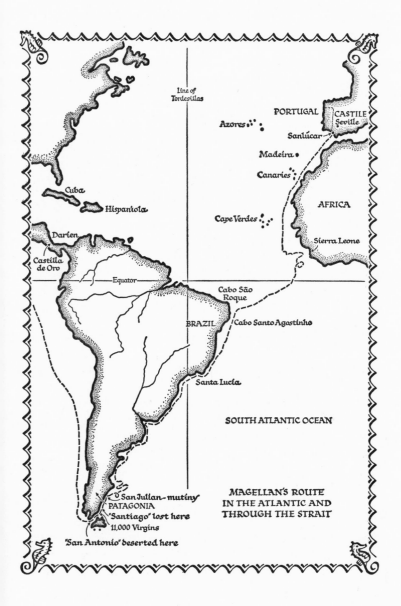

Line of
Tordesillas

PORTUGAL   CASTILE
Seville

Azores

Sanlúcar

Madeira

Canaries

AFRICA

Cape Verdes

Sierra Leone

Cuba

Hispaniola

Darien

Castilla
de Oro

Equator

Cabo São
Roque

BRAZIL   Cabo Santo Agostinho

Santa Lucía

SOUTH ATLANTIC OCEAN

San Julian – mutiny
PATAGONIA
"Santiago" lost here
11,000 Virgins

"San Antonio" deserted here

MAGELLAN'S ROUTE
IN THE ATLANTIC AND
THROUGH THE STRAIT

that he saw only two. If he took the more northern route, however, he could have gone from Clarion to the Marianas without seeing any, for the eastern Pacific north of the equator is almost empty of islands. The theory, moreover, fits the fact that Magellan was seeking Tarshish and Ophir, which he believed to lie in a northern latitude not far westward in the *Sinus*.

When we left that strait, if we had sailed continuously westward we would have circumnavigated the world without finding other land than the cape of the XI thousand Virgins. The latter is a cape of that strait at the Ocean Sea, straight east and west with Cape Deseado of the Pacific Sea. Both of those capes lie in a latitude of exactly fifty-two degrees toward the Antarctic Pole.

The Antarctic Pole is not so starry as the Arctic. Many small stars clustered together are seen, which have the appearance of two clouds of mist. There is but little distance between them, and they are somewhat dim. In the midst of them are two large and not very luminous stars, which move only slightly. Those two stars are the Antarctic Pole. Our loadstone, although it moved hither and thither, always pointed toward its own Arctic Pole, although it did not have so much strength as on its own side. And on that account when we were in that open expanse, the captain-general, asking all the pilots whether they were always sailing forward in the course which we had laid down on the maps, all replied: "By your course exactly as laid down." He answered them that they were pointing wrongly— which was a fact—and that it would be fitting to adjust the needle of navigation, for it was not receiving so much force from its side. When we were in the midst of that open expanse, we saw a cross with five extremely bright stars straight toward the west, those stars being exactly placed with regard to one another.

During those days we sailed west northwest, northwest by west, and northwest, until we reached the equinoctial line at the distance of one hundred and twenty-two degrees from the line of demarcation. The line of demarcation is thirty degrees from the meridian, and the meridian is three degrees eastward from Capo Verde. We passed while on that course, a short distance from two exceedingly rich islands, one in twenty degrees of the latitude of the Antarctic Pole, by name Cipangu, and the other in fifteen degrees, by name Sumbdit Pradit.[40] After we had passed the equinoctial line we sailed west northwest, and west by north, and then for two hundred leguas toward the west, changing our course to west by south until we reached thirteen degrees toward the Arctic Pole in order that we might approach nearer to the land of cape Gaticara. That cape [with the pardon of cosmographers, for they have not seen it], is not found where it is imagined to be, but to the north in twelve degrees or thereabouts.

About seventy leguas on the above course, and lying in twelve degrees of latitude and 146 in longi-

[40] Cipangu, of course, is Japan. No one has ascertained what Pigafetta meant by Sumbdit Pradit, but Da Mosto (*Raccolta Colombiana*, V, III, 67) suggests it is the island of Antillia, on Behaim's globe.

tude, we discovered on Wednesday, March 6, a small island to the northwest, and two others toward the southwest, one of which was higher and larger than the other two. The captain-general wished to stop at the large island and get some fresh food, but he was unable to do so because the inhabitants of that island entered the ships and stole whatever they could lay their hands on, so that we could not protect ourselves. The men were about to strike the sails so that we could go ashore, but the natives very deftly stole from us the small boat that was fastened to the poop of the flagship. Thereupon, the captain-general in wrath went ashore with forty armed men, who burned some forty or fifty houses together with many boats, and killed seven men. He recovered the small boat, and we departed immediately pursuing the same course. Before we landed, some of our sick men begged us if we should kill any man or woman to bring the entrails to them, as they would recover immediately.

When we wounded any of those people with our crossbow-shafts, which passed completely through their loins from one side to the other, they, looking at it, pulled on the shaft now on this and now on that side, and then drew it out, with great astonishment, and so died. Others who were wounded in the breast did the same, which moved us to great compassion. Those people seeing us departing followed us with more than one hundred boats for more than one legua. They approached the ships showing us fish, feigning that they would give them to us; but then threw stones at us and fled. And although the ships were under full sail, they passed between them and the small boats [fastened astern], very adroitly in those small boats of theirs. We saw some women in their boats who were crying out and tearing their hair, for love, I believe, of those whom we had killed.

Each one of those people lives according to his own will, for they have no seignior. They go naked, and some are bearded and have black hair that reaches to the waist. They wear small palmleaf hats, as do the Albanians. They are as tall as we, and well built. They have no worship. They are tawny, but are born white. Their teeth are red and black, for they think that is most beautiful. The women go naked except that they wear a narrow strip of bark as thin as paper, which grows between the tree and the bark of the palm, before their privies. They are goodlooking and delicately formed, and lighter complexioned than the men; and wear their hair which is exceedingly black, loose and hanging quite down to the ground. The women do not work in the fields but stay in the house, weaving mats, baskets, and other things needed in their houses, from palm leaves. They eat cocoanuts, camotes, birds, figs one palmo in length [bananas], sugarcane, and flying fish, besides other things. They anoint the body and the hair with cocoanut and beneseed oil. Their houses are all built of wood covered with planks and thatched with leaves of the fig-tree [banana-tree] two brazas long; and they have floors and windows.

The rooms and the beds are all furnished with the most beautiful palmleaf mats. They sleep on palm straw which is very soft and fine. They use no weapons, except a kind of a spear pointed with a fishbone at the end. Those people are poor, but ingenious and very thievish, on account of which we called those three islands the islands of Ladroni. Their amusement, men and women, is to plough the seas with those small boats of theirs. Those boats resemble *fucelere*, but are narrower, and some are black, [some] white, and others red. At the side opposite the sail, they have a large piece of wood pointed at the top, with poles laid across it and resting on the water, in order that the boats may sail more safely. The sail is made from palmleaves sewn together and is shaped like a lateen sail. For rudders they use a certain blade resembling a hearth shovel which have a piece of wood at the end. They can change stern and bow at will, and those boats resemble the dolphins which leap in the water from wave to wave. Those Ladroni thought, according to the signs which they made, that there were no other people in the world but themselves.[41]

At dawn on Saturday, March sixteen, 1521, we came upon a high land at a distance of three hundred leguas from the islands of Latroni—an island named Zamal. The following day, the captain-gen-

[41] There is no point in attempting to equate the inhabitants of the Marianas, or Ladrones, of Magellan's day with the present population, descendants of immigrants from the Philippines, Carolines, and Japan. All we can say is that the original islanders were Micronesian.

eral desired to land on another island which was uninhabited and lay to the right of the above mentioned island, in order to be more secure, and to get
water and have some rest. He had two tents set up
on the shore for the sick and had a sow killed for
them. On Monday afternoon, March 18, we saw a
boat coming toward us with nine men in it. Therefore, the captain-general ordered that no one should
move or say a word without his permission. When
those men reached the shore, their chief went immediately to the captain-general, giving signs of joy
because of our arrival. Five of the most ornately
adorned of them remained with us, while the rest
went to get some others who were fishing, and so
they all came. The captain-general seeing that they
were reasonable men, ordered food to be set before
them, and gave them red caps, mirrors, combs, bells,
ivory, bocasine, and other things. When they saw
the captain's courtesy, they presented fish, a jar of
palm wine, which they call *uraca*,[42] figs more than
one palmo long, and others which were smaller and
more delicate, and two cocoanuts. They had nothing
else then, but made us signs with their hands that
they would bring *umay* or rice, and cocoanuts and
many other articles of food within four days.

Cocoanuts are the fruit of the palmtree. Just as
we have bread, wine, oil, and milk, so those people
get everything from that tree. They get wine in the
following manner. They bore a hole into the heart

[42] Arrack, known all over the East, is not a wine but a distilled
drink of "incredible potency."

of the said palm at the top called *palmito,* from which distils a liquor which resembles white must. That liquor is sweet but somewhat tart, and [is gathered] in canes [of bamboo] as thick as the leg and thicker. They fasten the bamboo to the tree at evening for the morning, and in the morning for the evening. That palm bears a fruit, namely, the cocoanut, which is as large as the head or thereabouts. Its outside husk is green and thicker than two fingers. Certain filaments are found in that husk, whence is made cord for binding together their boats. Under that husk there is a hard shell, much thicker than the shell of the walnut, which they burn and make therefrom a powder that is useful to them. Under that shell there is a white marrowy substance one finger in thickness, which they eat fresh with meat and fish as we do bread; and it has a taste resembling the almond. It could be dried and made into bread. There is a clear, sweet water in the middle of that marrowy substance which is very refreshing. When that water stands for a while after having been collected, it congeals and becomes like an apple. When the natives wish to make oil, they take that cocoanut, and allow the marrowy substance and the water to putrefy. Then they boil it and it becomes oil like butter. When they wish to make vinegar, they allow only the water to putrefy, and then place it in the sun, and a vinegar results like [that made from] white wine. Milk can also be made from it for we made some. We scraped that marrowy substance and then mixed the scrapings with its own water which we strained through a cloth, and so obtained milk like goat's milk. Those palms resemble date-palms, but although not smooth they are less knotty than the latter. A family of X persons can be supported on two trees, by utilizing them week about for the wine; for if they did otherwise, the trees would dry up. They last a century.

Those people became very familiar with us. They told us many things, their names and those of some of the islands that could be seen from that place. Their own island was called Zuluan and it is not very large. We took great pleasure with them, for they were very pleasant and conversable. In order to show them greater honor, the captain-general took them to his ship and showed them all his merchandise—cloves, cinnamon, pepper, ginger, nutmeg, mace, gold, and all the things in the ship. He had some mortars fired for them, whereat they exhibited great fear, and tried to jump out of the ship. They made signs to us that the abovesaid articles grew in that place where we were going. When they were about to retire they took their leave very gracefully and neatly, saying that they would return according to their promise. The island where we were is called Humunu; [43] but inasmuch as we found two springs there of the clearest water, we called it Acquada da li buoni Segnialli ("the Watering-place of good Signs") , for there were the first signs of gold which we found in those districts. We found a great

[43] Now called Homonhon.

quantity of white coral there, and large trees with fruit a trifle smaller than the almond and resembling pine seeds. There are also many palms, some of them good and others bad. There are many islands in that district, and therefore we called them the archipelago of San Lazaro, as they were discovered on the Sabbath of St. Lazurus.[44] They lie in X degrees of latitude toward the Arctic Pole, and in a longitude of one hundred and sixty-one degrees from the line of demarcation.

At noon on Friday, March 22, those men came as they had promised us in two boats with cocoanuts, sweet oranges, a jar of palm-wine, and a cock, in order to show us that there were fowls in that district. They exhibited great signs of pleasure at seeing us. We purchased all those articles from them. Their seignior was an old man who was painted [tattooed]. He wore two gold earrings in his ears, and the others many gold armlets on their arms and kerchiefs about their heads. We stayed there one week, and during that time our captain went ashore daily to visit the sick, and every morning gave them cocoanut water from his own hand, which comforted them greatly. There are people living near that island who have holes in their ears so large that they can pass their arms through them. Those people are *caphri*, that is to say, heathen. They go naked, with a cloth woven from the bark of a tree about

[44] The name Felipinas, or Philippines, was later bestowed in honor of the heir-apparent of Spain, the future Philip II, born in 1527.

their privies, except some of the chiefs who wear cotton cloth embroidered with silk at the ends by means of a needle. They are dark, fat, and painted. They anoint themselves with cocoanut and with beneseed oil, as a protection against sun and wind. They have very black hair that falls to the waist, and use daggers, knives, and spears ornamented with gold, large shields, fascines, javelins, and fishing nets that resemble rizali; and their boats are like ours.

On the afternoon of holy Monday, the day of our Lady, March twenty-five, while we were on the point of weighing anchor, I went to the side of the ship to fish, and putting my feet upon a yard leading down into the storeroom, they slipped, for it was rainy, and consequently I fell into the sea, so that no one saw me. When I was all but under, my left hand happened to catch hold of the clew-garnet of the mainsail, which was dangling in the water. I held on tightly, and began to cry out so lustily that I was rescued by the small boat. I was aided, not, I believe, indeed, through my merits, but through the mercy of that font of charity [the Virgin]. That same day we shaped our course toward the west southwest between four small islands, namely, Cenalo, Hiunanghan, Ibusson, and Abarien.

On Thursday morning, March twenty-eight, as we had seen a fire on an island the night before, we anchored near it. We saw a small boat which the natives call *boloto* with eight men in it, approaching the flagship. A slave belonging to the captain-general, who was a native of Zamatra, which was formerly called Traprobana, spoke to them. They immediately understood him, came alongside the ship, unwilling to enter but taking a position at some little distance. The captain seeing that they would not trust us, threw them out a red cap and other things tied to a bit of wood. They received them very gladly, and went away quickly to advise their king. About two hours later we saw two *balanghai* coming. They are large boats and are so called [by those people]. They were full of men, and their king was in the larger of them, being seated under an awning of mats. When the king came near the flagship, the slave spoke to him. The king understood him, for in those districts the kings know more languages than the other people. He ordered some of his men to enter the ships, but he always remained in his *balanghai,* at some little distance from the ship, until his own men returned; and as soon as they returned he departed. The captain-general showed great honor to the men who entered the ship, and gave them some presents, for which the king wished before his departure to give the captain a large bar of gold and a basketful of ginger. The latter, however, thanked the king heartily but would not accept it. In the afternoon we went in the ships [and anchored] near the dwellings of the king.

Next day, holy Friday, the captain-general sent his slave, who acted as our interpreter, ashore in a small boat to ask the king if he had any food to have it carried to the ships; and to say that they would be well satisfied with us, for he [and his men] had come to the island as friends and not as enemies. The king came with six or eight men in the same boat and entered the ship. He embraced the captain-general to whom he gave three porcelain jars covered with leaves and full of raw rice, two very large *orade,* and other things. The captain-general gave the king a garment of red and yellow cloth made in the Turkish fashion, and a fine red cap; and to the others [the king's men], to some knives and to others mirrors. Then the captain-general had a collation spread for them, and had the king told through the slave that he desired to be *casi casi* with him, that is to say, brother. The king replied that he also wished to enter the same relations with the captain-general. Then the captain showed him cloth of various colors, linen, coral [ornaments], and many other articles of merchandise, and all the artillery, some of which he had discharged for him, whereat the natives were greatly frightened. Then the captain-general had a man armed as a soldier, and placed him in the midst of three men armed with swords and daggers, who struck him on all parts of the body. Thereby was the king rendered almost speechless. The captain-general told him through the slave that one of those armed men was worth one hundred of his own men. The king answered that that was a fact. The captain-general said that he had two hundred men in each ship who were armed in that manner.[45] He showed the king cuirasses, swords,

[45] This, of course, was a great exaggeration by Magellan, who at that time had less than half the manpower alleged.

138

and bucklers, and had a review made for him. Then
he led the king to the deck of the ship, that is located above at the stern; and had his sea-chart and
compass brought. He told the king through the interpreter how he had found the strait in order to
voyage thither, and how many moons he had been
without seeing land, whereat the king was astonished. Lastly, he told the king that he would like, if
it were pleasing to him, to send two of his men with
him so that he might show them some of his things.
The king replied that he was agreeable, and I went
in company with one of the other men.

When I reached shore, the king raised his hands
toward the sky and then turned toward us two. We
did the same toward him as did all the others. The
king took me by the hand; one of his chiefs took my
companion: and thus they led us under a bamboo
covering, where there was a *balanghai,* as long as
eighty of my palm lengths, and resembling a *fusta.*
We sat down upon the stern of that *balanghai,* constantly conversing with signs. The king's men
stood about us in a circle with swords, daggers,
spears, and bucklers. The king had a plate of pork
brought in and a large jar filled with wine. At every
mouthful, we drank a cup of wine. The wine that
was left [in the cup] at any time, although that happened but rarely, was put into a jar by itself. The
king's cup was always kept covered and no one else
drank from it but he and I. Before the king took the
cup to drink, he raised his clasped hands toward the
sky, and then toward me; and when he was about

to drink, he extended the fist of his left hand toward me (at first I thought that he was about to strike me) and then drank. I did the same toward the king. They all make those signs one toward another when they drink. We ate with such ceremonies and with other signs of friendship. I ate meat on holy Friday, for I could not help myself. Before the supper hour I gave the king many things which I had brought. I wrote down the names of many things in their language. When the king and the others saw me writing, and when I told them their words, they were all astonished. While engaged in that the supper hour was announced. Two large porcelain dishes were brought in, one full of rice and the other of pork with its gravy. We ate with the same signs and ceremonies, after which we went to the palace of the king which was built like a hayloft and was thatched with fig and palm leaves. It was built up high from the ground on huge posts of wood and it was necessary to ascend to it by means of ladders. The king made us sit down there on a bamboo mat with our feet drawn up like tailors. After a half-hour a platter of roast fish cut in pieces was brought in, and ginger freshly gathered, and wine. The king's eldest son, who was the prince, came over to us, whereupon the king told him to sit down near us, and he accordingly did so. Then two platters were brought in (one with fish and its sauce, and the other with rice), so that we might eat with the prince. My companion became intoxicated as a consequence of so much drinking and eating. They used the gum of a tree called *anime* wrapped in palm or fig leaves for lights. The king made us a sign that he was going to go to sleep. He left the prince with us, and we slept with the latter on a bamboo mat with pillows made of leaves. When day dawned the king came and took me by the hand, and in that manner we went to where we had had supper, in order to partake of refreshments, but the boat came to get us. Before we left, the king kissed our hands with great joy, and we his. One of his brothers, the king of another island, and three men came with us. The captain-general kept him to dine with us, and gave him many things.

Pieces of gold of the size of walnuts and eggs are found by sifting the earth in the island of that king who came to our ships. All the dishes of that king are of gold and also some portion of his house, as we were told by that king himself. According to their customs he was very grandly decked out, and the finest looking man that we saw among those people. His hair was exceedingly black, and hung to his shoulders. He had a covering of silk on his head, and wore two large golden earrings fastened in his ears. He wore a cotton cloth all embroidered with silk, which covered him from the waist to the knees. At his side hung a dagger, the haft of which was somewhat long and all of gold, and its scabbard of carved wood. He had three spots of gold on every tooth, and his teeth appeared as if bound with gold. He was perfumed with storax and benzoin. He was tawny and painted all over. That island of his was called Butuan and Calagan.[46] When those kings wished to see one another, they both went to hunt in that island where we were. The name of the first king is Raia Colambu, and the second Raia Siaui.

Early on the morning of Sunday, the last of March, and Easter-day, the captain-general sent the priest with some men to prepare the place where mass was to be said; together with the interpreter to tell the king that we were not going to land in order to dine with him, but to say mass. Therefore the king sent us two swine that he had had killed. When the hour for mass arrived, we landed with about fifty men, without our body armor, but carrying our other arms, and dressed in our best clothes. Before we reached the shore with our boats, six pieces were discharged as a sign of peace. We landed; the two kings embraced the captain-general, and placed him between them. We went in marching order to the place consecrated, which was not far from the shore. Before the commencement of mass, the captain sprinkled the entire bodies of the two kings with musk water. The mass was offered up. The kings went forward to kiss the cross as we did, but they did not offer the sacrifice. When the body of our Lord was elevated, they remained on their knees and worshiped Him with clasped hands. The ships fired all their artillery at once when the body of Christ was elevated, the signal having been given from the shore with muskets. After the conclusion of

[46] This king ruled Butuan and Caraga in northern Mindanao.

mass, some of our men took communion. The captain-general arranged a fencing tournament, at which the kings were greatly pleased. Then he had a cross carried in and the nails and a crown, to which immediate reverence was made. He told the kings through the interpreter that they were the standards given to him by the emperor his sovereign, so that wherever he might go he might set up those his tokens. [He said] that he wished to set it up in that place for their benefit, for whenever any of our ships came, they would know that we had been there by that cross, and would do nothing to displease them or harm their property. If any of their men were captured, they would be set free immediately on that sign being shown. It was necessary to set that cross on the summit of the highest mountain, so that on seeing it every morning, they might adore it; and if they did that, neither thunder, lightning, nor storms would harm them in the least. They thanked him heartily and [said] that they would do everything willingly. The captain-general also had them asked whether they were Moros or heathen, or what was their belief. They replied that they worshiped nothing, but that they raised their clasped hands and their face to the sky; and that they called their god "Abba." Thereat the captain was very glad, and seeing that, the first king raised his hands to the sky, and said that he wished that it were possible for him to make the captain see his love for him. The interpreter asked the king why there was so little to eat there. The latter replied that he did not live in that place except when he went hunting and to see his brother, but that he lived in another island where all his family were. The captain-general had him asked to declare whether he had any enemies, so that he might go with his ships to destroy them and to render them obedient to him. The king thanked him and said that he did indeed have two islands hostile to him, but that it was not then the season to go there. The captain told him that if God would again allow him to return to those districts, he would bring so many men that he would make the king's enemies subject to him by force. He said that he was about to go to dinner, and that he would return afterward to have the cross set up on the summit of the mountain. They replied that they were satisfied, and then forming in battalion and firing the muskets, and the captain having embraced the two kings, we took our leave.

After dinner we all returned clad in our doublets, and that afternoon went together with the two kings to the summit of the highest mountain there. When we reached the summit, the captain-general told them that he esteemed highly having sweated for them, for since the cross was there, it could not but be of great use to them. On asking them which port was the best to get food, they replied that there were three, namely, Ceylon, Zubu, and Calaghann, but that Zubu was the largest and the one with most trade. They offered of their own accord to give us pilots to show us the way. The captain-general thanked them, and determined to go there, for so did his unhappy fate will. After the cross was erected in position, each of us repeated a *Pater Noster* and an *Ave Maria,* and adored the cross; and the kings did the same. Then we descended through their cultivated fields, and went to the place where the *balanghai* was. The kings had some cocoanuts brought in so that we might refresh ourselves. The captain asked the kings for the pilots for he intended to depart the following morning, and [said] that he would treat them as if they were the kings themselves, and would leave one of us as hostage. The kings replied that every hour he wished the pilots were at his command, but that night the first king changed his mind, and in the morning when we were about to depart, sent word to the captain-general, asking him for love of him to wait two days until he should have his rice harvested, and other trifles attended to. He asked the captain-general to send him some men to help him, so that it might be done sooner; and said that he intended to act as our pilot himself. The captain sent him some men, but the kings ate and drank so much that they slept all the day. Some said to excuse them that they were slightly sick. Our men did nothing on that day, but they worked the next two days.

One of those people brought us about a porringer full of rice and also eight or ten figs fastened together to barter them for a knife which at the most was worth three catrini. The captain seeing that that native cared for nothing but a knife, called him to look at other things. He put his hand in his

145

purse and wished to give him one real for those
things, but the native refused it. The captain
showed him a ducado but he would not accept that
either. Finally the captain tried to give him a dop-
pione worth two ducados, but he would take nothing but a knife; and accordingly the captain had one
given to him. When one of our men went ashore
for water, one of those people wanted to give him
a pointed crown of massy gold, of the size of a
colona for six strings of glass beads, but the captain
refused to let him barter, so that the natives should
learn at the very beginning that we prized our merchandise more than their gold.

Those people are heathens, and go naked and
painted. They wear a piece of cloth woven from a
tree about their privies. They are very heavy drink-
ers. Their women are clad in tree cloth from their
waist down, and their hair is black and reaches to
the ground. They have holes pierced in their ears
which are filled with gold. Those people are constantly chewing a fruit which they call *areca*, and
which resembles a pear. They cut that fruit into
four parts, and then wrap it in the leaves of their
tree which they call *betre*. Those leaves resemble
the leaves of the mulberry. They mix it with a little
lime, and when they have chewed it thoroughly,
they spit it out. It makes the mouth exceedingly
red. All the people in those parts of the world use
it, for it is very cooling to the heart, and if they
ceased to use it they would die. There are dogs, cats,
swine, fowls, goats, rice, ginger, cocoanuts, figs,

oranges, lemons, millet, panicum, sorgo, wax, and a quantity of gold in that island. It lies in a latitude of nine and two-thirds degrees toward the Arctic Pole, and in a longitude of one hundred and sixty-two degrees from the line of demarcation. It is twenty-five from the Acquada, and is called Mazaua.

We remained there seven days, after which we laid our course toward the northwest, passing among five islands, namely, Ceylon, Bohol, Canighan, Baybai, and Gatighan.[47] In the last-named island of Gatighan, there are bats as large as eagles. As it was late we killed one of them, which resembled chicken in taste. There are doves, turtledoves, parrots, and certain black birds as large as domestic chickens, which have a long tail. The last mentioned birds lay eggs as large as the goose, and bury them under the sand, through the great heat of which they hatch out. When the chicks are born, they push up the sand, and come out. Those eggs are good to eat. There is a distance of twenty leguas from Mazaua to Gatighan. We set out westward from Gatighan, but the king of Mazaua could not follow us [closely], and consequently, we awaited him near three islands, namely, Polo, Ticobon, and Pozon. When he caught up with us he was greatly astonished at the rapidity with which we sailed. The captain-general had him come into his ship with several of his chiefs at which they were pleased. Thus did we go to Zubu from Gatighan, the distance to Zubu being fifteen leguas.

[47] Leyte, Bohol, Canigao, the northern part of Leyte, and an island impossible to identify. Masaua is now called Limasaua.

At noon on Sunday, April seven, we entered the port of Zubu,[48] passing by many villages, where we saw many houses built upon logs. On approaching the city, the captain-general ordered the ships to fling their banners. The sails were lowered and arranged as if for battle, and all the artillery was fired, an action which caused great fear to those people. The captain sent a foster-son of his as ambassador to the king of Zubu with the interpreter. When they reached the city, they found a vast crowd of people together with the king, all of whom had been frightened by the mortars. The interpreter told them that that was our custom when entering into such places, as a sign of peace and friendship, and that we had discharged all our mortars to honor the king of the village. The king and all of his men were reassured, and the king had us asked by his governor what we wanted. The interpreter replied that his master was a captain of the greatest king and prince in the world, and that he was going to discover Malucho; but that he had come solely to visit the king because of the good report which he had heard of him from the king of Mazaua, and to buy food with his merchandise. The king told him that he was welcome, but that it was their custom for all ships that entered their ports to pay tribute, and that it was but four days since a junk from Ciama laden with gold and slaves had paid him tribute. As proof of his statement the king pointed out to the interpreter a merchant from Ciama, who had remained

[48] Cebu, on the island of the same name.

148

to trade the gold and slaves. The interpreter told the king that, since his master was the captain of so great a king, he did not pay tribute to any seignior in the world, and that if the king wished peace he would have peace, but if war instead, war. Thereupon, the Moro merchant said to the king *Cata raia chita,* that is to say, "Look well, sire." "These men are the same who have conquered Calicut, Malaca, and all India Magiore. If they are treated well, they will give good treatment, but if they are treated evil, evil and worse treatment, as they have done to Calicut and Malaca." The interpreter understood it all and told the king that his master's king was more powerful in men and ships than the king of Portogalo, that he was the king of Spagnia and emperor of all the Christians, and that if the king did not care to be his friend he would next time send so many men that they would destroy him. The Moro related everything to the king, who said thereupon that he would deliberate with his men, and would answer the captain on the following day. Then he had refreshments of many dishes, all made from meat and contained in porcelain platters, besides many jars of wine brought in. After our men had refreshed themselves, they returned and told us everything. The king of Mazaua, who was the most influential after that king and the seignior of a number of islands, went ashore to speak to the king of the great courtesy of our captain-general.

Monday morning, our notary, together with the interpreter, went to Zubu. The king, accompanied by his chiefs, came to the open square where he had our men sit down near him. He asked the notary whether there were more than one captain in that company, and whether that captain wished him to pay tribute to the emperor his master. The notary replied in the negative, but that the captain wished only to trade with him and with no others. The king said that he was satisfied, and that if the captain wished to become his friend, he should send him a drop of blood from his right arm, and he himself would do the same [to him] as a sign of the most sincere friendship. The notary answered that the captain would do it. Thereupon, the king told him that all the captains who came to that place, were wont to give presents one to the other, and asked whether our captain or he ought to commence. The interpreter told the king that since he desired to maintain the custom, he should commence, and so he did.

Tuesday morning the king of Mazaua came to the ships with the Moro. He saluted the captain-general in behalf of the king [of Zubu], and said that the king of Zubu was collecting as much food as possible to give to him, and that after dinner he would send one of his nephews and two others of his chief men to make peace. The captain-general had one of his men armed with his own arms, and had the Moro told that we all fought in that manner. The Moro was greatly frightened, but the captain told him not to be frightened for our arms were soft toward our friends and harsh toward our enemies; and as handkerchiefs wipe off the sweat so did our arms overthrow and destroy all our adversaries, and those who hate our faith. The captain did that so that the Moro who seemed more intelligent than the others, might tell it to the king.

After dinner the king's nephew, who was the prince, came to the ships with the king of Mazaua, the Moro, the governor, the chief constable, and eight chiefs, to make peace with us. The captain-general was seated in a red velvet chair, the principal men on leather chairs, and the others on mats upon the floor. The captain-general asked them through the interpreter whether it were their custom to speak in secret or in public, and whether that prince and the king of Mazaua had authority to make peace. They answered that they spoke in public, and that they were empowered to make peace. The captain-general said many things concerning peace, and that he prayed God to confirm it in heaven. They said that they had never heard any one speak such words, but that they took great pleasure in hearing them. The captain seeing that they listened and answered willingly, began to advance arguments to induce them to accept the faith. Asking them who would succeed to the seigniory after the death of the king, he was answered that the king had no sons but only daughters, the eldest of whom was the wife of that nephew of his, who therefore was the prince. [They said that] when the fathers and mothers grew old, they received no further honor, but their children commanded

151

them. The captain told them that God made the sky, the earth, the sea, and everything else, and that He had commanded us to honor our fathers and mothers, and that whoever did otherwise was condemned to eternal fire; that we are all descended from Adam and Eva, our first parents; that we have an immortal spirit; and many other things pertaining to the faith. All joyfully entreated the captain to leave them two men, or at least one, to instruct them in the faith, and [said] that they would show them great honor. The captain replied to them that he could not leave them any men then, but that if they wished to become Christians, our priest would baptize them, and that he would next time bring priests and friars who would instruct them in our faith. They answered that they would first speak to their king, and that then they would become Christians, [whereat] we all wept with great joy. The captain-general told them that they should not become Christians for fear or to please us, but of their own free wills; and that he would not cause any displeasure to those who wished to live according to their own law, but that the Christians would be better regarded and treated than the others. All cried out with one voice that they were not becoming Christians through fear or to please us, but of their own free will. Then the captain told them that if they became Christians, he would leave a suit of armor, for so had his king commanded him; that we could not have intercourse with their women without committing a very great sin, since they were pagans; and that he assured them that if they became Christians, the devil would no longer appear to them except in the last moment at their death. They said that they could not answer the beautiful words of the captain, but that they placed themselves in his hands, and that he should treat them as his most faithful servants. The captain embraced them weeping, and clasping one of the prince's hands and one of the king's between his own, said to them that, by his faith in God and to his sovereign, the emperor, and by the habit which he wore, he promised them that he would give them perpetual peace with the king of Spagnia. They answered that they promised the same. After the conclusion of the peace, the captain had refreshments served to them. Then the prince and the king [of Mazaua] presented some baskets of rice, swine, goats, and fowls to the captain-general on behalf of their king, and asked him to pardon them, for such things were but little [to give] to one such as he. The captain gave the prince a white cloth of the finest linen, a red cap, some strings of glass beads, and a gilded glass drinking cup. Those glasses are greatly appreciated in those districts. He did not give any present to the king of Mazaua, for he had already given him a robe of Cambaya, besides other articles. To the others he gave now one thing and now another. Then he sent to the king of Zubu through me and one other a yellow and violet silk robe, made in Turkish style, a fine red cap, some strings of glass beads, all in a silver dish, and two

gilt drinking cups in our hands. When we reached
the city we found the king in his palace surrounded
by many people. He was seated on a palm mat on
the ground, with only a cotton cloth before his privies, and a scarf embroidered with the needle about
his head, a necklace of great value hanging from his
neck, and two large gold earrings fastened in his ears
set round with precious gems. He was fat and short,
and tattooed with fire in various designs. From another mat on the ground he was eating turtle eggs
which were in two porcelain dishes, and he had four
jars full of palm wine in front of him covered with
sweet-smelling herbs and arranged with four small
reeds in each jar by means of which he drank. Having duly made reverence to him, the interpreter
told the king that his master thanked him very
warmly for his present, and that he sent this present
not in return for his present but for the intrinsic
love which he bore him. We dressed him in the
robe, placed the cap on his head, and gave him the
other things; then kissing the beads and putting
them upon his head, I presented them to him. He
doing the same [kissing them] accepted them. Then
the king had us eat some of those eggs and drink
through those slender reeds. The others, his men,
told him in that place, the words of the captain concerning peace and his exhortation to them to become Christians. The king wished to have us stay
to supper with him, but we told him that we could
not stay then. Having taken our leave of him, the
prince took us with him to his house, where four

young girls were playing [instruments—one, on a drum like ours, but resting on the ground; the second was striking two suspended gongs alternately with a stick wrapped somewhat thickly at the end with palm cloth; the third, one large gong in the same manner; and the last, two small gongs held in her hand, by striking one against the other, which gave forth a sweet sound. They played so harmoniously that one would believe they possessed good musical sense. Those girls were very beautiful and almost as white as our girls and as large. They were naked except for tree cloth hanging from the waist and reaching to the knees. Some were quite naked and had large holes in their ears with a small round piece of wood in the hole, which keeps the hole round and large. They have long black hair, and wear a short cloth about the head, and are always barefoot. The prince had three quite naked girls dance for us. We took refreshments and then went to the ships. Those gongs are made of brass and are manufactured in the regions about the Signio Magno which is called China. They are used in those regions as we use bells and are called *aghon*.

On Wednesday morning, as one of our men had died during the previous night, the interpreter and I went to ask the king where we could bury him. We found the king surrounded by many men, of whom, after the due reverence was made, I asked it. He replied, "If I and my vassals all belong to your sovereign, how much more ought the land." I told the king that we would like to consecrate the place, and to set up a cross there. He replied that he was quite satisfied, and that he wished to adore the cross as did we. The deceased was buried in the square with as much pomp as possible, in order to furnish a good example. Then we consecrated the place, and in the evening buried another man. We carried a quantity of merchandise ashore which we stored in a house. The king took it under his care as well as four men who were left to trade the goods by wholesale. Those people live in accordance with justice, and have weights and measures. They love peace, ease, and quiet. They have wooden balances, the bar of which has a cord in the middle by which it is held. At one end is a bit of lead, and at the other marks like quarter-libras, third-libras, and libras. When they wish to weigh they take the scales which has three wires like ours, and place it above the marks, and so weigh accurately. They have very large measures without any bottom. The youth play on pipes made like ours which they call *subin*. Their houses are constructed of wood, and are built of planks and bamboo, raised high from the ground on large logs, and one must enter them by means of ladders. They have rooms like ours; and under the house they keep their swine, goats, and fowls. Large sea snails, beautiful to the sight, are found there which kill whales. For the whale swallows them alive, and when they are in the whale's body, they come out of their shells and eat the whale's heart. Those people afterward find them alive near the dead whale's heart. Those creatures have black teeth and skin and a white shell, and the flesh is good to eat. They are called *laghan*.[49]

On Friday we showed those people a shop full of our merchandise, at which they were very much surprised. For metals, iron, and other large merchandise they gave us gold. For the other smaller articles they gave us rice, swine, goats, and other food. Those people gave us X pieces of gold for XIIII libras of iron (one piece being worth about one and one-half ducados). The captain-general did not wish to take too much gold, for there would have been some sailors who would have given all that they owned for a small amount of gold, and would have spoiled the trade for ever. On Saturday, as the captain had promised the king to make him a Christian on Sunday, a platform was built in the consecrated square, which was adorned with hangings and palm branches for his baptism. The captain-general sent men to tell the king not to be afraid of the pieces that would be discharged in the morning, for it was our custom to discharge them at our greater feasts without loading with stones.

On Sunday morning, April fourteen, forty men of us went ashore, two of whom were completely armed and preceded the royal banner. When we reached land all the artillery was fired. Those people followed us hither and thither. The captain and the king embraced. The captain told the king that the royal banner was not taken ashore except with fifty men armed as were those two, and with fifty

[49] Lagan. Robertson says the shell resembles mother-of-pearl.

musketeers; but so great was his love for him that he had thus brought the banner. Then we all approached the platform joyfully. The captain and the king sat down in chairs of red and violet velvet, the chiefs on cushions, and the others on mats. The captain told the king through the interpreter that he thanked God for inspiring him to become a Christian; and that [now] he would more easily conquer his enemies than before. The king replied that he wished to become a Christian, but that some of his chiefs did not wish to obey, because they said that they were as good men as he. Then our captain had all the chiefs of the king called, and told them that, unless they obeyed the king as their king, he would have them killed and would give their possessions to the king. They replied that they would obey him. The captain told the king that he was going to Spagnia, but that he would return again with so many forces that he would make him the greatest king of those regions, as he had been the first to express a determination to become a Christian. The king, lifting his hands to the sky, thanked the captain, and requested him to let some of his men remain [with him], so that he and his people might be better instructed in the faith. The captain replied that he would leave two men to satisfy him, but that he would like to take two of the children of the chiefs with him, so that they might learn our language, who afterward on their return would be able to tell the others the wonders of Spagnia. A large cross was set up in the middle of the square.

The captain told them that if they wished to become Christians as they had declared on the previous days, that they must burn all their idols and set up a cross in their place. They were to adore that cross daily with clasped hands, and every morning after their [the Spaniards'] custom, they were to make the sign of the cross (which the captain showed them how to make) ; and they ought to come hourly, at least in the morning, to that cross, and adore it kneeling. The intention that they had already declared, they were to confirm with good works. The king and all the others wished to confirm it thoroughly. The captain-general told the king that he was clad all in white to demonstrate his sincere love toward them. They replied that they could not respond to his sweet words. The captain led the king by the hand to the platform while speaking these good words in order to baptize him. He told the king that he would call him Don Carlo, after his sovereign the emperor; the prince, Don Fernando, after the emperor's brother; the king of Mazaua, Johanni; a chief, Fernando, after our chief, that is to say, the captain; the Moro, Christoforo; and then the others, now one name, and now another. Five hundred men were baptized before mass. After the conclusion of mass, the captain invited the king and some of the other chiefs to dinner, but they refused, accompanying us, however, to the shore. The ships discharged all the mortars; and embracing, the king and chiefs and the captain took leave of one another.

After dinner the priest and some of the others went ashore to baptize the queen, who came with forty women. We conducted her to the platform, and she was made to sit down upon a cushion, and the other women near her, until the priest should be ready. She was shown an image of our Lady, a very beautiful wooden child Jesus, and a cross. Thereupon, she was overcome with contrition, and asked for baptism amid her tears. We named her Johanna, after the emperor's mother; her daughter, the wife of the prince, Catherina; the queen of Mazaua, Lisabeta; and the others, each their [distinctive] name. Counting men, women, and children, we baptized eight hundred souls. The queen was young and beautiful, and was entirely covered with a white and black cloth. Her mouth and nails were very red, while on her head she wore a large hat of palm leaves in the manner of a parasol, with a crown about it of the same leaves, like the tiara of the pope; and she never goes any place without such a one. She asked us to give her the little child Jesus to keep in place of her idols; and then she went away. In the afternoon, the king and queen, accompanied by numerous persons, came to the shore. Thereupon, the captain had many trombs of fire and large mortars discharged, by which they were most highly delighted. The captain and the king called one another brothers. That king's name was Raia Humabon. Before that week had gone, all the persons of that island, and some from the other islands, were baptized. We burned one hamlet which was located in a neighboring island, because it refused to obey the king or us. We set up the cross there for those people were heathen. Had they been Moros, we would have erected a column there as a token of greater hardness, for the Moros are much harder to convert than the heathen.

The captain-general went ashore daily during those days to hear mass, and told the king many things regarding the faith. One day the queen came with great pomp to hear mass. Three girls preceded her with three of her hats in their hands. She was dressed in black and white with a large silk scarf, crossed with gold stripes thrown over her head, which covered her shoulders; and she had on her hat. A great number of women accompanied her, who were all naked and barefoot, except that they had a small covering of palm-tree cloth before their privies, and a small scarf upon the head, and all with hair flowing free. The queen, having made the due reverence to the altar, seated herself on a silk embroidered cushion. Before the commencement of the mass, the captain sprayed her and some of her women with musk rosewater, for they delighted exceedingly in such perfumes. The captain knowing that the queen was very much pleased with the child Jesus, gave it to her, telling her to keep it in place of her idols, for it was in memory of the son of God. Thanking him heartily she accepted it.

Before mass one day, the captain-general had the king come clad in his silk robe, and the chief men of the city, [to wit], the king's brother and

prince's father, whose name was Bendara; another
of the king's brothers, Cadaio; and certain ones
called Simiut, Sibuaia, Sisacai, Maghalibe, and many
others whom I shall not name in order not to be
tedious. The captain made them all swear to be obedient to their king, and they kissed the latter's hand.
Then the captain had the king declare that he
would always be obedient and faithful to the king of
Spagnia, and the king so swore. Thereupon, the
captain drew his sword before the image of our
Lady, and told the king that when anyone so swore,
he should prefer to die rather than to break such
an oath, if he swore by that image, by the life of the
emperor his sovereign, and by his habit to be ever
faithful. After the conclusion of that the captain
gave the king a red velvet chair, telling him that
wherever he went he should always have it carried
before him by one of his nearest relatives; and he
showed him how it ought to be carried. The king
responded that he would do that willingly for love
of him, and he told the captain that he was making
a jewel to give to him, namely, two large earrings of
gold to fasten in his ears, two armlets to put on his
arms, above the elbows, and two other rings for the
feet above the ankles, besides other precious gems
to adorn the ears. Those are the most beautiful or-
naments which the kings of those districts can wear.
They always go barefoot, and wear a cloth garment
that hangs from the waist to the knees.

One day the captain-general asked the king and
the other people why they did not burn their idols

as they had promised when they became Christians; and why they sacrificed so much flesh to them. They replied that what they were doing was not for themselves, but for a sick man who had not spoken now for four days, so that the idols might give him health. He was the prince's brother, and the bravest and wisest man in the island. The captain told them to burn their idols and to believe in Christ, and that if the sick man were baptized, he would quickly recover; and if that did not so happen they could behead him [the captain] then and there. Thereupon, the king replied that he would do it, for he truly believed in Christ. We made a procession from the square to the house of the sick man with as much pomp as possible. There we found him in such condition that he could neither speak nor move. We baptized him and his two wives, and X girls. Then the captain had him asked how he felt. He spoke immediately and said that by the grace of our Lord he felt very well. That was a most manifest miracle [that happened] in our times. When the captain heard him speak, he thanked God fervently. Then he made the sick man drink some almond milk, which he had already made for him. Afterward he sent him a mattress, a pair of sheets, a coverlet of yellow cloth, and a pillow. Until he recovered his health, the captain sent him almond milk, rosewater, oil of roses, and some sweet preserves. Before five days the sick man began to walk. He had an idol that certain old women had concealed in his house burned in the presence of the king and all the people. He had many shrines along the seashore destroyed, in which the consecrated meat was eaten. The people themselves cried out "Castiglia! Castiglia!" and destroyed those shrines. They said that if God would lend them life, they would burn all the idols that they could find, even if they were in the king's house. Those idols are made of wood, and are hollow, and lack the back parts. Their arms are open and their feet turned up under them with the legs open. They have a large face with four huge tusks like those of the wild boar; and are painted all over.

There are many villages in that island. Their names, those of their inhabitants, and of their chiefs are as follows: Cinghapola, and its chiefs, Cilaton, Ciguibucan, Cimaningha, Cimatichat, and Cicanbul; one, Mandaui, and its chief, Apanoaan; one Lalan, and its chief, Theteu; one, Lalutan, and its chief, Tapan; one Cilumai; and one, Lubucun. All those villages rendered obedience to us, and gave us food and tribute. Near that island of Zubu was an island called Matan, which formed the port where we were anchored.[50] The name of its village was Matan, and its chiefs were Zula and Cilapulapu. That city which we burned was in that island and was called Bulaia.

In order that your most illustrious Lordship may know the ceremonies that those people use in consecrating the swine, they first sound those large

[50] Mactan. It forms the port in the sense that it provides Cebu harbor with a cover from the open sea.

gongs. Then three large dishes are brought in; two with roses and with cakes of rice and millet, baked and wrapped in leaves, and roast fish; the other with cloth of Cambaia is spread on the ground. Then two very old women come, each of whom has a bamboo trumpet in her hand. When they have stepped upon the cloth they make obeisance to the sun. Then they wrap the cloths about themselves. One of them puts a kerchief with two horns on her forehead, and takes another kerchief in her hands, and dancing and blowing upon her trumpet, she thereby calls out to the sun. The other takes one of the standards and dances and blows on her trumpet. They dance and call out thus for a little space, saying many things between themselves to the sun. She with the kerchief takes the other standard, and lets the kerchief drop, and both blowing on their trumpets for a long time, dance about the bound hog. She with the horns always speaks covertly to the sun, and the other answers her. A cup of wine is presented to her of the horns, and she dancing and repeating certain words, while the other answers her, and making pretense four or five times of drinking the wine, sprinkles it upon the heart of the hog. Then she immediately begins to dance again. A lance is given to the same woman. She shaking it and repeating certain words, while both of them continue to dance, and making motions four or five times of thrusting the lance through the heart of the hog, with a sudden and quick stroke, thrusts it through from one side to the other. The wound is quickly

165

stopped with grass. The one who has killed the hog, taking in her mouth a lighted torch, which has been lighted throughout that ceremony, extinguishes it. The other one dipping the end of her trumpet in the blood of the hog, goes around marking with blood with her finger first the foreheads of their husbands, and then the others; but they never came to us. Then they divest themselves and go to eat the contents of those dishes, and they invite only women [to eat with them]. The hair is removed from the hog by means of fire. Thus no one but old women consecrate the flesh of the hog, and they do not eat it unless it is killed in this way.

Those people go naked, wearing but one piece of palm-tree cloth about their privies. The males, large and small, have their penis pierced from one side to the other near the head, with a gold or tin bolt as large as a goose quill. In both ends of the same bolt, some have what resembles a spur, with points upon the ends; others like the head of a cart nail. I very often asked many, both old and young, to see their penis, because I could not credit it. In the middle of the bolt is a hole, through which they urinate. The bolt and the spurs always hold firm. They say that their women wish it so, and that if they did otherwise they would not have communication with them. When the men wish to have communication with their women, the latter themselves take the penis not in the regular way and commence very gently to introduce it [into their vagina], with the spur on top first, and then the other part. When it is inside it takes its regular position; and thus the penis always stays inside until it gets soft, for otherwise they could not pull it out. Those people make use of that device because they are of a weak nature. They have as many wives as they wish, but one of them is the principal wife. Whenever any of our men went ashore, both by day and by night, every one invited him to eat and to drink. Their viands are half cooked and very salty. They drink frequently and copiously from the jars through those small reeds, and one of their meals lasts for five or six hours. The women loved us very much more than their own men. All of the women from the age of six years and upward, have their vaginas gradually opened because of the men's penises.[51]

They practice the following ceremonies when one of their chiefs dies. First all the chief women of the place go to the house of the deceased. The deceased is placed in the middle of the house in a box. Ropes are placed about the box in the manner of a palisade, to which many branches of trees are attached. In the middle of each branch hangs a cotton cloth like a curtained canopy. The most principal women sit under those hangings, and are all covered with white cotton cloth, each one by a girl who fans her with a palm-leaf fan. The other women sit about the room sadly. Then there is one woman who cuts off the hair of the deceased very slowly with a knife.

[51] Lord Stanley omits most of the previous paragraph. Lagôa (II, 104) again falls back on Pigafetta's Italian.

Another who was the principal wife of the deceased, lies down upon him, and places her mouth, her hands, and her feet upon those of the deceased. When the former is cutting off the hair, the latter weeps; and when the former finishes the cutting, the latter sings. There are many porcelain jars containing fire about the room, and myrrh, storax, and bezoin, which make a strong odor through the house, are put on the fire. They keep the body in the house for five or six days during those ceremonies. I believe that the body is anointed with camphor. Then they bury the body and the same box which is shut in a log by means of wooden nails and covered and enclosed by logs of wood. Every night about midnight in that city, a jet black bird as large as a crow was wont to come, and no sooner had it thus reached the houses than it began to screech, so that all the dogs began to howl; and that screeching and howling would last for four or five hours, but those people would never tell us the reason of it.

On Friday, April twenty-six, Zula, a chief of the island of Matan, sent one of his sons to present two goats to the captain-general, and to say that he would send him all that he had promised, but that he had not been able to send it to him because of the other chief Cilapulapu, who refused to obey the king of Spagnia. He requested the captain to send him only one boatload of men on the next night, so that they might help him and fight against the other chief. The captain-general decided to go thither with three boatloads. We begged him repeatedly not to go, but he, like a good shepherd, refused to abandon his flock. At midnight, sixty men of us set out armed with corselets and helmets, together with the Christian king, the prince, some of the chief men, and twenty or thirty *balanguais*. We reached Matan three hours before dawn. The captain did not wish to fight then, but sent a message to the natives by the Moro to the effect that if they would obey the king of Spagnia, recognize the Christian king as their sovereign, and pay us our tribute, he would be their friend; but that if they wished otherwise, they should wait to see how our lances wounded. They replied that if we had lances they had lances of bamboo and stakes hardened with fire. [They asked us] not to proceed to attack them at once, but to wait until morning, so that they might have more men. They said that in order to induce us to go in search of them; for they had dug certain pitholes between the houses in order that we might fall into them. When morning came fortynine of us leaped into the water up to our thighs, and walked through water for more than two crossbow flights before we could reach the shore. The boats could not approach nearer because of certain rocks in the water. The other eleven men remained behind to guard the boats. When we reached land, those men had formed in three divisions to the number of more than one thousand five hundred persons. When they saw us, they charged down upon us with exceeding loud cries, two divisions on our flanks and the other on our front. When the captain saw that, he formed us into two divisions, and thus did we begin to fight. The musketeers and crossbowmen shot from a distance for about a half-hour, but uselessly; for the shots only passed through the shields which were made of thin wood and the arms [of the bearers]. The captain cried to them, "Cease firing! cease firing!" but his order was not at all heeded. When the natives saw that we were shooting our muskets to no purpose, crying out they determined to stand firm, but they redoubled their shouts. When our muskets were discharged, the natives would never stand still, but leaped hither and thither, covering themselves with their shields. They shot so many arrows at us and hurled so many bamboo spears (some of them tipped with iron) at the captain-general, besides pointed stakes hardened with fire, stones, and mud, that we could scarcely defend ourselves. Seeing that, the captain-general sent some men to burn their houses in order to terrify them. When they saw their houses burning, they were roused to greater fury. Two of our men were killed near the houses, while we burned twenty or thirty houses. So many of them charged down upon us that they shot the captain through the right leg with a poisoned arrow. On that account, he ordered us to retire slowly, but the men took to flight, except six or eight of us who remained with the captain. The natives shot only at our legs, for the latter were bare; and so many were the

170

spears and stones that they hurled at us, that we could offer no resistance. The mortars in the boats could not aid us as they were too far away. So we continued to retire for more than a good crossbow flight from the shore always fighting up to our knees in the water. The natives continued to pursue us, and picking up the same spear four or six times, hurled it at us again and again. Recognizing the captain, so many turned upon him that they knocked his helmet off his head twice, but he always stood firmly like a good knight, together with some others. Thus did we fight for more than one hour, refusing to retire farther. An Indian hurled a bamboo spear into the captain's face, but the latter immediately killed him with his lance, which he left in the Indian's body. Then, trying to lay hand on sword, he could draw it out but halfway, because he had been wounded in the arm with a bamboo spear. When the natives saw that, they all hurled themselves upon him. One of them wounded him on the left leg with a large cutlass, which resembles a scimitar, only being larger. That caused the captain to fall face downward, when immediately they rushed upon him with iron and bamboo spears and with their cutlasses, until they killed our mirror, our light, our comfort, and our true guide. When they wounded him, he turned back many times to see whether we were all in the boats. Thereupon, beholding him dead, we, wounded, retreated, as best we could, to the boats, which were already pulling off. The Christian king would have aided us, but the captain charged him before we landed, not to leave his *balanghai,* but to stay to see how we fought. When the king learned that the captain was dead, he wept. Had it not been for that unfortunate captain, not a single one of us would have been saved in the boats, for while he was fighting the others retired to the boats. I hope through [the efforts of] your most illustrious Lordship that the fame of so noble a captain will not become effaced in our times. Among the other virtues which he possessed, he was more constant than ever any one else in the greatest of adversity. He endured hunger better than all the others, and more accurately than any man in the world did he understand sea charts and navigation. And that this was the truth was seen openly, for no other had had so much natural talent nor the boldness to learn how to circumnavigate the world, as he had almost done. That battle was fought on Saturday, April twenty-seven, 1521. The captain desired to fight on Saturday, because it was the day especially holy to him. Eight of our men were killed with him in that battle, and four Indians, who had become Christians and who had come afterward to aid us were killed by the mortars of the boats. Of the enemy, only fifteen were killed, while many of us were wounded. In the afternoon the Christian king sent a message with our consent to the people of Matan, to the effect that if they would give us the captain and the other men who had been killed, we would give them as much merchandise as they wished. They answered that they would not give up such a man, as we imagined [they would do], and that they would not give him for all the riches in the world, but that they intended to keep him as a memorial.

On Saturday, the day on which the captain was killed, the four men who had remained in the city to trade, had our merchandise carried to the ships. Then we chose two commanders, namely, Duarte Barboza, a Portuguese and a relative of the captain, and Johan Seranno, a Spaniard. As our interpreter, Henrich by name, was wounded slightly, he would not go ashore any more to attend to our necessary affairs, but always kept his bed. On that account, Duarte Barboza, the commander of the flagship, cried out to him and told him, that although his master, the captain, was dead, he was not therefore free; on the contrary he [Barboza) would see to it that when we should reach Espagnia, he should still be the slave of Doña Beatrice, the wife of the captain-general. And threatening the slave that if he did go ashore, he would be flogged, the latter arose, and, feigning to take no heed to those words, went ashore to tell the Christian king that we were about to leave very soon, but that if he would follow his advice, he could gain the ships and all our merchandise. Accordingly, they arranged a plot, and the slave returned to the ship, where he showed that he was more cunning than before.

On Wednesday morning, the first of May, the Christian king sent word to the commanders that the jewels which he had promised to send to the king of Spagnia were ready, and that he begged them and their other companions to come to dine with him that morning, when he would give them the jewels. Twenty-four men went ashore, among whom was our astrologer, San Martín de Sivilla. I could not go because I was all swollen up by a wound from a poisoned arrow which I had received in my face. Jovan Carvaio and the constable returned, and told us that they saw the man who had been cured by a miracle take the priest to his house. Consequently, they had left that place, because they suspected some evil. Scarcely had they spoken those words when we heard loud cries and lamentations. We immediately weighed anchor and discharging many mortars into the houses, drew in nearer to the shore. While thus discharging [our pieces] we saw Johan Seranno in his shirt bound and wounded, crying to us not to fire any more, for the natives would kill him. We asked him whether all the others and the interpreter were dead. He said that they were all dead except the interpreter. He begged us earnestly to redeem him with some of the merchandise; but Johan Carvaio, his boon companion, [and others] would not allow the boat to go ashore so that they might remain masters of the ships. But although Johan Serrano weeping asked us not to set sail so quickly, for they would kill him, and said that he prayed God to ask his soul of Johan Carvaio, his comrade, in the day of judgement, we immediately departed.[52] I do not know whether he is dead or alive.

In that island are found dogs, cats, rice, millet, panicum, sorgo, ginger, figs, oranges, lemons, sugar-cane, garlic, honey, cocoanuts, nangcas, gourds, flesh of many kinds, palm wine, and gold. It is a large island, and has a good port with two entrances—one to the west and the other to the east northeast. It lies in X degrees of latitude toward the Arctic Pole, and in a longitude of one hundred and sixty-four degrees from the line of demarcation. Its name is Zubu. We heard of Malucho there before the death of the captain-general. Those people play a violin with copper strings.

Words of those heathen people

for Man	lac
for Woman	paranpaon
for Young woman	beni beni
for Married woman	babay
for Hair	boho
for Face	guay
for Eyelids	pilac
for Eyebrows	chilei
for Eye	matta
for Nose	ilon
for Jaws	apin
for Lips	olol
for Mouth	baba
for Teeth	nipin

[52] Pigafetta obviously blames Carvalho for failing to rescue Serrano, but another account suggests that the rescue could not have been attempted without endangering all the European lives.

for Gums	leghex
for Tongue	dilla
for Ears	delengan
for Throat	liogh
for Neck	tangip
for Chin	queilan
for Beard	bonghot
for Shoulders	bagha
for Spine	licud
for Breast	dughan
for Body	tiam
for Armpit	ilot
for Arm	botchen
for Elbow	sico
for Pulse	molanghai
for Hand	camat
for the Palm of the hand	palan
for Finger	dudlo
for Fingernail	coco
for Navel	pusut
for Penis	utin
for Testicles	boto
for Vagina	billat
for to have Communication with women	jiam
for Buttocks	samput
for Thigh	paha
for Knee	tuhud
for Shin	bassag bassag
for Calf of the leg	bitis
for Ankle	bolbol
for Heel	tiochid
for Sole of the foot	lapa lapa
for Gold	balaoan
for Silver	pilla
for Brass	concach
for Iron	butan
for Sugarcane	tube

176

for Spoon	gandan
for Rice	bughax baras
for Honey	deghex
for Wax	talho
for Salt	acin
for Wine	tuba nio nipa
for to Drink	minuncubil
for to Eat	macan
for Hog	babui
for Goat	candin
for Chicken	monoch
for Millet	humas
for Sorgo	batat
for Panicum	dana
for Pepper	manissa
for Cloves	chianche
for Cinnamon	mana
for Ginger	luia
for Garlic	laxuna
for Oranges	acsua
for Egg	silog
for Cocoanut	lubi
for Vinegar	zlucha
for Water	tubin
for Fire	clayo
for Smoke	assu
for to Blow	tigban
for Balances	tinban
for Weight	tahil
for Pearl	mutiara
for Mother of pearl	tipay
for Pipe (a musical instrument)	subin
for Disease of St. Job	alupalan
Bring me	palatin comorica
for certain Rice cakes	tinapai
Good	main
No	tidale

177

Antonio Pigafetta

for Knife	capol, sundan
for Scissors	catle
to Shave	chunthinch
for a well adorned Man	pixao
for Linen	balandan
for the Cloth with which they cover themselves	abaca
for hawk'sbell	coloncolon
for Pater nosters of all classes	tacle
for Comb	cutlei, missamis
for to Comb	monssughud
for Shirt	sabun
for Sewing-needle	daghu
for to Sew	mamis
for Porcelain	mobuluc
for Dog	aian, ydo
for Cat	epos
for their Scarfs	gapas
for Glass Beads	balus
Come here	marica
for House	ilaga, balai
for Timber	tatamue
for the Mats on which they sleep	tagichan
for Palm-mats	bani
for their Leaf cushions	uliman
for Wooden platters	dulan
for their God	abba
for Sun	adlo
for Moon	songhot
for Star	bolan, bunthun
for Dawn	mene
for Morning	uema
for Cup	tagha
Large	bassal
for Bow	bossugh
for Arrow	oghon

178

for Shields	calassan
for Quilted garments used for fighting	baluti
for their daggers	calix, baladao
for their Cutlasses	campilan
for Spear	bancan
for Like	tuan
for Figs (bananas)	saghin
for Gourds	baghin
for the Cords of their violins	gotzap
for River	tau
for Fishing-net	pucat, laia
for small Boat	sampan
for large Canes	cauaghan
for the small ones	bonbon
for their large Boats	balanghai
for their small Boats	boloto
for Crabs	cuban
for Fish	icam, yssida
for a Fish that is all colored	panapsapan
for another red (Fish)	timuan
for a certain other (kind of fish)	pilax
for another (kind of Fish)	emaluan
All the same	siama siama
for a Slave	bonsul
for Gallows	bolle
for Ship	benaoa
for a King or Captain-General	raia

Numbers

One	uzza
two	dua
three	tolo
four	upat
five	lima
six	onom

179

seven	pitto
eight	gualu
nine	ciam
ten	polo

In the midst of that archipelago, at a distance of eighteen leguas from that island of Zubu, at the head of the other island called Bohol, we burned the ship "Conceptione," for too few men of us were left [to work it]. We stowed the best of its contents in the other two ships, and then laid our course toward the south southwest, coasting along the island called Panilongon, where black men like those in Etiopia live.[53] Then we came to a large island, whose king in order to make peace with us, drew blood from his left hand marking his body, face, and the tip of his tongue with it as a token of the closest friendship, and we did the same. I went ashore alone with the king in order to see that island. We had no sooner entered a river than many fishermen offered fish to the king. Then the king removed the cloths which covered his privies, as did some of his chiefs; and began to row while singing past many dwellings which were upon the river. Two hours after nightfall we reached the king's house. The distance from the beginning of the river where our ships were to the king's house was two leguas. When we entered the house, we came upon many torches of cane and palm leaves, which were of the *anime,* of which mention was made above. Until the supper was brought in, the king with two

[53] Panglao, whose inhabitants are Negritos.

of his chiefs and two of his beautiful women drank the contents of a large jar of palm wine without eating anything. I, excusing myself as I had supped, would only drink but once. In drinking they observed all the same ceremonies that the king of Mazaua did. Then the supper, which consisted of rice and very salt fish, and was contained in porcelain dishes, was brought in. They ate their rice as if it were bread, and cook it after the following manner. They first put in an earthen jar like our jars, a large leaf which lines all of the jar. Then they add the water and the rice, and after covering it allow it to boil until the rice becomes as hard as bread, when it is taken out in pieces. Rice is cooked in the same way throughout those districts. When we had eaten, the king had a reed mat and another of palm leaves, and a leaf pillow brought in so that I might sleep on them. The king and his two women went to sleep in a separate place, while I slept with one of his chiefs. When day came and until the dinner was brought in, I walked about that island. I saw many articles of gold in those houses but little food. After that we dined on rice and fish, and at the conclusion of dinner, I asked the king by signs whether I could see the queen. He replied that he was willing, and we went together to the summit of a lofty hill, where the queen's house was located. When I entered the house, I made a bow to the queen, and she did the same to me, whereupon I sat down beside her. She was making a sleeping mat of palm leaves. In the house there was hanging a number of porcelain jars

181

and four metal gongs—one of which was larger than
the second, while the other two were still smaller—
for playing upon. There were many male and female slaves who served her. Those houses are constructed like those already mentioned. Having taken
our leave, we returned to the king's house, where
the king had us immediately served with refreshments of sugarcane. The most abundant product of
that island is gold. They showed me certain large
valleys, making me a sign that the gold there was
as abundant as the hairs of their heads, but they
have no iron with which to dig it, and they do not
care to go to the trouble [to get it]. That part of
the island belongs to the same land as Butuan and
Calaghan, and lies toward Bohol, and is bounded
by Mazaua. As we shall return to that island again,
I shall say nothing further [now]. The afternoon
having waned, I desired to return to the ships. The
king and the other chief men wished to accompany
me, and therefore we went in the same *balanghai*.
As we were returning along the river, I saw, on the
summit of a hill at the right, three men suspended
from one tree, the branches of which had been cut
away. I asked the king what was the reason for that,
and he replied that they were malefactors and rob-
bers. Those people go naked as do the others above
mentioned. The king's name is Raia Calanao. The
harbor is an excellent one. Rice, ginger, swine,
goats, fowls, and other things are to be found there.
That port lies in a latitude of eight degrees toward
the Arctic Pole, and in a longitude of one hundred

and sixty-seven degrees from the line of demarcation. It is fifty leguas from Zubu, and is called Chipit.[54] Two days' journey thence to the northwest is found a large island called Lozon,[55] where six or eight junks belonging to the Lequian people go yearly.

Leaving there and laying our course west southwest, we cast anchor at an island not very large and almost uninhabited. The people of that island are Moros and were banished from an island called Burne. They go naked as do the others. They have blowpipes and small quivers at their side, full of arrows and a poisonous herb. They have daggers whose hafts are adorned with gold and precious gems, spears, bucklers, and small cuirasses of buffalo horn. They called us holy beings. Little food was to be found in that island, but [there were] immense trees. It lies in a latitude of seven and one half degrees toward the Arctic Pole, and is forty-three leguas from Chippit. Its name is Caghaian.[56]

About twenty-five leguas to the west northwest from the above island we found a large island, where rice, ginger, swine, goats, fowls, figs one-half braza long and as thick as the arm (they are excellent; and certain others are one palmo and less in length, and are much better than all the others), cocoanuts, camotes, sugarcane, and roots resembling turnips in taste, are found. Rice is cooked there under

[54] Quipit, located near the western end of Mindanao.

[55] This is of course Luzon, though two days' sail from Quipit would hardly have sufficed to reach it.

[56] Cagayan, in the Sulu Sea.

the fire in bamboos or in wood; and it lasts better
than that cooked in earthen pots. We called that
land the land of promise, because we suffered great
hunger before we found it. We were often on the
point of abandoning the ships and going ashore in
order that we might not die of hunger. The king
made peace with us by gashing himself slightly in
the breast with one of our knives, and upon bleed-
ing, touching the tip of his tongue and his forehead
in token of the truest peace, and we did the same.
That island lies in a latitude of nine and one-third
degrees toward the Arctic Pole, and a longitude of
one hundred and seventy-one and one-third degrees
from the line of demarcation. [It is called] Pulaoan.[57]

Those people of Polaoan go naked as do the
others. Almost all of them cultivate their fields.
They have blowpipes with thick wooden arrows
more than one palmo long, with harpoon points,
and others tipped with fishbones, and poisoned with
an herb; while others are tipped with points of
bamboo like harpoons and are poisoned. At the
end of the arrow they attach a little piece of soft
wood, instead of feathers. At the end of their blowpipes they fasten a bit of iron like a spear head; and
when they have shot all their arrows they fight with
that. They place a value on brass rings and chains,
bells, knives, and still more on copper wire for binding their fishhooks. They have large and very tame
cocks, which they do not eat because of a certain

[57] Palawan.

184

veneration that they have for them. Sometimes they make them fight with one another, and each one puts up a certain amount on his cock, and the prize goes to him whose cock is the victor. They have distilled rice wine which is stronger and better than that made from the palm.

Ten leguas southwest of that island, we came to an island, which, as we coasted by, seemed to us to be going upward. After entering the port, the holy body [*i. e.,* St. Elmo's fire] appeared to us through the pitchy darkness. There is a distance of fifty leguas from the beginning of that island to the port. On the following day, July nine, the king of that island sent a very beautiful prau to us, whose bow and stern were worked in gold. At the bow flew a white and blue banner surmounted with peacock feathers. Some men were playing on musical instruments and drums. Two *almadies* came with that prau. Praus resemble fustas,[58] while the *almadies* are their small fishing boats. Eight old men, who were chiefs, entered the ships and took seats in the stern upon a carpet. They presented us with a painted wooden jar full of betel and *areca* (the fruit which they chew continually), and jessamine and orange blossoms, a covering of yellow silk cloth, two cages full of fowls, a couple of goats, three jarsful of distilled rice wine, and some bundles of sugarcane. They did the same to the other ship, and embracing

[58] The European fusta Pigafetta had in mind was a lateen-sail craft, delicately built, with one or two masts and moved partly by oars.

us took their leave. The rice wine is as clear as water, but so strong that it intoxicated many of our men. It is called *arach*.

Six days later the king again sent three praus with great pomp, which encircled the ships with musical instruments playing and drums and brass gongs beating. They saluted us with their peculiar cloth caps which cover only the top of their heads. We saluted them by firing our mortars without [loading with] stones. Then they gave us a present of various kinds of food, made only of rice. Some were wrapped in leaves and were made in somewhat longish pieces, some resembled sugar-loaves, while others were made in the manner of tarts with eggs and honey. They told us that their king was willing to let us get water and wood, and to trade at our pleasure. Upon hearing that seven of us entered their prau bearing a present to their king, which consisted of a green velvet robe made in the Turkish manner, a violet velvet chair, five brazas of red cloth, a cap, a gilded drinking glass, a covered glass vase, three writing-books of paper, and a gilded writing-case. To the queen [we took] three brazas of yellow cloth, a pair of silvered shoes, and a silvered needlecase full of needles. [We took] three brazas of red cloth, a cap, and a gilded drinking-glass to the governor. To the herald who came in the prau we gave a robe of red and green cloth, made in the Turkish fashion, a cap, and a writing book of paper; and to the other seven chief men, to one a bit of cloth, and to another a cap, and to all of them a writing book of paper. Then we immediately departed [for the land].

When we reached the city,[59] we remained about two hours in the prau, until the arrival of two elephants with silk trappings, and twelve men each of whom carried a porcelain jar covered with silk in which to carry our presents. Thereupon, we mounted the elephants while those twelve men preceded us afoot with the presents in the jars. In this way we went to the house of the governor, where we were given a supper of many kinds of food. During the night we slept on cotton mattresses, whose lining was of taffeta, and the sheets of Cambaia. Next day we stayed in the house until noon. Then we went to the king's palace upon elephants, with our presents in front as on the preceding day. All the streets from the governor's to the king's house were full of men with swords, spears, and shields, for such were the king's orders. We entered the courtyard of the palace mounted on the elephants. We went up a ladder accompanied by the governor and other chiefs, and entered a large hall full of many nobles, where we sat down upon a carpet with the presents in the jars near us. At the end of that hall there is another hall higher but somewhat smaller. It was all adorned with silk hangings, and two windows, through which light entered the hall and hung with two brocade curtains, opened from it. There were three hundred footsoldiers with naked rapiers at their thighs in that hall to guard

[59] The travelers were now in the city of Brunei in Borneo.

the king. At the end of the small hall was a large window from which a brocade curtain was drawn aside so that we could see within it the king seated at a table with one of his young sons chewing betel. No one but women were behind him. Then a chief told us that we could not speak to the king, and that if we wished anything, we were to tell it to him, so that he could communicate it to one of higher rank. The latter would communicate it to a brother of the governor who was stationed in the smaller hall, and this man would communicate it by means of a speaking-tube through a hole in the wall to one who was inside with the king. The chief taught us the manner of making three obeisances to the king with our hands clasped above the head, raising first one foot and then the other and then kissing the hands toward him, and we did so, that being the method of the royal obeisance. We told the king that we came from the king of Spagnia, and that the latter desired to make peace with him and asked only for permission to trade. The king had us told that since the king of Spagnia desired to be his friend, he was very willing to be his, and said that we could take water and wood, and trade at our pleasure. Then we gave him the presents, on receiving each of which he nodded slightly. To each one of us was given some brocaded and gold cloth and silk, which were placed upon our left shoulders, where they were left but a moment. They presented us with refreshments of cloves and cinnamon, after which the curtains were drawn to and the windows closed.

The men in the palace were all attired in cloth of gold and silk which covered their privies, and carried daggers with gold hafts adorned with pearls and precious gems, and they had many rings on their hands. We returned upon the elephants to the governor's house, seven men carrying the king's presents to us and always preceding us. When we reached the house, they gave each one of us his present, placing them upon our left shoulders. We gave each of those men a couple of knives for his trouble. Nine men came to the governor's house with a like number of large wooden trays from the king. Each tray contained ten or twelve porcelain dishes full of veal, capons, chickens, peacocks, and other animals, and fish. We supped on the ground upon a palm mat from thirty or thirty-two different kinds of meat besides the fish and other things. At each mouthful of food we drank a small cupful of their distilled wine from a porcelain cup the size of an egg. We ate rice and other sweet food with gold spoons like ours. In our sleeping quarters there during those two nights, two torches of white wax were kept constantly alight in two rather tall silver candlesticks, and two large lamps full of oil with four wicks apiece and two men to snuff them continually. We went elephant-back to the seashore, where we found two praus which took us back to the ships. That city is entirely built in salt water, except the houses of the king and certain chiefs. It contains twenty-five thousand fires [families]. The houses are all constructed of wood and built up from the ground on tall pillars. When the tide is high the women go in boats through the settlement selling the articles necessary to maintain life. There is a large brick wall in front of the king's house with towers like a fort, in which were mounted fifty-six bronze pieces, and six of iron. During the two days of our stay there, many pieces were discharged. That king is a Moro and his name is Raia Siripada. He was forty years old and corpulent. No one serves him except women who are the daughters of chiefs. He never goes outside of his palace, unless when he goes hunting, and no one is allowed to talk with him except through the speaking tube. He has X scribes, called Xiritoles, who write down his deeds on very thin tree bark.

On Monday morning, July twenty-nine, we saw more than one hundred praus divided into three squadrons and a like number of *tunguli* (which are their small boats) coming toward us. Upon catching sight of them, imagining that there was some trickery afoot, we hoisted our sails as quickly as possible, abandoning an anchor in our haste. We expected especially that we were to be captured in between certain junks which had anchored behind us on the preceding day. We immediately turned upon the latter, capturing four of them and killing many persons. Three or four of the junks sought flight by beaching. In one of the junks which we captured was the son of the king of the island of Lozon. He was the captain-general of the king of Burne, and came with those junks from a large city named Laoe, which is located at the end of that island [Borneo] toward Java Major. He had destroyed and sacked that city because it refused to obey the king [of Burne], but the king of Java Major instead. Giovan Carvaio, our pilot, allowed that captain and the junks to go without our consent, for a certain sum of gold, as we learned afterward. Had the pilot not given up the captain to the king, the latter would have given us whatever we had asked, for that captain was exceedingly feared throughout those regions, especially by the heathens, as the latter are very hostile to that Moro king. In that same port there is another city inhabited by heathens, which is larger than that of the Moros, and built like the latter in salt water. On that account the two peoples have daily combats together in that same harbor. The heathen king is as powerful as the Moro king, but is not so haughty, and could be converted easily to the Christian faith. When the Moro king heard how we had treated the junks, he sent us a message by one of our men who was ashore to the effect that the praus were not coming to do us any harm, but that they were going to attack the heathens. As a proof of that statement, the Moros showed him some heads of men who had been killed, which they declared to be the heads of heathens. We sent a message to the king, asking him to please allow two of our men who were in the city for purposes of trade and the son of Johan Carvaio, who had been born in the country of Verzin, to come to us, but the king

191

refused. That was the consequences of Johan Carvaio letting the above captain go. We kept sixteen of the chiefest men [of the captured junks] to take them to Spagnia, and three women in the queen's name, but Johan Carvaio usurped the latter for himself.

Junks are their ships and are made in the following manner. The bottom part is built about two palmos above the water and is of planks fastened with wooden pegs, which are very well made; above that they are entirely made of very large bamboos. They have a bamboo as a counterweight. One of those junks carries as much cargo as a ship. Their masts are of bamboo, and the sails of the bark of trees. Their porcelain is a sort of exceedingly white earth which is left for fifty years under the earth before it is worked, for otherwise it would not be fine. The father buries it for the son. If [poison] is placed in a dish made of fine porcelain, the dish immediately breaks. The money made by the Moros in those regions is of bronze pierced in the middle in order that it may be strung. On only one side of it are four characters, which are letters of the great king of Chiina. We call that money *picis*.[60] They gave us six porcelain dishes for one *cathil*[61] (which is equivalent to two of our libras) of quicksilver; one hundred *picis* for one book of writing paper; one small porcelain vase for one hundred and sixty *cathils* of bronze; one porcelain vase for three

[60] Small coins of brass, copper, tin, or zinc, called *pichis*.
[61] Properly *kati*. A weight rather than a piece of money.

knives; one *bahar* (which is equivalent to two hundred and three *cathils*) of wax for 160 *cathils* of bronze; one *bahar* of salt for eighty *cathils* of bronze; one *bahar* of *anime* to calk the ships (for no pitch is found in those regions) for forty *cathils* of bronze. Twenty *tahils* [62] make one *cathil*. At that place the people highly esteem bronze, quicksilver, glass, cinnabar, wool cloth, linens, and all our other merchandise, although iron and spectacles more than all the rest. Those Moros go naked as do the other peoples [of those regions]. They drink quicksilver—the sick man drinks it to cleanse himself, and the well man to preserve his health.

The king of Burne has two pearls as large as two hen's eggs. They are so round that they will not stand still on a table. I know that for a fact, for when we carried the king's presents to him, signs were made for him to show them to us, but he said that he would show them next day. Afterward some chiefs said that they had seen them.

Those Moros worship Mahomet. The latter's law orders them not to eat pork; as they wash the buttocks with the left hand, not to use that hand in eating; not to cut anything with the right hand; to sit down to urinate; not to kill fowls or goats without first addressing the sun; to cut off the tops of the wings with the little bits of skin that stick up from under and the feet of fowls; then to split them in twain; to wash the face with the right hand, but not to cleanse the teeth with the fingers; and not to

[62] The Chinese *tael*.

eat anything that has been killed unless it be by themselves. They are circumcised like the Jews.

Camphor, a kind of balsam, is produced in that island. It exudes between the wood and the bark, and the drops are as small as [grains of] wheat bran. If it is exposed it gradually evaporates. Those people call it *capor*. Cinnamon, ginger, mirabolans, oranges, lemons, nangcas, watermelons, cucumbers, gourds, turnips, cabbages, scallions, cows, buffaloes, swine, goats, chickens, geese, deer, elephants, horses, and other things are found there. That island is so large that it takes three months to sail round it in a prau. It lies in a latitude of five and one-fourth degrees toward the Arctic Pole, and in a longitude of one hundred and seventy-six and two-thirds degrees from the line of demarcation, and its name is Burne.

Leaving that island, we turned back in order to find a suitable place to calk the ships, for they were leaking. One ship ran on to some shoals of an island called Bibalon,[63] because of the carelessness of its pilot, but by the help of God we freed it. A sailor of that ship incautiously snuffed a candle into a barrel full of gunpowder, but he quickly snatched it out without any harm. Then pursuing our course, we captured a prau laden with cocoanuts on its way to Burne. Its crew sought refuge on an islet, until we captured it. Three other praus escaped behind certain islets.

At the head of Burne between it and an island called Cimbonbon, which lies in [a latitude of]

[63] Cape Sampanmangio, the northern extremity of Borneo.

eight degrees and seven minutes, is a perfect port for repairing ships.[64] Consequently, we entered it; but as we lacked many things for repairing the ships, we delayed there for forty-two days. During that time, each one of us labored hard, one at one thing and one at another. Our greatest fatigue however was to go barefoot to the woods for wood. In that island there are wild boars, of which we killed one which was going by water from one island to another [by pursuing it] with the small boat. Its head was two and one-half palmos long, and its teeth were large. There are found large crocodiles, both on land and sea, oysters and shellfish of various kinds. Among the last named we found two, the flesh of one of which weighed twenty-six libras, and the other forty-four. We caught a fish, which had a head like that of a hog and two horns. Its body consisted entirely of one bone, and on its back it resembled a saddle; and it was small. Trees are also found there which produce leaves which are alive when they fall, and walk. Those leaves are quite like those of the mulberry, but are not so long. On both sides near the stem, which is short and pointed, they have two feet. They have no blood, but if one touches them they run away. I kept one of them for nine days in a box. When I opened the box, that leaf went round and round it. I believe those leaves live on nothing but air.[65]

[64] This port cannot be identified, but was probably on Borneo itself.

[65] The jumping leaves were insects.

Having left that island, that is, the port, we met at the head of the island of Pulaoan a junk which was coming from Burne, on which was the governor of Pulaoan. We made them a signal to haul in their sails, and as they refused to haul them in, we captured the junk by force, and sacked it. [We told] the governor [that] if [he] wished his freedom, he was to give us, inside of seven days, four hundred measures of rice, twenty swine, twenty goats, and one hundred and fifty fowls. After that he presented us with cocoanuts, figs, sugarcanes, jars full of palm wine, and other things. Seeing his liberality, we returned some of his daggers and arquebuses to him, giving him in addition, a flag, a yellow damask robe, and XV brazas of cloth; to his son, a cloak of blue cloth; to a brother of the governor, a robe of green cloth and other things; and we parted from them as friends. We turned our course back between the island of Cagaian and the port of Cippit, and laid our course east by south in order that we might find the islands of Malucho. We passed by certain reefs near which we found the sea to be full of grass, although the depth was very great. When we passed through them, it seemed as though we were entering another sea. Leaving Chipit to the east, we found two islands, Zolo and Taghima,[66] which lie toward the west, and near which pearls are found. The two pearls of the king of Burne were found there, and the king got them, as was told us, in the following manner. That king took to wife a daugh-

[66] Sulu, or Jolo, and some island near Basilan.

ter of the king of Zolo, who told him that her father had those two pearls. The king determined to get possession of them by hook or by crook. Going one night with five hundred praus, he captured the king and two of his sons, and took them to Burne with him. [He told] the king of Zolo that if he wished freedom, he must surrender the two pearls to him.

Then we laid our course east by north between two settlements called Cauit and Subanin, and an inhabited island called Monoripa, located X leguas from the reefs.[67] The people of that island make their dwellings in boats and do not live otherwise. In those two settlements of Cavit and Subanin, which are located in the island of Butuan and Calaghan, is found the best cinnamon that grows. Had we stayed there two days, those people would have laden our ships for us, but as we had a wind favorable for passing a point and certain islets which were near that island, we did not wish to delay. While under sail we bartered two large knives which we had taken from the governor of Pulaoan for seventeen libras [of cinnamon]. The cinnamon tree grows to a height of three or four cubits, and as thick as the fingers of the hand. It has but three or four small branches and its leaves resemble those of the laurel. Its bark is the cinnamon, and it is gathered twice per year. The wood and leaves are as strong as the cinnamon when they are green. Those people call it *caiu mana*. *Caiu* means wood, and *mana*, sweet, hence, "sweet wood."

[67] These are all points on the approach to Zamboanga.

197

Laying our course toward the northeast, and going to a large city called Maingdanao, which is located in the island of Butuan and Calaghan, so that we might gather information concerning Maluco, we captured by force a *bigniday*, a vessel resembling a prau, and killed seven men. It contained only eighteen men, and they were as well built as any whom we had seen in those regions. All were chiefs of Maingdanao, among them being one who told us that he was a brother of the king of Maingdanao, and that he knew the location of Malucho. Through his directions we discontinued our course toward the northeast, and took that toward the southeast. At a cape of that island of Butuan and Caleghan, and near a river, are found shaggy men who are exceedingly great fighters and archers. They use swords one palmo in length, and eat only raw human hearts with the juice of oranges or lemons. Those shaggy people are called Benaian.[68] When we took our course toward the southeast, we lay in a latitude of six degrees and seven minutes toward the Arctic Pole, and thirty leguas from Cavit.

Sailing toward the southeast, we found four islands, [namely], Ciboco, Biraham Batolach, Sarangani, and Candighar.[69] One Saturday night, October twenty-six, while coasting by Birahan Batolach, we encountered a most furious storm. Thereupon, praying God, we lowered all the sails. Immediately

[68] Da Mosto (*Raccolta,* V, III, 91) reports the custom of heart eating, though without citrus-fruit juice, among the Manobos of eastern Mindanao.
[69] Sibuco, Virano, Batolaque, Sarangani, and Balut.

Magellan's Voyage Around the World

our three saints appeared to us and dissipated all the darkness. St. Elmo remained for more than two hours on the maintop, like a torch; St. Nicholas on the mizzentop; and St. Clara on the foretop. We promised a slave to St. Elmo, St. Nicholas, and St. Clara, and gave alms to each one. Then continuing our voyage, we entered a harbor between the two islands of Saranghani and Candighar, and anchored to the eastward near a settlement of Sarangani, where gold and pearls are found. Those people are heathens and go naked as do the others. That harbor lies in a latitude of five degrees nine minutes, and is fifty leguas from Cavit.

Remaining one day in that harbor, we captured two pilots by force, in order that they might show us where Malucho lay. Then laying our course south southwest, we passed among eight inhabited and desert islands, which were situated in the manner of a street. Their names are Cheaua, Cauiao, Cabiao, Camanuca, Cabaluzao, Cheai, Lipan, and Nuza.[70] Finally we came to an island at their end, which was very beautiful to look at. As we had a contrary wind, so that we could not double a point of that island, we sailed hither and thither near it. Consequently, one of the men whom we had captured at Saranghai, and the brother of the king of Maingdanao who took with him his small son, escaped during the night by swimming to that island. But the boy was drowned, for he was unable to hold tightly to his father's shoulder. Being unable to dou-

[70] Small islands, some of which are in the Talantse group.

199

ble the said point, we passed below the island where there were many islets. That island has four kings, [namely], Raia Matandatu, Raia Lalagha, Raia Bapti, and Raia Parabu. The people are heathens. The island lies in a latitude of three and one-half degrees toward the Arctic Pole and is 27 leguas from Saranghany. Its name is Sanghir.

Continuing the same course, we passed near six islands, [namely], Cheama, Carachita, Para, Zanghalura, Ciau [which is ten leguas from Sanghir, and has a high but not large mountain, and whose king is called Raia Ponto], and Paghinzara. The latter is located eight leguas from Ciau, and has three high mountains. The name of its king is Raia Babintan. [Then we found the island] Talaut; and we found twelve leguas to the east of Paghinzara two islands, not very large, but inhabited, called Zoar and Meau. After passing those two islands, on Wednesday, the sixth of November, we discovered four lofty islands fourteen leguas east of the two [above-mentioned islands]. The pilot who still remained with us told us that those four islands were Maluco. Therefore, we thanked God and as an expression of our joy discharged all our artillery. It was no wonder that we were so glad, for we had passed twenty-seven months less two days in our search for Malucho. Among all those islands, even to Malucho, the shallowest bottom that we found was at a depth of one or two hundred brazas, notwithstanding the assertion of the Portuguese that that region could not be navigated because of the

numerous shoals and the dark sky as they have imagined.

Three hours before sunset on Friday, November eight, 1521, we entered into a harbor of an island called Tadore, and anchoring near the shore
in twenty brazas we fired all our artillery. Next day
the king came to the ships in a prau, and circled
about them once. We immediately went to meet
him in a small boat, in order to show him honor.
He made us enter his prau and seat ourselves
near him. He was seated under a silk awning which
sheltered him on all sides. In front of him was one of
his sons with the royal scepter, and two persons with
two gold jars to pour water on his hands, and two
others with two gilded caskets filled with their betel.
The king told us that we were welcome there, and
that he had dreamt some time ago that some ships
were coming to Maluco from remote parts; and that
for more assurance he had determined to consult
the moon, whereupon he had seen the ships were
coming, and that we were they. Upon the king entering our ships all kissed his hand and then we led
him to the stern. When he entered inside there, he
would not stoop, but entered from above. Causing
him to sit down in a red velvet chair, we clothed
him in a yellow velvet robe made in the Turkish
fashion. In order to show him greater honor, we sat
down on the ground near him. Then when all were
seated, the king began to speak and said that he and
all his people desired ever to be the most loyal
friends and vassals to our king of Spagnia. He re-

ceived us as his children, and we could go ashore as
if in our own houses, for from that time thenceforth,
his island was to be called no more Tadore but Castiglia, because of the great love which he bore to our
king, his sovereign. We made him a present which
consisted of the robe, the chair, a piece of delicate
linen, four brazas of scarlet cloth, a piece of brocaded silk, a piece of yellow damask, some Indian
cloth embroidered with gold and silk, a piece of
berania (the white linen of Cambaia) , two caps, six
strings of glass beads, twelve knives, three large mirrors, six pairs of scissors, six combs, some gilded
drinking-cups, and other articles. To his son we
gave an Indian cloth of gold and silk, a large mirror,
a cap, and two knives; and to each of nine others—
all of them his chiefs—a silk cloth, caps, and two
knives; and to many others caps or knives. We kept
giving presents until the king bade us desist. After
that he declared to us that he had nothing else except his own life to send to the king his sovereign.
We were to approach nearer to the city, and whoever came to the ships at night, we were to kill with
our muskets. In leaving the stern, the king would
never bend his head. When he took his leave we
discharged all the guns. That king is a Moro and
about forty-five years old. He is well built and has
a royal presence, and is an excellent astrologer. At
that time he was clad in a shirt of the most delicate
white stuff with the ends of the sleeves embroidered
in gold, and in a cloth that reached from his waist
to the ground. He was barefoot, and had a silk scarf

wrapped about his head, and above it a garland of flowers. His name is Raia Sultan Manzor.[71]

On Sunday, November X, that king desired us to tell him how long it was since we had left Spagnia, and what pay and quintalada [72] the king gave to each of us. He requested us to give him a signature of the king and a royal banner, for then and thenceforth, he would cause it that his island and another called Tarenate [provided that he were able to crown one of his grandsons, named Calonaghapi] would both belong to the king of Spagnia; and for the honor of his king he was ready to fight to the death, and when he could no longer resist, he would go to Spagnia with all his family in a junk which he was having built new, carrying the royal signature and banner; and therefore he was the king's servant for a long time. He begged us to leave him some men so that he might constantly be reminded of the king of Spagnia. He did not ask for merchandise because the latter would not remain with him. He told us that he would go to an island called Bachian, in order sooner to furnish the ships with cloves, for there were not enough dry cloves in his island to load the two ships. As that day was Sunday, it was decided not to trade. The festive day of those people is our Friday.

In order that your most illustrious Lordship may know the islands where cloves grow, they are

[71] Elsewhere called Almanzor, which is the Spanish version of the Moslem name Al Mansur.

[72] The percentage of the freight allotted to the officers and crew of an expedition. It may also mean prize money.

five, [namely], Tarenatte, Tadore, Mutir, Machian, and Bachian. Tarenate is the chief one, and when its king was alive, he ruled nearly all the others. Tadore, the one where we were, has a king. Mutir and Machian have no king but are ruled by the people, and when the two kings of Tarenate and of Tadore engage in war, those two islands furnish them with men. The last island is Bachian, and it has a king. That entire province where cloves grow is called Malucho. At that time it was not eight months since one Francesco Seranno had died in Tarenate. [He was] a Portuguese and the captain-general of the king of Tarenate and opposed the king of Tadore. He did so well that he constrained the king of Tadore to give one of his daughters to wife to the king of Tarenate, and almost all the sons of the chiefs as hostages. The above mentioned grandson of the king of Tadore was born to that daughter. Peace having been made between the two kings, and when Francesco Seranno came one day to Tadore to trade cloves, the king of Tadore had him poisoned with the said betel leaves. He lived only four days. His king wished to have him buried according to his law [with Mahometan rites], but three Christians who were his servants would not consent to it. He left a son and a daughter, both young, born by a woman whom he had taken to wife in Java Major, and two hundred *bahars* of cloves. He was a close friend and a relative of our royal captain-general, and was the cause of inciting the latter to undertake that enterprise, for when our captain was

at Malacha, he had written to him several times
that he was in Tarenate. As Don Manuel, then king
of Portugal, refused to increase our captain-general's
pension by only a single testoon per month for his
merits, the latter went to Spagnia, where he had obtained everything for which he could ask from his
sacred Majesty. Ten days after the death of
Francesco Seranno, the king of Tarenate, by name,
Raya Abuleis,[73] having expelled his son-in-law, the
king of Bachian, was poisoned by his daughter, the
wife of the latter king, under pretext of trying to
bring about peace between the two kings. The king
lingered but two days, and left nine principal sons,
whose names are Chechili Momuli, Jadore Vunighi,
Chechili de Roix, Cili Manzur, Cili Pagi, Chialin,
Chechilin Cathara, Vaiechu Serich, and Calano
Ghapi.

On Monday, November XI, one of the sons of
the king of Tarenate, (to wit) , Chechili de Roix,
came to the ships clad in red velvet. He had two
praus and his men were playing upon the abovementioned gongs. He refused to enter the ship at
that time. He had [charge of] the wife and children,
and the other possessions of Francesco Seranno.
When we found out who he was, we sent a message
to the king, asking him whether we should receive
Chechili de Roix, since we were in his port, and he
replied to us that we could do as we pleased. But
the son of the king, seeing that we were hesitating,
moved off somewhat from the ships. We went to

[73] Boleyse. See Introduction, page 16.

him with the boat in order to present him an Indian cloth of gold and silk, and some knives, mirrors, and scissors. He accepted them somewhat haughtily, and immediately departed. He had a Christian Indian with him named Manuel, the servant of one Petro Alfonso de Lorosa,[74] a Portuguese who went from Bandan to Tarenate, after the death of Francesco Seranno. As the servant knew how to talk Portuguese, he came aboard our ship, and told us that, although the sons of the king of Tarenate were at enmity with the king of Tadore, yet they were always at the service of the king of Spagnia. We sent a letter to Pietro Alfonso de Lorosa, through his servant, [telling him] that he could come without any hesitation.

Those kings have as many women as they wish, but only one chief wife, whom all the others obey. The abovesaid king of Tadore had a large house outside of the city, where two hundred of his chief women lived with a like number of women to serve them. When the king eats, he sits alone or with his chief wife in a high place like a gallery whence he can see all the other women who sit about the gallery; and he orders her who best pleases him to sleep with him that night. After the king has finished eating, if he orders those women to eat together, they do so, but if not, each one goes to eat in her own chamber. No one is allowed to see those women without permission from the king, and if anyone is found near the king's house by day or by night, he

[74] See Introduction.

is put to death. Every family is obliged to give the king one or two of its daughters. That king had twenty-six children, eight sons, and the rest daughters. Lying next that island there is a very large island, called Giailolo, which is inhabited by Moros and heathens. Two kings are found there among the Moros, one of them, as we were told by the king, having had six hundred children, and the other five hundred and twenty-five. The heathens do not have so many women; nor do they live under so many superstitions, but adore for all that day the first thing that they see in the morning when they go out of their houses. The king of those heathens, called Raya Papua, is exceedingly rich in gold, and lives in the interior of the island. Reeds as thick around as the leg and filled with water that is very good to drink, grow on the flinty rocks in the island of Giaiallo. We bought many of them from those people.

On Tuesday, November twelve, the king had a house built for us in the city in one day for our merchandise. We carried almost all of our goods thither, and left three of our men to guard them. We immediately began to trade in the following manner. For X brazas of red cloth of very good quality, they gave us one *bahar* of cloves, which is equivalent to four quintals and six libras; for fifteen brazas of cloth of not very good quality, one quintal and one hundred libras; for fifteen hatchets, one *bahar;* for thirty-five glass drinking-cups, one *bahar* (the king getting them all) ; for seventeen *cathils* of cinnabar, one *bahar;* for seventeen *cathils* of quicksilver, one *bahar;* for twenty-six brazas of linen, one *bahar;* for twenty-five brazas of finer linen, one *bahar;* for one hundred and fifty knives, one *bahar;* for fifty pairs of scissors, one *bahar;* for forty caps, one *bahar;* for X pieces of Guzerat cloth, one *bahar;* for three of those gongs of theirs, two *bahars;* for one quinta of bronze, one *bahar.* [Almost] all the mirrors were broken, and the few good ones the king wished for himself. Many of those things [that we traded] were from the abovementioned junks which we had captured. Our haste to return to Spagnia made us dispose of our merchandise at better bargains [to the natives] than we should have done. Daily so many boatloads of goats, fowls, figs [bananas], cocoanuts, and other kinds of food were brought to the ships, that we were surprised. We supplied the ships with good water, which issues forth hot [from the ground], but if it stands for the space of an hour outside its spring, it becomes very cold, the reason therefor being that it comes from the mountain of cloves. This is quite the opposite from the assertion in Spagnia that water must be carried to Maluco from distant parts.

On Wednesday, the king sent his son, named Mossahap, to Mutir, so that they might supply us more quickly. On that day we told the king that we had captured certain Indians. The king thanked God heartily, and asked us to do him the kindness to give him their persons, so that he might send them back to their land, with five of his own men, in order that they might make the king of Spagnia and his fame known. Then we gave him the three women who had been captured in the queen's name for the reason already advanced. Next day, we gave the king all the prisoners, except those from Burne, for which he thanked us fervently. Thereupon, he asked us, in order thereby to show our love for him, to kill all the swine that we had in the ships, in return for which he would give us an equal number of goats and fowls. We killed them in order to show him a pleasure, and hung them up under the deck. When those people happen to see any swine they cover their faces in order that they might not look upon them or catch their odor.

In the afternoon of that same day, Pietro Alfonso, the Portuguese, came in a prau. He had not disembarked before the king sent to summon him and told him banteringly to answer us truly in whatever we should ask him, even if he did come from Tarennate. He told us that he had been sixteen years in India, but X in Maluco, for Maluco had been discovered secretly for that time. It was a year all but one fortnight, since a large ship had arrived at that place from Malaca, and had left laden with cloves, but had been obliged to remain in Bandan for some months because of bad weather. Its captain was Tristan de Meneses, a Portuguese. When he asked the latter what was the news back in Christendom, he was told that a fleet of five ships had left Siviglia to discover Maluco in the name of the king of Spagnia under command of Fernando de Magallianes, a Portuguese; that the king of Portugallo, angered that a Portuguese should be opposed to him, had sent some ships to the cape of Bonna Speransa, and a like number to the cape of Sancta Maria, where the cannibals live, in order to prevent their passage, but that he was not found. Then the king of Portagalo had heard that the said captain had passed into another sea, and was on his way to Malucho. He immediately wrote directing his chief captain of India, one Diego Lopes de Sichera, to send six ships to Maluco. But the latter did not send them because the Grand Turk was coming to Malacha, for he was obliged to send sixty sail to oppose him at the strait of Mecha in the land of Juda.[75] They found only a few galleys that had been beached on the shore of the strong and beautiful city of Adem, all of which they burned. After that the chief captain sent a large galleon with two tiers of guns to Malucho to oppose us, but it was unable to proceed because of certain shoals and currents of water near Malaca, and contrary winds. The captain of that galleon was Francesco Faria, a Portuguese. It was but a few days since a caravel with two junks had been in that place to get news of us. The junks went to Bachian for a cargo of cloves with seven Portuguese. As those Portuguese did not respect the women of the king and of his subjects, although the king told them often not to act so, and since they refused to discontinue, they were put to death. When the men in the caravel heard that, they immediately returned to Malaca abandoning the junks

[75] Not Judah, but Jidda, the seaport serving Mecca.

with four hundred *bahars* of cloves, and sufficient merchandise to purchase one hundred *bahars* more. Every year a number of junks sail from Malaca to Bandan for mace and nutmeg, and from Bandan to Malucho for cloves. Those people sail in three days in those junks of theirs from Maluco to Bandan, and in a fortnight from Bandan to Malaca. The king of Portagalo had enjoyed Malucho already for X years secretly, so that the king of Spagnia might not learn of it. That Portuguese remained with us until three in the morning, and told us many other things. We plied him so well, promising him good pay, that he promised to return to Spagnia with us.

On Friday, November fifteen, the king told us that he was going to Bachian to get the cloves abandoned there by the Portuguese. He asked us for two presents so that he might give them to the two governors of Mutir in the name of the king of Spagnia. Passing in between the ships he desired to see how we fired our musketry, crossbows, and the culverins, which are larger than an arquebus. He shot three times with a crossbow, for it pleased him more than the muskets. On Saturday, the Moro king of Giailolo came to the ships with a considerable number of praus. To some of the men we gave some green damask silk, two brazas of red cloth, mirrors, scissors, knives, combs, and two gilt drinking cups. That king told us that since we were friends of the king of Tadore, we were also his friends, for he loved that king as one of his own sons; and whenever any of our men would go to his land, he would show him

211

the greatest honor. That king is very aged and is feared among all those islands, for he is very powerful. His name is Raia Jessu. That island of Jayalolo is so large that it takes four months to circumnavigate it in a prau.[76] On Sunday morning that same king came to the ships and desired to see how we fought and how we discharged our guns. He took the greatest pleasure in it. After they had been discharged he immediately departed. He had been a great fighter in his youth as we were told.

That same day, I went ashore to see how the clove grows. The clove tree is tall and as thick as a man's body or thereabout. Its branches spread out somewhat widely in the middle, but at the top they have the shape of a summit. Its leaves resemble those of the laurel, and the bark is of a dark color. The cloves grow at the end of the twigs, ten or twenty in a cluster. Those trees have generally more cloves on one side than on the other, according to the season. When the cloves sprout they are white, when ripe, red, and when dried, black. They are gathered twice per year, once at the nativity of our Savior, and the other at the nativity of St. John the Baptist; for the climate is more moderate at those two seasons, but more so at the time of the nativity of our Savior. When the year is very hot and there is little rain, those people gather three or four hundred *bahars* [of cloves] in each of those islands. Those trees grow only in the mountains, and if any

[76] Gilolo, also called Halmahera, is large, but this statement must be an exaggeration.

of them are planted in the lowlands near the mountains, they do not live. The leaves, the bark, and the green wood are as strong as the cloves. If the latter are not gathered when they are ripe, they become large and so hard that only their husk is good. No cloves are grown in the world except in the five mountains of those five islands, except that some are found in Gialilolo and in a small island between Tadore and Mutir, by name Mare, but they are not good. Almost every day we saw a mist descend and encircle now one and now another of those mountains, on account of which those cloves become perfect. Each of those people possesses clove trees, and each one watches over his own trees although he does not cultivate them. Some nutmeg trees are found in that island. The tree resembles our walnut tree, and has leaves like it. When the nut is gathered it is as large as a small quince, with the same sort of down, and it is of the same color. Its first rind is as thick as the green rind of our walnut. Under that there is a thin layer, under which is found the mace. The latter is a brilliant red and is wrapped about the rind of the nut, and within that is the nutmeg. The houses of those people are built like those of the others, but are not raised so high from the ground, and are surrounded with bamboos like a hedge. The women there are ugly and go naked as do the others, [covered only] with those cloths made from the bark of trees. Those cloths are made in the following manner. They take a piece of bark and leave it in the water until it becomes soft. Then they beat it with bits of wood and [thus] make it as long and as wide as they wish. It becomes like a veil of raw silk, and has certain threads within it, which appear as if woven. They eat wooden bread made from a tree resembling the palm, which is made as follows. They take a piece of that soft wood from which they take certain long black thorns. Then they pound the wood, and so make the bread. They use that bread, which they call *saghu* [sago], almost as their sole food at sea. The men there go naked as do the others [of those regions], but they are so jealous of their wives that they do not wish us to go ashore with our drawers exposed; for they assert that their women imagine that we are always in readiness.

A number of boats came from Tarenate daily laden with cloves, but, as we were awaiting the king, we did not barter for anything except food. The men who came from Tarenate were very sorry because we refused to trade with them. On Sunday night, November twenty-four, and toward Monday, the king came with gongs a-playing, and passed between the ships, [whereat] we discharged many pieces. He told us that cloves would be brought in quantity within four days. Monday the king sent us seven hundred and ninety-one *cathils* of cloves, without reckoning the tare. The tare is to take the spices for less than they weigh, for they become dryer daily. As those were the first cloves which we had laden in our ships, we fired many pieces. Cloves are called *ghomode* there; in Saranghani where we captured the two pilots, *bongalauan;* and in Malaca, *chianche.*

On Tuesday, November twenty-six, the king told us that it was not the custom of any king to leave his island, but that he had left [his] for the love that he bore the king of Castiglia, and so that we might go to Spagnia sooner and return with so many ships that we could avenge the murder of his father who was killed in an island called Buru, and then thrown into the sea. He told us that it was the custom, when the first cloves were laden in the ships or in the junks, for the king to make a feast for the crews of the ships, and to pray their God that He would lead those ships safe to their port. He also wished to do it because of the king of Bachian and one of his brothers who were coming to visit him. He had the streets cleaned. Some of us imagining that some treachery was afoot, because three Portuguese in the company of Francesco Seranno had been killed in the place where we took in water, by certain of those people who had hidden in the thickets, and because we saw those Indians whispering with our prisoners, declared in opposition to some who wished to go to the feast that we ought not go ashore for feasts, for we remembered that other so unfortunate one. We were so urgent that it was concluded to send a message to the king asking him to come soon to the ships, for we were about to depart, and would give him the four men whom we had promised him, besides some other merchandise. The king came immediately and entered the ships.

He told some of his men that he entered them with
as great assurance as into his own houses. He told us
that he was greatly astonished at our intention of
departing so soon, since the limit of time for lading
the ships was thirty days; and that he had not left
the island to do us any harm, but to supply the ships
with cloves sooner. He said that we should not depart then for that was not the season for sailing
among those islands, both because of the many
shoals found about Bandan and because we might
easily meet some Portuguese ships [in those seas].
However, if it were our determination to depart
then, we should take all our merchandise, for all
the kings roundabout would say that the king of
Tadore had received so many presents from so great
a king, and had given nothing in return; and that
they would think that we had departed only for fear
of some treachery, and would always call him a
traitor. Then he had his koran brought, and first
kissing it and placing it four or five times about his
head, and saying certain words to himself as he did
so (which they call *zambahean*) , he declared in the
presence of all, that he swore by Allah and by the
koran which he had in his hand, that he would
always be a faithful friend to the king of Spagnia. He
spoke all those words nearly in tears. In return for
his good words, we promised to wait another fortnight. Thereupon, we gave him the signature of the
king and the royal banner. None the less we heard
afterward on good authority that some of the chiefs
of those islands had proposed to him to kill us, say-

ing it would be doing the greatest kind of pleasure to the Portuguese, and that the latter would forgive those of Bachian. But the king had replied that he would not do it under any consideration, since he had recognized the king of Spagnia and had made peace with him.

After dinner on Wednesday, November twenty-seven, the king had an edict proclaimed that all those who had cloves could bring them to the ships. All that and the next day we bartered for cloves with might and main. On Friday afternoon, the governor of Machian came with a considerable number of praus. He refused to disembark, for his father and one of his brothers who had been banished from Machian were living in Tadore. Next day, our king and his nephew, the governor, entered the ships. As we had no more cloth, the king sent to have three brazas of his brought and gave it to us, and we gave it with other things to the governor. At his departure we discharged many pieces. Afterward the king sent us six brazas of red cloth, so that we might give it to the governor. We immediately presented it to the latter, and he thanked us heartily for it, telling us that he would send us a goodly quantity of cloves. That governor's name is Humar, and he was about twenty-five years old.

On Sunday, the first of December, that governor departed. We were told that the king of Tadore had given him some silk cloth and some of those gongs so that he might send the cloves quicker. On Monday the king went out of the island to get cloves. On Wednesday morning, as it was the day of St. Barbara, and because the king came, all the artillery was discharged. At night the king came to the shore, and asked to see how we fired our rockets and fire bombs, at which he was highly delighted. On Thursday and Friday we bought many cloves, both in the city and in the ships. For four brazas of ribbon, they gave us one *bahar* of cloves; for two brass chains, worth one marcello, they gave us one hundred libras of cloves. Finally, when we had no more merchandise, one man gave his cloak, another his doublet, and another his shirt, besides other articles of clothing, in order that they might have their share in the cargo. On Saturday, three of the sons of the king of Tarenate and their three wives, the daughters of our king, and Pietro Alfonso, the Portuguese, came to the ships. We gave each of the three brothers a gilt glass drinkingcup, and scissors and other things to the women. Many pieces were discharged at their departure. Then we sent ashore many things to the daughter of our king, now the wife of the king of Tarennatte, as she refused to come to the ships with the others. All those people, both men and women, always go barefoot.

On Sunday, December eight, as it was the day of the conception, we fired many pieces, rockets, and fire bombs. On Monday afternoon the king came to the ships with three women, who carried his betel for him. No one except the king can take women with him. Afterward the king of Jailolo came and wished to see us fight together again. Several days later our king told us that he was like a child at the breast who knew his dear mother, who departing would leave him alone. Especially would he be disconsolate, because now he had become acquainted with us, and enjoyed some of the products of Spagnia. Inasmuch as our return would be far in the future, he earnestly entreated us to leave him some of our culverins for his defense. He advised us to sail only by day when we left, because of the numerous shoals amid those islands. We replied to him that if we wished to reach Spagnia we would have to sail day and night. Thereupon, he told us that he would pray daily to his God for us, asking Him to conduct us in safety. He told us that the king of Bachian was about to come to marry one of his brothers to one of his [the king of Tidore's] daughters, and asked us to invent some entertainment in token of joy; but that we should not fire the large pieces, because they would do great damage to the ships as they were laden. During that time, Pietro Alfonso, the Portuguese, came with his wife and all his other possessions to remain in the ships. Two days later, Chechili de Roix, son of the king of Tarennate, came in a well-manned prau, and asked the Portuguese to go down into it for a few moments. The Portuguese answered that he would not go down, for he was going to Spagnia with us, whereupon the king's son tried to enter the ship, but we refused to allow him to come aboard, as he was a close friend to the Portuguese captain of Malaca, and had come to seize the Portuguese. He severely scolded those who lived near the Portuguese because they had allowed the latter to go without his permission.

On Sunday afternoon, December fifteen, the king of Bachian and his brother came in a prau with three tiers of rowers at each side. In all there were one hundred and twenty rowers, and they carried many banners made of white, yellow, and red parrot feathers. There was much sounding of those gongs, for the rowers kept time in their rowing to those sounds. He brought two other praus filled with girls to present them to his betrothed. When they passed near the ships, we saluted them by firing pieces, and they in order to salute us went round the ships and the port. Our king came to congratulate him as it is not the custom for any king to disembark on the land of another king. When the king of Bachian saw our king coming, he rose from the carpet on which he was seated, and took his position at one side of it. Our king refused to sit down upon the carpet, but on its other side, and so no one occupied the carpet. The king of Bachian gave our king five hundred *patols,* because the latter was giving his daughter to wife to the former's brother. The said *patols* are cloths of gold and silk manufactured in Chiina, and are highly esteemed among them. Whenever one of those people dies the other members of his family clothe themselves in those cloths in order to show him more honor. They give three *bahars* of cloves for one of those robes or thereabouts, according to the [value of the] robe.

On Monday our king sent a banquet to the king of Bachian by fifty women all clad in silk garments from the waist to the knees. They went two by two with a man between each couple. Each one bore a large tray filled with other small dishes which contained various kinds of food. The men carried nothing but the wine in large jars. Ten of the oldest women acted as macebearers. Thus did they go quite to the prau where they presented everything to the king who was sitting upon the carpet under a red and yellow canopy. As they were returning, those women captured some of our men and it was necessary to give them some little trifle in order to regain their freedom. After that our king sent us goats, cocoanuts, wine, and other things. That day we bent the new sails in the ships. On them was a cross of St. James of Galitia, with an inscription which read: "This is the sign of our good fortune."

On Tuesday, we gave our king certain pieces of artillery resembling arquebuses, which we had captured among those India [islands], and some of our culverins, together with four barrels of powder. We took aboard at that place eighty butts of water in each ship. Five days previously the king had sent one hundred men to cut wood for us at the island of Mare, by which we were to pass. On that day the king of Bachian and many of his men came ashore to make peace with us. Before the king walked four men with drawn daggers in their hands. In the presence of our king and of all the others he said that he would always remain in the service of the

king of Spagnia, and that he would save in his name
the cloves left by the Portuguese until the arrival of
another of our fleets, and he would never give them
to the Portuguese without our consent. He sent as a
present to the king of Spagnia a slave, two *bahars* of
cloves (he sent X, but the ships could not carry
them as they were so heavily laden), and two extremely beautiful dead birds. Those birds are as
large as thrushes, and have a small head and a long
beak. Their legs are a palmo in length and as thin
as a reed, and they have no wings, but in their stead
long feathers of various colors, like large plumes.
Their tail resembles that of the thrush. All the rest
of the feathers except the wings are of a tawny color.
They never fly except when there is wind. The
people told us that those birds came from the terrestrial paradise, and they call them *bolon diuata*,
that is to say, "birds of God." On that day each one
of the kings of Maluco wrote to the king of Spagnia
[to say] that they desired to be always his true
subjects. The king of Bachian was about seventy
years old. He observed the following custom,
namely, whenever he was about to go to war or to
undertake any other important thing, he first had it
done two or three times on one of his servants whom
he kept for no other purpose.

One day our king sent to tell our men who were
living in the house with the merchandise not to go
out of the house by night, because of certain of his
men who anoint themselves and roam abroad by
night. They appear to be headless, and when any of

them meets any other man, he touches the latter's hand, and rubs a little of the ointment on him. The man falls sick very soon, and dies within three or four days. When such persons meet three or four together, they do nothing else than to deprive them of their senses. [The king said] that he had had many of them hanged. When those people build a new house, before they go to dwell there they make a fire round about it and hold many feasts. Then they fasten to the roof of the house a trifle of everything found in the island so that such things may never be wanting to the inhabitants. Ginger is found throughout those islands. We ate it green like bread. Ginger is not a tree, but a small plant which puts forth from the ground certain shoots a palmo in length, which resembles reeds, and whose leaves resembled those of the reed, except that they are narrower. Those shoots are worthless, but the roots form the ginger. It is not so strong green as dry. Those people dry it in lime, for otherwise it would not keep.

On Wednesday morning as we desired to depart from Malucho, the king of Tadore, the king of Jaialolo, the king of Bachian, and a son of the king of Tarennate, all came to accompany us to the island of Mare. The ship "Victoria" set sail, and stood out a little awaiting the ship "Trinitade." But the latter not being able to weigh anchor, suddenly began to leak in the bottom. Thereupon, the "Victoria" returned to its anchorage, and we immediately began to lighten the "Trinitade" in order to see whether we could repair it. We found that the water was rushing in as through a pipe, but we were unable to find where it was coming in. All that and the next day we did nothing but work the pump, but we availed nothing. When our king heard of it, he came immediately to the ships, and went to considerable trouble in his endeavors to locate the leak. He sent five of his men into the water to see whether they could discover the hole. They remained more than one-half hour under water, but were quite unable to find the leak. The king seeing that he could not help us and that the water was increasing hourly, said almost in tears that he would send to the head of the island for three men, who could remain under water a long time. Our king came with the three men early on Friday morning. He immediately sent them into the water with their hair hanging loose so that they could locate the leak by that means. They stayed a full hour under water but were quite unable to locate it.[77] When the king saw that he could be of no assistance, he asked us weeping who of us would go "to Spagnia to my sovereign, and give him news of me." We replied to him that the "Victoria" would go there in order not to lose the east winds which were beginning to blow, while the other ship until being refitted would await the west winds and would go then to Darien which is located in the other part of the sea in the country of Diucatan [Yucatan]. The king told us that he had two hundred and twenty-five carpenters who would

[77] We must assume that they came up occasionally for air.

224

do all the work, and that he would treat all who re-mained here as his sons. They would not suffer any fatigue beyond two of them to boss the carpenters in their work. He spoke those words so earnestly that he made us all weep. We of the ship "Victoria," mistrusting that the ship might open, as it was too heavily laden, lightened it of sixty quintals of cloves, which we had carried into the house where the other cloves were. Some of the men of our ship desired to remain there, as they feared that the ship would not last out the voyage to Spagnia, but much more for fear lest they perish of hunger.

On the day of St. Thomas, Saturday, December twenty-one, our king came to the ships, and assigned us the two pilots whom we had paid to conduct us out of those islands. They said that it was the proper time to leave then, but as our men [who stayed behind] were writing to Spagnia, we did not leave until noon. When that hour came, the ships bid one another farewell amid the discharge of the cannon, and it seemed as though they were bewailing their last departure. Our men [who were to remain] accompanied us in their boats a short distance, and then with many tears and embraces we departed. The king's governor accompanied us as far as the island of Mare. We had no sooner arrived at that island than we bought four praus laden with wood, and in less than one hour we stowed it aboard the ship and then immediately laid our course toward the southwest. Johan Carvaio stayed there with fifty-three of our men, while we comprised forty-

225

seven men and thirteen Indians. The said island of Tadore has a bishop, and he who then exercised that office had forty wives and a multitude of children.

Throughout those islands of Malucho are found cloves, ginger, sago (which is their wood bread), rice, goats, geese, chickens, cocoanuts, figs [bananas], almonds larger than ours, sweet and tasty pomegranates, oranges, lemons, camotes, honey produced by bees as small as ants, which make their honey in the trees, sugarcane, cocoanut oil, beneseed oil, watermelons, wild cucumbers, gourds, a refreshing fruit as large as cucumbers called *comulicai,* another fruit, like the peach called *guava,* and other kinds of food. One also finds there parrots of various colors, and among the other varieties, some white ones called *cathara,* and some entirely red called *nori.* One of those red ones is worth one *bahar* of cloves, and that class speak with greater distinctness than the others. Those Moros have lived in Malucho for about fifty years. Heathens lived there before,[78] but they did not care for the cloves. There are still some of the latter, but they live in the mountains where the cloves grow.

The island of Tadore lies in a latitude of twenty-seven minutes toward the Arctic Pole, and in a longitude of one hundred and sixty-one degrees from the line of demarcation. It is nine and one-half degrees south of the first island of the archipelago

[78] This refers to the comparative recency of the conversion of the Moluccas to Islam, not to an entire population change.

called Zamal, and extends north by east and south by west. Tarenate lies in a latitude of two-thirds of a degree toward the Arctic Pole. Mutir lies exactly under the equinoctial line. Machian lies in one-quarter degree toward the Antarctic Pole, and Bachian also toward the Antarctic Pole in one degree. Tarenate, Tadore, Mutir, and Machian are four lofty and peaked mountains where the cloves grow. When one is in those four islands, he cannot see Bachian, but it is larger than any of those four islands. Its clove mountain is not so sharp as the others, but it is larger.

Words of those Moro People

for their God	Alla
for Christian	naceran
for Turk	rumno
for Moro	musulman; isilam
for Heathen	caphre
for their Mosque	mischit
for their Priests	maulana catip mudin
for their Wise Men	horan pandita
for their Devout Men	mossai
for their Ceremonies	zambahehan de ala meschit
for Father	bapa
for Mother	mama ambui
for Son	anach
for Brother	saudala
for the Brother of so and so	capatin muiadi
for Cousin	saudala sopopu
for Grandfather	niny
for Father-in-law	minthua
for Son-in-law	mi nanthu
for Man	horan
for Woman	poran poan

for Hair	lambut
for Head	capala
for Forehead	dai
for Eye	matta
for Eyebrows	quilai
for Eyelids	cenin
for Nose	idon
for Mouth	mulut
for Lips	bebere
for Teeth	gigi
for Cheeks	issi
for Tongue	lada
for Palate	langhi
for Chin	aghai
for Beard	janghut
for Mustaches	missai
for Jaw	pipi
for Ear	talingha
for Throat	laher
for Neck	tun dun
for Shoulders	balachan
for Breast	dada
for Heart	atti
for Teat	sussu
for Stomach	parut
for Body	tun dunbutu
for Penis	botto
for Vagina	bucchii
for to have communication with women	amput
for Buttocks	buri
for Thighs	taha
for Leg	mina
for the Shinbone of the Leg	tula
for its Calf	tilor chaci
for Ankle	buculati
for Heel	tumi
for Foot	batis

for the Sole of the Foot	empachaqui
for Fingernail	cuchu
for Arm	langhan
for Elbow	sichu
for Hand	tanghan
for the large Finger of the hand (thumb)	idun tanghan
for the Second Finger	tungu
for the Third	geri
for the Fourth	mani
for the Fifth	calinchin
for Rice	bugax
for Cocoanut in Malucho and Burne	biazzao
[for Cocoanut] in Lozon	nior
[for Cocoanut] in Java Major	calambil
for Fig [banana]	pizan
for Sugarcane	tubu
for Camotes	gumbili
for the Roots like turnips	ubi
for Nangca	mandicai sicui
for Melon	antimon
for Cucumbers	labu
for Cow	lambu
for Hog	babi
for Buffalo	carban
for Sheep	biri
for She-goat	cambin
for Cock	sambunghan
for Hen	aiambatina
for Capon	gubili
for Egg	talor
for Gander	itich
for Goose	ansa
for Bird	bolon
for Elephant	gagia
for Horse	cuda

229

for Lion	huriman
for Deer	roza
for Reeds	cuiu
for Bees	haermadu
for Honey	gulla
for Wax	lelin
for Candle	dian
for its Wick	sumbudian
for Fire	appi
for Smoke	asap
for Cinders	abu
for Cooked	azan
for well cooked	lambech
for Water	tubi
for Gold	amax
for Silver	pirac
for the Precious Gem	premata
for Pearl	mutiara
for Quicksilver	raza
for Copper [*metalo*]	tumbaga
for Iron	baci
for Lead	tima
for their Gongs	agun
for Cinnabar	galuga sadalinghan
for Silver [color *or* cloth?]	soliman danas
for Silk Cloth	cain sutra
for red Cloth	cain mira
for Black Cloth	cain ytam
for White Cloth	cain pute
for Green Cloth	cain igao
for Yellow Cloth	cain cunin
for Cap	cophia
for Knife	pixao
for Scissors	guntin
for Mirror	chiela min
for Comb	sissir
for Glass Bead	manich
for Bell	giringirin

for Ring	sinsin
for Cloves	ghianche
for Cinnamon	caiumanis
for Pepper	lada
for Long Pepper	sabi
for Nutmeg	buapala gosoga
for Copper Wire	canot
for Dish	pinghan
for Earthen Pot	prin
for Porringer	manchu
for Wooden Dish	dulan
for Shell	calunpan
for their Measures	socat
for Land [*terra*]	buchit
for Mainland	buchit tana
for Mountain	gonun
for Rock	batu
for Island	polan
for a Point of Land (a Cape)	taniun buchit
for River	songhai
What is so-and-so's name?	apenamaito?
for Cocoanut oil	mignach
for Beneseed oil	lana lingha
for Salt	garan sira
for Musk and Its Animal	castori
for the wood eaten by the castors	comaru
for Leech	linta
for Civet	jabat
for the Cat which makes the Civet	mozan
for Rhubarb	calama
for Demon	saytan
for World	bumi
for Wheat	gandun
for to Sleep	tidor
for Mats	tical

231

for Cushion	bantal
for Pain	sachet
for Health	bay
for Brush	cupia
for Fan	chipas
for their Cloths	chebun
for Shirts	bain
for their Houses	pati alam
for Year	tanu
for Month	bullan
for Day	alli
for Night	mallan
for Afternoon	malamari
for Noon	tam hahari
for Morning	patan patan
for Sun	mata hari
for Moon	bulan
for Half moon	tanam patbulan
for Stars	bintan
for Sky	languin
for Thunder	gunthur
for Merchant	sandgar
for City	naghiri
for Castle	cuta
for House	rinna
for to Sit	duodo
sit down, sir	duodo orancaia
sit down, honest fellow	duodo horandai et anan
Lord	tuan
for Boy	cana cana
for one of their Foster-children	lascar
for Slave	alipin
for Yes	ca
for No	tida
for to Understand	thao
for not to Understand	tida taho
Do not look at me	tida liat

Look at me	liat
to be one and the same thing	casi casi; siama siama
for to Kill	mati
for to Eat	macan
for Spoon	sandoch
for Harlot	sondal
Large	bassal
Long	pangian
Small	chechil
Short	pandach
for to Have	ada
for not to Have	tida hada
listen, sir	tuan diam
Where is the junk going?	dimana ajun?
for Sewing-needle	jalun
for to Sew	banan
for Sewing-thread	pintal banan
for Woman's headdress	dastar capala
for King	raia
for Queen	putli
for Wood	caiu
for to Work	caraiar
for to take Recreation	buandala
for Vein of the arm where one bleeds himself	urat paratanghan
for the Blood that comes from the arm	dara carnal
for good Blood	dara
When they sneeze, they say	ebarasai
for Fish	ycam
for Polypus	calabutan
for Meat	dagin
for Sea-snail	cepot
Little	serich
Half	satanha sapanghal
for Cold	dinghin
for Hot	panas

233

For	jan
for Truth	benar
for Lie	dusta
for to Steal	manchiuri
for Scab	codis
Take	na
Give me	ambil
Fat	gannich
Thin	golos
for Hair	tundun capala
How many?	barapa?
Once	satu chali
One braza	dapa
for to Speak	catha
for Here	siui
for There	sana datan
good day	salamalichum
for the Answer [to good day]	alichum salam
sir, may good fortune attend you	mali horancaia mancan
I have eaten already	suda macan
fellow, betake yourself off	pandan chita horan
for to Desire	banunchan
good evening	sabalchaer
for the Answer (to good evening)	chaer sandat
for to Give	minta
To give to someone	bri pocol
for Iron Fetters	balanghu
oh, what a smell!	bosso chini
for Young man	horan muda
for Old man	tua
for Scribe	xiritoles
for Writing-paper	cartas
for to Write	mangurat
for Pen	calam
for Ink	dauat

for Writing-desk	padantan
for Letter	surat
I do not have it	guala
Come here	camari
What do you want?	appa man?
Who sent you?	appa ito?
for Seaport	labuan
for Galley	gurap
for Ship	capal
for Bow (of a boat)	asson
for Stern (of a boat)	biritan
for to Sail	belaiar
for the Ship's mast	tian
for Yard [of a ship]	laiar
for the Rigging	tamira
for Sail	leier
for Maintop	sinbulaia
for the Anchor rope	danda
for Anchor	san
for Boat	sanpan
for Oar	daiun
for Mortar [cannon]	badil
for Wind	anghin
for Sea	laut
fellow, come here	horan itu datan
for their Daggers	calix golog
for their Dagger hilt	daga nan
for Sword	padan gole
for Blowpipe	sumpitan
for their Arrows	damach
for the poisonous Herb	ypu
for Quiver	bolo
for Bow (weapon)	bolsor
for its Arrows	anat paan
for Cats	cochin puchia
for Rat	ticus
for Lizard	buaia
for Shipworms	capan lotos

for Fishhook	matacanir
for Fishbait	unpan
for Fishline	tunda
for to Wash	mandi
Not to be afraid	tangan tacut
Fatigue	lala
a pleasant cup	sadap manis
for Friend	sandara
for Enemy	sanbat
I am certain	zonhu
for to Barter	biniaga
I have not	anis
to be a friend	pugna
Two things	malupho
If	oue
for Crowd (?)	zoroan pagnoro
to give pleasure to one	mamain
to be stiff with cold	amala
for Madman	gila
for Interpreter	giorobaza
How many languages do you know?	barapa bahasa tan?
Many	bagna
for to speak of Malaca	chiaramalain
Where is so and so?	dimana horan?
for Flag	tonghol
Now	sacaran
Tomorrow	hezoch
The next day	luza
Yesterday	calamari
for Palm-mallet	colbasi
for Nail	pacu
for Mortar	lozon
for Rammer for crushing (rice?)	atan
for to Dance	manari
for to Pay	baiar
for to Call	panghil

236

Unmarried	ugan
Married	suda babini
All one	sannia
for Rain	ugian
for Drunken	moboch
for Skin	culit
for Anger	ullat
for to Fight	guzar
Sweet	manis
Bitter	azon
How are you?	appa giadi?
Well	bay
Poorly	sachet
Bring me that	biriacan
This man is a coward	giadi hiat horan itu
Enough	suda

The Winds

for the North	iraga
for the South	salatan
for the East	timor
for the West	baratapat
for the Northwest	utara
for the Southwest	berdaia
for the Northwest	bardaut
for the Southeast	tunghara

Numbers

One	satus
Two	dua
Three	tiga
Four	ampat
Five	lima
Six	anam
Seven	tugu
Eight	duolappan
Nine	sambilan

Ten	sapolo
Twenty	duapolo
Thirty	tigapolo
Forty	ampatpolo
Fifty	limapolo
Sixty	anampolo
Seventy	tuguppolo
Eighty	dualapanpolo
Ninety	sambilampolo
One hundred	saratus
Two hundred	duaratus
Three hundred	tigaratus
Four hundred	anamparatus
Five hundred	limaratus
Six hundred	anambratus
Seven hundred	tugurattus
Eight hundred	dualapanratus
Nine hundred	sambilanratus
One thousand	salibu
Two thousand	dualibu
Three thousand	tigalibu
Four thousand	ampatlibu
Five thousand	limalibu
Six thousand	anamlibu
Seven thousand	tugulibu
Eight thousand	dualapanlibu
Nine thousand	sambilanlibu
Ten thousand	salacza
Twenty thousand	dualacza
Thirty thousand	tigalacza
Forty thousand	ampatlacza
Fifty thousand	limalacza
Sixty thousand	anamlacza
Seventy thousand	tugulacza
Eighty thousand	dualapanlacza
Ninety thousand	sambilanlacza
One hundred thousand	sacati
Two hundred thousand	duacati

Three hundred thousand	tigacati
Four hundred thousand	ampatcati
Five hundred thousand	limacati
Six hundred thousand	anamcati
Seven hundred thousand	tugacati
Eight hundred thousand	dualapancati
Nine hundred thousand	sambilancati
One million [*literally:* ten times one hundred thousand]	sainta

All the hundreds, the thousands, the tens of thousands, the hundreds of thousands, and the millions are joined with the numbers, satus, dua, etc.

Proceeding on our way we passed amid those islands [those of] Caioan, Laigoma, Sico, Giogi, and Caphi. In the said island of Caphi is found a race as small as dwarfs, who are amusing people, and are pigmies. They have been subjected by force to our king of Tadore. [We also passed the islands of] Laboan, Toliman, Titameti, Bachian, of which we have already spoken, Lalalata, Tabobi, Maga, and Batutiga. Passing outside the latter on its western side, we laid our course west southwest, and discovered some islets toward the south. And inasmuch as the Malucho pilots told us to go thither, for we were pursuing our course among many islands and shoals, we turned toward the southeast, and encountered an island which lies in a latitude of two degrees toward the Antarctic Pole, and fifty-five leguas from Maluco. It is called Sulach, and its inhabitants are heathens. They have no king, and eat human flesh. They go naked, both men and

women, only wearing a bit of bark two fingers wide
before their privies. There are many islands thereabout where the inhabitants eat human flesh. The
names of some of them are as follows: Silan, Nose-
lao, Biga, Atulabaou, Leitimor, Tenetun, Gondia,
Pailarurun, Manadan, and Benaia. Then we coasted
along two islands called Lamatola [79] and Tenetun,
lying about X leguas from Sulach. In that same
course we encountered a very large island where
one finds rice, swine, goats, fowls, cocoanuts, sugarcane, sago, a food made from one of their varieties
of figs called *chanali,* and *chiacare,* which are called
nangha. Nangcas are a fruit resembling the cucumber. They are knotty on the outside, and inside they
have a certain small red fruit like the apricot. It
contains no stone, but has instead a marrowy substance resembling a bean but larger. That marrowy substance has a delicate taste like chestnuts.
[There is] a fruit like the pineapple. It is yellow
outside, and white inside, and when cut it is like a
pear, but more tender and much better. Its name
is *connilicai.* The inhabitants of that island go
naked as do those of Solach. They are heathens and
have no king. That island lies in a latitude of three
and one-half degrees toward the Antarctic Pole, and
is seventy-five leguas from Malucho. Its name is
Buru. Ten leguas east of the above island is a large
island which is bounded by Jiaalolo. It is inhabited
by Moros and heathens. The Moros live near the

[79] Robertson suggests that this was Lisamatula, rather close to
the Moluccas.

240

sea, and the heathens in the interior. The latter eat human flesh. The products mentioned are produced in that island. It is called Ambon. Between Buru and Ambon are found three islands surrounded by reefs, called Vudia, Cailaruri, and Benaia; and near Buru, and about four leguas to the south, is a small island, called Ambalao.

About thirty-five leguas to the south by west of the above island of Buru, are found Bandan. Bandan consists of twelve islands. Mace and nutmeg grow in six of them. Their names are as follows: Zoroboa, the largest of them all, and the others, Chelicel, Samianapi, Pulac, Pulurun, and Rosoghin. The other six are as follows: Unuueru, Pulanbaracon, Lailaca, Manucan, Man, and Meut. Nutmeg is not found in them, but only sago, rice, cocoanuts, figs, and other fruits.[80] Those islands are located near together, and their inhabitants are Moros, who have no king. Bandan lies in a latitude of six degrees toward the Antarctic Pole, and in a longitude of one hundred and sixty-three and one-half degrees from the line of demarcation. As it was a trifle outside of our course we did not go there.

Leaving the above mentioned island of Baru, and taking the course toward the southwest by west, we reached, [after sailing through] about eight degrees of longitude, three islands, quite near together, called Zolot, Nocemamor, and Galiau.[81]

[80] Pigafetta does not mean to deny that nutmeg grows in the Bandas, but merely says that it is not found in the last six islands he has named.

[81] In the vicinity of Flores.

While sailing amid them, we were struck by a fierce storm, which caused us to make a pilgrimage to our Lady of Guidance.[82] Running before the storm we landed at a lofty island, but before reaching it we were greatly worn out by the violent gusts of wind that came from the mountains of that island, and the great currents of water. The inhabitants of that island are savage and bestial, and eat human flesh. They have no king, and go naked, wearing only that bark as do the others, except that when they go to fight they wear certain pieces of buffalo hide before, behind, and at the sides, which are ornamented with small shells, boars' tusks, and tails of goat skins fastened before and behind. They wear their hair done up high and held by certain long reed pins which they pass from one side to the other, which keep the hair high. They wear their beards wrapped in leaves and thrust into small bamboo tubes—a ridiculous sight. They are the ugliest people who live in those Indias. Their bows and arrows are of bamboo. They have a kind of a sack made from the leaves of a tree in which their women carry their food and drink. When those people caught sight of us, they came to meet us with bows, but after we had given them some presents, we immediately became their friends. We remained there a fortnight in order to calk the sides of the ship. In that island are found fowls, goats, cocoanuts, wax (of which they gave us fifteen libras for one libra of old iron) , and pepper, both long and round. The long pepper re-

[82] Pigafetta means that they promised to make this pilgrimage.

sembles the first blossoms of the hazelnut in winter. Its plant resembles ivy, and it clings to trees as does that plant; but its leaves resemble those of the mulberry. It is called *luli*. The round pepper grows like the former, but in ears like Indian corn, and is shelled off; and it is called *lada*. The fields in those regions are full of this [last variety of] pepper, planted to resemble arbors. We captured a man in that place so that he might take us to some island where we could lay in provisions. That island lies in a latitude of eight and one-half degrees toward the Antarctic Pole, and a longitude of one hundred and sixty-nine and two-thirds degrees from the line of demarcation; and is called Malua.

Our old pilot from Maluco told us that there was an island nearby called Arucheto, the men and women of which are not taller than one cubit, but who have ears as long as themselves. With one of them they make their bed and with the other they cover themselves. They go shaven close and quite naked, run swiftly, and have shrill voices. They live in caves underground, and subsist on fish and a substance which grows between the wood and the bark [of a tree], which is white and round like preserved coriander, which is called *ambulon*. However, we did not go there because of the strong currents of water, and the numerous shoals.

On Saturday, January 25, MCCCCCXXII, we left the island of Malua. On Sunday, the twenty-sixth, we reached a large island [83] which lies five

[83] Timor.

leguas to the south southwest of Malua. I went ashore alone to speak to the chief of a city called Amaban to ask him to furnish us with food. He told me that he would give us food. He told me that he would give me buffaloes, swine, and goats, but we could not come to terms because he asked many things for one buffalo. Inasmuch as we had but few things, and hunger was constraining us, we retained in the ship a chief and his son from another village called Balibo. He for fear lest we kill him, immediately gave us six buffaloes, five goats, and two swine; and to complete the number of ten swine and ten goats [which we had demanded] they gave us one [additional] buffalo. For thus had we placed the condition [of their ransom]. Then we sent them ashore very well pleased with linen, Indian cloth of silk and cotton, hatchets, Indian knives, scissors, mirrors, and knives. That chief to whom I went to talk had only women to serve him. All the women go naked as do the other women [of the islands]. In their ears they wear small earrings of gold, with silk tassels pendant from them. On their arms they wear many gold and brass armlets as far as the elbow. The men go as the women, except that they fasten certain gold articles, round like a trencher, about their necks, and wear bamboo combs adorned with gold rings in their hair. Some of them wear the necks of dried gourds in their ears in place of gold rings.

White sandal wood is found in that island and

nowhere else. [There is also] ginger, buffaloes, swine, goats, fowls, rice, figs [bananas], sugarcane, oranges, lemons, wax, almonds, kidney-beans, and other things, as well as parrots of various colors. On the other side of the island are four brothers, who are the kings of that island. Where we were, there were cities and some of their chiefs. The names of the four settlements of the kings are as follows: Oibich, Lichsana, Suai, and Cabanaza. Oibich is the largest. There is a quantity of gold found in a mountain in Cabanaza, according to the report given us, and its inhabitants make all their purchases with little bits of gold. All the sandal wood and wax that is traded by the inhabitants of Java and Malaca is traded for in that region. We found a junk from Lozon there, which had come thither to trade in sandal wood. Those people are heathens. When they go to cut the sandal wood, the devil (according to what were told), appears to them in various forms, and tells them that if they need anything they should ask him for it. They become ill for some days as a result of that apparition. The sandal wood is cut at a certain time of the moon, for otherwise it would not be good. The merchandise valued in exchange for sandal wood there is red cloth, linen, hatchets, iron, and nails. That island is inhabited in all parts, and extends for a long distance east and west, but is not very broad north and south. It lies in a latitude of ten degrees toward the Antarctic Pole, and in a longitude of one hundred and seventy-four and one-half degrees from the line of demarcation, and is called Timor. The disease of St. Job was to be found in all of the islands which we encountered in that archipelago, but more in that place than in others. It is called *foi franchi* that is to say "Portuguese disease." [84]

A day's journey thence toward the west northwest, we were told that we would find an island where quantities of cinnamon grow, by name Ende. Its inhabitants are heathens, and have no king. [We were told] also that there are many islands in the same course, one following the other, as far as Java Major, and the cape of Malaca. The names of those islands are as follows: Ende, Tanabutun, Creuo, Chile, Bimacore, Aranaran, Mani, Zumbaua, Lomboch, Chorum, and Java Major. Those inhabitants do not call it Java but Jaoa. The largest cities are located in Java, and are as follows: Magepaher (when its king was alive, he was the most powerful in all those islands, and his name was Raia Patiunus); Sunda, where considerable pepper grows; Daha; Dama; Gagiamada; Minutaranghan; Cipara; Sidaiu; Tuban; Cressi; Cirubaia; and Balli. [We were told] also that Java Minor is the island of Madura, and is located near to Java Major, [being only] one-half legua away. We were told also that when one of the chief men of Java dies, his body is burned. His principal wife adorns herself with garlands of flowers and has herself carried on a chair

[84] St. Job's disease is syphilis, but the implication that Europeans introduced it into the East is erroneous.

through the entire village by three or four men. Smiling and consoling her relatives who are weeping, she says: "Do not weep, for I am going to sup with my dear husband this evening, and to sleep with him this night." Then she is carried to the fire, where her husband is being burned. Turning toward her relatives, and again consoling them, she throws herself into the fire, where her husband is being burned.[85] Did she not do that, she would not be considered an honorable woman or a true wife to her dead husband. When the young men of Java are in love with any gentlewoman, they fasten certain little bells between their penis and the foreskin. They take a position under their sweetheart's window, and making a pretense of urinating, and shaking their penis, they make the little bells ring, and continue to ring them until their sweetheart hears the sound. The sweetheart descends immediately, and they take their pleasure; always with those little bells, for their women take great pleasure in hearing those bells ring from the inside. Those bells are covered, and the more they are covered the louder they sound. Our oldest pilot told us that in an island called Acoloro, which lies below Java Major, there are found no persons but women, and that they become pregnant from the wind. When they bring forth, if the offspring is a male, they kill it, but if it is a female they rear it. If men

[85] This extension of the Hindu *sati* custom of widow burning applied to Bali rather than to Java itself. The Balinese widow, for economy reasons, was more often stabbed than burned.

go to that island of theirs, they kill them if they are able to do so.[86]

They also told us that a very huge tree is found below Java Major toward the north, in the gulf of Chiina (which the ancients call Signo Magno), in which live birds called *garuda*.[87] Those birds are so large that they carry a buffalo or an elephant to the place [called Puzathaer], of that tree, which is called *cam panganghi,* and its fruit *bua panganghi.* The latter is larger than a cucumber. The Moros of Burne whom we had in our ship told us that they had seen them, for their king had had two of them sent to him from the kingdom of Siam. No junk or other boat can approach to within three or four leguas of the place of the tree, because of the great whirlpools in the water round about it. The first time that anything was learned of that tree was [from] a junk which was driven by the winds into the whirlpool. The junk having been beaten to pieces, all the crew were drowned except a little boy, who, having been tied to a plank, was miraculously driven near that tree. He climbed up into the tree without being discovered, where he hid under the wing of one of those birds. Next day the bird having gone ashore and having seized a buffalo, the boy came out from under the wing as best he could.

[86] This is a version of the Greek Amazon myth, and the story in different forms was told about many lands. Marco Polo picked up an eastern account similar to this on his travels. Leonardo Olschki, *Marco Polo's Asia,* Berkeley and Los Angeles, 1960, p. 232.

[87] The garuda bird is the mythical phoenix of the Buddhist faith, but belief in it is older than Buddhism and goes back to primitive India.

The story was learned from him, and then the people nearby knew that the fruit which they found in the sea came from that tree.

The cape of Malacha lies in one and one-half degrees toward the Antarctic Pole. Along the coast east of that cape are many villages and cities. The names of some of them are as follows: Cinghapola, which is located on the cape; Pahan; Calantan; Patani; Bradlun; Benan; Lagon; Cheregigharan; Tumbon; Phran; Cui; Brabri; Bangha; India; which is the city where the king of Siam, by name Siri Zacabedera, lives; Jandibum; Lanu; and Long-honpifa. Those cities are built like ours, and are subject to the king of Siam. On the shores of the rivers of that kingdom of Siam, live, as we are told, large birds which will not eat of any dead animal that may have been carried there, unless another bird comes first to eat its heart, after which they eat it. Next to Siam is found Camogia, whose king is called Saret Zacabedera; then Chiempa, whose king is Raia Brahaun Maitri. Rhubarb which is found in the following manner grows there. Twenty or twenty-five men assemble and go together into the jungles. Upon the approach of night, they climb trees, both to see whether they can catch the scent of the rhubarb, and also for fear of the lions, elephants, and other wild beasts. The wind bears to them the odor of the rhubarb from the direction in which it is to be found. When morning dawns they go in that direction whence the wind has come, and seek the rhubarb until they find it. The rhubarb is a large rotten tree; and unless it has become rotten, it gives off no odor. The best part of that tree is the root, although the wood is also rhubarb which is called *calama*. Next is found Cochi, whose king is called Raia Seribumni Pala. After that country is found Great Chiina, whose king is the greatest in all the world, and is called Santhoa Raia. He has seventy crowned kings subject to himself, and some of the latter have ten or fifteen kings subject to them. His port is called Guantan. [i.e., Canton]. Among the multitude of other cities, there are two principal ones called Nanchin [i.e., Nanking] and Comlaha where the above king lives.[88] He keeps his four principal men near his palace—one toward the west, one toward the east, one toward the south, and one toward the north. Each one of those four men gives audience only to those who come from his own quarter. All the kings and seigniors of greater and upper India obey that king; and in token that they are his true vassals, each one has an animal which is stronger than the lion, and called *chinga,* carved in marble in the middle of his square. That *chinga* is the seal of the said king of Chiina, and all those who go to Chiina must have that animal carved in wax [or] on an elephant's tooth, for otherwise they would not be allowed to enter his harbor. When any seignior is disobedient to that king, he is ordered to be flayed, and his skin dried in the sun

[88] This is another name for Peking, called Khanbaliq by the Mongols of the thirteenth and fourteenth centuries and Kanbalu by Marco Polo.

and salted. Then the skin is stuffed with straw or other substance, and placed head downward in a prominent place in the square, with the hands clasped above the head, so that he may be seen then to be performing *zonghu,* that is, obeisance. That king never allows himself to be seen by anyone. When he wishes to see his people, he rides about the palace on a skilfully made peacock, a most elegant contrivance, accompanied by six of his most principal women clad like himself; after which he enters a serpent called *nagha,* which is as rich a thing as can be seen, and which is kept in the greatest court of the palace. The king and the women enter it so that he may not be recognized among his women. He looks at his people through a large glass which is in the breast of the serpent. He and the women can be seen, but one cannot tell which is the king.[89] The latter is married to his sisters, so that the blood royal may not be mixed with others. Near his palace are seven encircling walls, and in each of those circular places are stationed ten thousand men for the guard of the palace [who remain there] until a bell rings, when ten thousand other men come for each circular space. They are changed in this manner each day and each night. Each circle of the wall has a gate. At the first stands a man with a large hook in his hand, called *satu horan* with *satu*

[89] The Ming Emperor of China to whom this refers must have been Wu-tsung (1505–1521). No such remarkable methods of perambulation as this are ascribed to him by Chinese authorities, but he did have a reputation for going about in disguise to inspect the condition of the people.

bagan; in the second, a dog, called *satu hain;* in the third, a man with an iron mace, called *satu horan* with *pocum becin;* in the fourth, a man with a bow in his hand called *satu horan* with *anat panan;* in the fifth, a man with a spear, called *satu horan* with *tumach;* in the sixth, a lion, called *satu horiman;* in the seventh, two white elephants, called two *gagia pute.* That palace has seventy-nine halls which contain only women who serve the king. Torches are always kept lighted in the palace, and it takes a day to go through it. In the upper part of it are four halls, where the principal men go sometimes to speak to the king. One is ornamented with copper, both below and above; one all with silver; one all with gold; and the fourth with pearls and precious gems. When the king's vassals take him gold or any other precious things as tribute, they are placed in those halls, and they say: "Let this be for the honor and glory of our Santhoa Raia." All the above and many other things were told us by a Moro who had seen them. The inhabitants of Chiina are light complexioned, and wear clothes. They eat at tables as we do, and have the cross, but it is not known for what purpose. Musk is produced in that country of Chiina. Its animal is a cat like the civet cat. It eats nothing except a sweet wood as thick as the finger, called *chamaru.* When the Chinese wish to make the musk, they attach a leech to the cat, which they leave fastened there, until it is well distended with blood. Then they squeeze the leech out into a dish and put the blood in the sun for four or five days. After that they sprinkle it with urine, and as often as they do that they place it in the sun. Thus it becomes perfect musk. Whoever owns one of those animals has to pay a certain sum to the king. Those grains which seem to be grains of musk are of kid's flesh crushed in the real musk and not the blood. Although the blood can be made into grains, it evaporates. The musk and the cat are called *castor* and the leech *lintha*. Many peoples are to be found as one follows the coast of that country of Chiina, who are as follows. The Chienchii inhabit islands where pearls and cinnamon grow. The Lechii live on the mainland; above their port stretches a mountain, so that all the junks and ships which desire to enter that port must unstep their masts. The king on the mainland [is called] Mom. He has twenty kings under him and is subordinate to the king of Chiina. His city is called Baranaci. The great Oriental catayo is located there.[90] Han [is] a cold, lofty island where copper, silver, pearls, and silk are produced, whose king is called Raia Zotru; Mli Ianla, whose king is called Raia Chetisqnuga; Gnio, and its king, Raia Sudacali. All three of the above places are cold and are located on the mainland. Triaganba and Trianga [are] two islands where pearls, copper, silver, and silk are produced, and whose king is Raia Rrom. Bassi Bassa [is] on the mainland; and then [follow] two islands, Sumbdit and Pradit, which are

---

[90] Catayo is Marco Polo's Cathay (Kitai), but in Pigafetta's day Europeans did not correctly identify the recently discovered China with this land.

exceedingly rich in gold, whose inhabitants wear a large gold ring around the legs at the ankle. On the mainland near that point live a race in some mountains who kill their fathers and mothers as age comes on, so that they may have no further trouble. All the peoples of those districts are heathens.

On Tuesday night as it drew near Wednesday, February eleven, 1522, we left the island of Timor and took to the great open sea called Laut Chidol. Laying our course toward the west southwest, we left the island of Zamatra, formerly called Traprobana,[91] to the north on our right hand, for fear of the king of Portoghala; [as well as] Pegu, Bengala, Uriza, Chelin where the Malabars live, who are subject to the king of Narsingha, Calicut, subject to the same king, Cambaia, where the Guzerati live, Cananor, Ghoa, Armus, and all the rest of the coast of India Major.[92] Six different classes of people inhabit India Major: Nairi, Panichali, Yranai, Pangelini, Macuai, and Poleai. The Nairi are the chiefs; and the Panichali are the townspeople: those two classes of men have converse together. The Iranai gather the palm wine and figs. The Pangelini are the sailors. The Macuai are the fishermen. The Poleai are the farmers and harvest the rice. These last always live in the country, although they enter the city at times. When anything is given them it is

[91] Pigafetta here mistakenly identifies Trapobana, or Taprobane, with Sumatra instead of Ceylon.

[92] This is an attempt to survey the Indian Ocean coast from Burma to the Persian Gulf. Armus is Hormuz, now of minor importance but once the metropolis of the Persian Gulf.

laid on the ground, and then they take it. When they go through the streets they call out *Po! po! po!* that is "Beware of me!" It happened, as we were told, that a Nair once had the misfortune to be touched by a Polea, for which the Nair immediately had the latter killed so that he might erase that disgrace. In order that we might double the cape of Bonna Speranza, we descended to forty-two degrees on the side of the Antarctic Pole. We were nine weeks near that cape with our sails hauled down because we had the west and northwest winds on our bow quarter and because of a most furious storm. That cape lies in a latitude of thirty-four and one-half degrees, and is one thousand six hundred leguas from the cape of Malaca. It is the largest and most dangerous cape in the world. Some of our men, both sick and well, wished to go to a Portuguese settlement called Mozanbich,[92] because the ship was leaking badly, because of the severe cold, and especially because we had no other food than rice and water; for as we had no salt, our provisions of meat had putrefied. Some of the others however, more desirous of their honor than of their own life, determined to go to Spagnia living or dead. Finally by God's help, we doubled that cape on May six at a distance of five leguas. Had we not approached so closely, we could never have doubled it. Then we sailed northwest for two months continually without taking on any fresh food or water. Twenty-one

[93] Correctly Moçambique, the Portuguese-held island off the mainland of east Africa.

men died during that short time. When we cast them into the sea, the Christians went to the bottom face upward, while the Indians always went down face downward.[94] Had not God given us good weather we would all have perished of hunger. Finally, constrained by our great extremity, we went to the islands of Capo Verde. Wednesday, July nine, we reached one of those islands called Sancto Jacobo, and immediately sent the boat ashore for food, with the story for the Portuguese that we had lost our foremast under the equinoctial line (although we had lost it upon the cape of Bonna Speranza), and when we were restepping it, our captain-general had gone to Spagnia with the other two ships. With those good words and with our merchandise, we got two boatloads of rice. We charged our men when they went ashore in the boat to ask what day it was, and they told us that it was Thursday with the Portuguese. We were greatly surprised for it was Wednesday with us, and we could not see how we had made a mistake; for as I had always kept well, I had set down every day without any interruption. However, as was told us later, it was no error, but as the voyage had been made continually toward the west and we had returned to the same place as does the sun, we had made that gain of twenty-four hours, as is clearly seen. The boat having returned to the shore again for rice, thirteen men and the boat were detained, because

[94] Other authorities also record this phenomenon but have no explanation to offer.

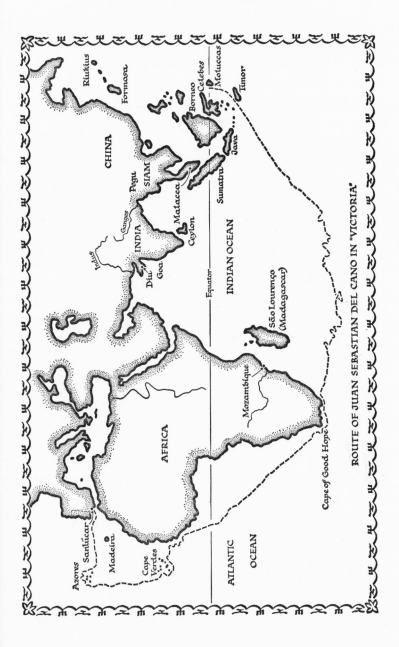

ROUTE OF JUAN SEBASTIAN DEL CANO IN "VICTORIA"

one of them, as we learned afterward in Spagnia, told the Portuguese that our captain was dead, as well as others, and that we were not going to Spagnia. Fearing lest we also be taken prisoners by certain caravels, we hastily departed. On Saturday, September six, 1522, we entered the bay of San Lucar with only eighteen men and the majority of them sick, all that were left of the sixty men who left Malucho. Some died of hunger; some deserted at the island of Timor; and some were put to death for crimes. From the time we left that bay [of San Lucar] until the present day [of our return], we had sailed fourteen thousand four hundred and sixty leguas, and furthermore had completed the circumnavigation of the world from east to west. On Monday, September eight, we cast anchor near the quay of Seviglia, and discharged all our artillery. Tuesday, we all went in shirts and barefoot, each holding a candle, to visit the shrine of Santa Maria de la Victoria, and that of Santa Maria de l'Antiqua.

Leaving Seviglia, I went to Vagliadolit [Valladolid], where I presented to his sacred Majesty, Don Carlo, neither gold nor silver, but things very highly esteemed by such a sovereign. Among other things I gave him a book, written by my hand, concerning all the matters that had occurred from day to day during our voyage. I left there as best I could and went to Portagalo where I spoke with King Johanni of what I had seen. Passing through Spagnia, I went to Fransa where I made a gift of certain things from the other hemisphere to the mother of the most Christian king, Don Francisco, Madame the regent. Then I came to Italia, where I established my permanent abode, and devoted my poor labors to the famous and most illustrious lord, Phillipo de Villers Lisleadam, the most worthy grand master of Rhodi.

The Cavalier

ANTONIO PAGAPHETTA

JUAN SEBASTIÁN DEL CANO

History has not assigned a very illustrious place to this Basque navigator who completed the first voyage around the world. Pigafetta, who sailed under his command from the East Indies to Sanlúcar, devotes only two pages to this culminating part of the great adventure and never mentions the name of the "Victoria's" commander. John Fiske, in the nineteenth century, called El Cano a "weak man who had ill deserved such honour." [95] Recently Charles McKew Parr has said that "he did not have the respect of his men, [and] there were mutinies and desertions en route." [96] But surely the man who conducted a leaky, overladen ship, with a frequently starving crew, through unfamiliar waters nearly halfway around the globe could not have been so bad a commander as these remarks imply.

Juan Sebastián del Cano was born at Guetaria in Gipúzcoa, probably in 1487.[97] We know little of his career before the Magellan voyage beyond the fact that he had commanded a ship in the Mediterranean. In 1519 at Seville he enlisted as mate of the "Concepción" under the direct orders of Gaspar de Quesada. Little is heard of El Cano before the fleet arrived at San Julián, where he took part

[95] *The Discovery of America,* Boston and New York, 1898, II, 211.

[96] *So Noble a Captain,* p. 370.

[97] José de Arteche, *Elcano,* Madrid, 1942, p. 23.

in the mutiny—doing so, according to his own later testimony, "to obey the commandments of the king." [98] With the mutiny suppressed, El Cano escaped the death penalty and presumably continued as second in command of the ship. Again there is silence about his part in the expedition until after Magellan's death in battle, though we know that El Cano took no part in the fighting because he lay ill at the time.

After the sad termination of Magellan's career, the survivors immediately chose Duarte Barbosa and Juan Rodríguez Serrano as their leaders, but both were killed a few days later when their supposed ally, the recently baptized king of Cebu, massacred all the white men he could entice on shore. Next the Portuguese, João Lopes Carvalho, took command. From May 1 to September 21, 1521, he conducted the fleet in an aimless manner around the East Indies, apparently trying to reach the Moluccas but unable to find them. He burned the "Concepción" on Bohol with the approval of the others, then turned virtually to piracy, capturing and plundering native craft and setting up a harem of stolen native women aboard the flagship. [99] His leadership, in the judgment of all the officers and crew members, was getting the expedition simply nowhere. When they reached a haven in northern Borneo where they calked the ships and examined the hulls, all hands agreed to depose Carvalho. There was no mutiny; they merely let him know that his captaincy had ended. Gonzalo Gómez de Espinosa, whose courage had broken the San Julián mutiny for Magellan, received command of the "Trinidad" and El Cano that of the "Victoria." These two, with the purser of the expedition, Martín Méndez, became a triumvirate exercising the high command. As neither of the others understood navigation, El Cano became *de facto* head of the whole undertaking from this point.

The aimlessness and indecision that had marked Carvalho's leadership now gave way to decisive and business-

[98] Navarrete, *Colección,* IV, 261.
[99] Melón, p. 670.

like procedure. El Cano did not know the way to the Moluccas but learned what he needed to know when, off Mindanao, he captured a pirogue manned by native warriors. They saved their lives by indicating the proper route. The ships took a course slightly east of south and, after passing various islands, entered the port of Tidore, the neighbor of Ternate, on November 8, 1521.[100] El Cano quickly made friends with Almanzor, kinglet of the island, who gladly furnished in trade all the cloves the Spaniards wanted and agreed to become the vassal of King Charles. They soon learned that Magellan's friend Serrão had died of poison eight months earlier, though different stories existed as to just how and by whom it had been administered.[101] They did, however, find a living Portuguese, Pedro Afonso de Lorosa, who had evidently come to the islands a decade earlier and remained as a trader. Lorosa had kept in touch with Malacca and could tell the Spaniards that King Manuel, gravely disturbed by the threat of the Magellan expedition, had issued orders for the safeguarding of his own supremacy in the Moluccas. The governor of India, who was Magellan's old commander Diogo Lopes de Sequeira, had received instructions to go in person to the islands or send a fleet there to destroy the Spaniards should they arrive.[102] The Portuguese expedition, then, might come at any time. As El Cano's ships were in no condition to resist it and as the commander recognized Almanzor for a fair weather friend only, Lorosa's news furnished an incentive to speed the loading of cargo and the departure. The trader, who knew himself to be in bad odor with his own countrymen, embarked with his native wife aboard the "Trinidad" and prepared to share the further fortunes of the expedition.

When the last consignments of spices, coconuts, palm

[100] Medina, III, cccv.

[101] Compare the story that Serrão was poisoned by a native woman at Portuguese instigation with the charge that the king of Tidore ordered the poisoning. Melón, p. 682.

[102] The report was mainly true, though Lorosa's details do not altogether agree with Barros'.

wine, rice, and goats had been taken aboard, it was found that the "Trinidad" leaked badly and could not sail without repairs. El Cano, whose "Victoria" was in better condition, did not wish to wait because he had decided to go home by way of the Cape of Good Hope and needed the seasonal easterly winds that were then beginning. Accordingly he left on December 21, 1521, guided by Moluccan pilots who would direct him during the opening stages of the long voyage.[103] The "Trinidad," still commanded by Gómez de Espinosa and piloted by Leone Pancaldo, did not get under way until April 6, 1522. It had been decided that this ship, instead of following El Cano, should recross the Pacific and try to make the coast of Darien, where Pedrarias Dávila still commanded and where González and Niño were known to have orders to prepare a fleet to sail westward along the northern coast of the *Sinus*.[104]

Espinosa left Tidore with a total complement of fifty-four persons and a heavy load of cloves. He worked his way through the East Indies, discovered several of the Caroline islands, and by mid-June was off the coast of Agrigan in the Marianas. From there he sailed northward and an undetermined distance eastward to 43° N., where he encountered a storm lasting twelve days. The winds continued unfavorable after the tempest. Meanwhile food and water ran short, the cold grew intense, and the undernourished seamen sickened and died.[105] It was now August, four months since leaving Tidore. Espinosa realized that he could never make Panama and that his only hope lay in turning back. He accordingly backtracked to Saipan, where he received some food from the natives and where three of his men deserted. One of them, Gonzalo de Vigo, was picked up on Saipan by the expedition of Garcia Jofré de Loaisa in 1526.[106] Espinosa continued toward the Moluccas, his men dying at the rate of one every three days. Less than half his

[103] Medina, III, cccxii.
[104] Alvarez Rubiano, *Pedrarias,* p. 322; Herrera, III, 52.
[105] Medina, III, cccxxxiii.
[106] *Ibid.,* p. ccccliv.

original number remained when he cast anchor early in November at an island neighboring on Ternate and Tidore.[107] The comfort awaiting the Spaniards here was certainly very slight. Since their departure in April, a Portuguese force commanded by António de Brito had moved into Ternate, captured the few men left there by the expedition as traders, and destroyed their place of business. Espinosa wrote Brito a letter describing his own desperate condition and asking for help, but received in reply only a demand for instant surrender. Barros says of the envoy sent to Espinosa by Brito:

Finally, on entering the ship, when Duarte de Meneses saw its people, he was seized by great pity, because the majority of them were so bent that they could not move without assistance: they were almost paralytics, and thirty-seven of them were already dead, and the ship was so contaminated by illness, besides the work of hunger and lack of necessities, that our people, when D. Garcia came, were as afraid to enter it as if it had been a pest house.[108]

Espinosa of course surrendered, and Barros emphasizes the humane feelings of his good friend António de Brito by saying that he "sent supplies to heal and take care of those people, as if they had been natives of his own country." [109] This hardly agrees with Brito's own statement to the new king of Portugal, John III, to whom he wrote concerning the captured captain, notary, and pilot, "It would be performing the best service to Your Highness if I commanded their heads to be cut off. . . . I detained them in the Moluccas because it is an unhealthy place, to see if the climate would kill them: I did not venture to order them killed because I did not know the will of Your Highness in this matter." [110] He decapitated Lorosa as a traitor, however, and forced the Spanish prisoners to work on a fortress the Portuguese were constructing on Ternate. They were then moved from place to place in the East, and

[107] *Ibid.*, cccxxxv.
[108] Barros, III, 296–97.
[109] *Ibid.*, p. 297.
[110] *Alguns documentos,* pp. 473–74.

after most of them had died, a few survivors, including Espinosa, were taken to Lisbon and finally allowed to go to Spain.[111]

In the meantime El Cano and his ship had completed the homeward voyage. After leaving Tidore, the "Victoria" proceeded by easy stages to Timor, where Pigafetta, at the captain's order, went ashore and obtained permission from the local ruler to trade for food, white sandalwood, and cinnamon. Here El Cano lost two men by desertion,[112] which reduced his company to 45 Europeans and 13 East Indians. Pigafetta, as will be seen from his narrative, busied himself with acquiring both information and interesting misinformation concerning the surrounding islands of the Indian seas. On February 11, 1522, El Cano considered the ship as ready as it would ever be for the voyage to Spain, and set sail upon the Indian Ocean. For the next five months, until he reached the Cape Verde Islands, he deviated as far as possible from the customary sailing routes and seldom sighted land. It was necessary to keep out of sight of other ships, because these would have been Portuguese and he was sailing seas forbidden to Spain by the Treaty of Tordesillas.

El Cano unquestionably performed here one of the greatest feats in maritime history. Magellan had crossed the Pacific, but he did so with three ships, still in fair condition and favored by good weather all the way. The "Victoria" had by now been twice damaged and patched, and its hull was in such shape as to make even a short voyage risky. The weather frequently turned bad; the provisions acquired at Tidore and Timor gave out, except for some spoiling rice; and the water supply ran short long before the end of the voyage. The men no longer had the warm European clothing that had sustained them in Patagonia and Magellan's strait, and there was fever aboard.

Rounding the Cape of Good Hope was known to be difficult. As they approached it, many on board, including

[111] Medina, III, cccxxxviii.
[112] Melón, p. 700.

Pigafetta, desired to put in at the Portuguese post of Mozambique because their food had run low, the ship leaked, and the cold had become almost insufferable. At this point El Cano proved his courage and leadership by refusing to consider the idea. To enter Mozambique would mean being taken prisoners, which would bring their glorious enterprise to the tamest of conclusions. His will carried the day, and he persuaded or browbeat the faint hearts into rounding the Cape regardless of danger. El Cano did not know these waters and at first thought the chances would be better if he went well below the Cape to 42° S. and made his circumnavigation effort there. He accordingly tried this, but it proved to be the wrong method. The winds blew against him and any progress made with hours of labor was lost in minutes by wildly augmented gusts. He spent weeks advancing and retreating while the slender stock of provisions diminished and the crew grew weaker. El Cano then decided to attack his problem the other way and sail close to the African coast, even at the risk of being blown ashore and wrecked. He found Good Hope to be a zone of turbulent waters, where currents clashed from different directions and the winds seemed to battle each other. Details of the final rounding are lost. All we can say is that El Cano at last accomplished it on May 6, 1522, and that Pigafetta considered that the achievement required the help of God. Once around the Cape, in Saldanha Bay just north of the modern Cape Town, the "Victoria" met a Portuguese ship bound for India. The two hailed each other, and El Cano took the risk of telling the Portuguese captain, Pedro Cuaresma, who he was and from where he had come. It did not occur to Cuaresma that it was his patriotic duty to sink the "Victoria" to prevent her return to Castile, so the two vessels went their respective ways.[113]

El Cano sailed northward through the Atlantic, hunger and privation taking a fearful toll of his men. Dead bodies were thrown in the ocean with little formality, and Pigafetta made the interesting observation that the Christians

[113] See p. 327.

sank with faces turned to the sky and the East Indians with faces downward in the water. It required two months of daily suffering to bring the "Victoria" from the Cape to the harbor of Rio Grande at the island of São Tiago in the Portuguese-owned Cape Verde Islands. There could be no doubt this time that the mariners, now reduced to about thirty-five, must risk entering the port or perish. El Cano therefore ordered the stop, and Pigafetta explains how the commander attempted to deceive the Portuguese authorities with a made-up story of where the ship had been—a story that worked until the Spaniards passed off East Indian spices in exchange for provisions. Pigafetta also says that the voyagers here learned they were a day off in their reckoning, mistaking Thursday for Wednesday and only later receiving a proper explanation. Peter Martyr, who helped Charles receive El Cano at Valladolid, was greatly interested in the time discrepancy and took some pains to discover the reason. He sought the help of Gaspare Contarini, the learned Venetian ambassador at the court of Charles, and the two worked out an answer as follows:

The Spanish fleet, leaving the Gorgades [Cape Verde] Islands, proceeded straight to the west, that is to say, it followed the sun, and each day was a little longer than the preceding, according to the distance covered. Consequently, when the tour of the world was finished—which the sun makes in twenty-four hours from its rising to its setting,— the ship had gained an entire day; that is to say, one less than those who remain all that time in the same place. Had a Portuguese fleet, sailing towards the east, continued in the same direction, following the same route first discovered, it is positive that when it got back to the Gorgades it would have lost a little time each day, in making the circuit of the world: it would consequently have to count one day more.[114]

[114] *De orbe novo,* II, 171. Herrera (IV, 189) says, ". . . and so it happened that they ate meat on Thursdays and celebrated Easter on Monday," but both could not be true. He gives an accurate explanation, however, which is the one offered by Jusepe de Acosta, a Jesuit.

El Cano, after taking some food aboard, pushed off in haste when it became evident that the Portuguese had learned his identity and meant to seize the ship. He left thirteen men ashore, and it is quite possible that one or more of these sailors had added to the suspicion aroused by the oriental spices by becoming too talkative in the presence of the Portuguese.[115] The fifty-four days spent in sailing from São Tiago to Sanlúcar proved almost the hardest of all. Hunger was less acute now, thanks to the food obtained at the island before the awakening of Portuguese suspicions, but the thirteen men who had been left there as prisoners were probably the strongest and healthiest members of the crew. El Cano had expected to buy slaves at São Tiago to work the pumps, as the "Victoria" leaked badly, but there had been no time to procure these. Nineteen white men, counting the captain and Pigafetta, aided by four surviving Orientals, had to do this work as well as handle the sails.

El Cano followed approved maritime practice by sailing north-northwest from the Cape Verdes to the Azores. The first of these islands was sighted on August 4, and two days later the body of the Breton Etienne Villon was thrown in the Atlantic [116]—the last burial of this kind that was necessary. Turning eastward to Europe, the mariners beheld Cape St. Vincent on September 4, and two days later they passed the bar of Sanlúcar, guided by the local pilot, Pedro Sordo, who boarded the ship to perform this service.[117] Their voyage had lasted three years minus fourteen days, and eighteen ragged Europeans, whose names have all been preserved,[118] besides three unnamed East Indians, descended from the ship.

[115] Medina, III, 95–99.

[116] *Colección de documentos inéditos para la historia de Chile*, collected by J. T. Medina, 30 vols., Santiago de Chile, 1888, I, 177. He appears here under the name Estéban Breton.

[117] Medina, IV, 128.

[118] A list is given in Medina, III, cccxx.

Maximilian of Transylvania

This writer was probably born in Brussels, though the "Transylvania" part of his name suggests that he had lived in Hungary. He served as secretary to Charles V and absorbed an interest in overseas affairs partly from Peter Martyr, who had made a lifelong study of the subject, and partly from Cristóbal de Haro, whose niece he married.[1] Being at Valladolid when El Cano arrived there, he interrogated him and his two companions, Albo and Bustamante. If Maximilian spoke with Pigafetta he could not have been much influenced by him, for in many details he obviously takes his data from another source. He shows an interest in the diplomatic background of the whole subject and a taste for classical learning that he might have obtained from his own studies but more likely owes to Martyr. He wrote the letter to Cardinal-Archbishop Lang of Salzburg, whose natural son he was, partly to give himself practice in writing Latin and partly to enhance his own fame.[2]

We are not well informed concerning other geographical activities of Maximilian. He is credited by a Flemish monk, Franciscus Monachus, with having made a terrestrial globe, surpassing all others of the time, on which he indicated with precision the results of the Magellan expedition.[3] Johann Schöner, the map- and globe-maker, was influenced by the letter to Lang, but we do not know whether Maxi-

[1] Denucé, *Magellan*, p. 27.
[2] Henry Stevens, *Johann Schöner*, ed. E. H. Coote, London, 1888, pp. xxi–ii.
[3] Denucé, *Magellan*, p. 28.

milian ever met the famous geographer. Maximilian was dead by 1526, evidently at an early age and with a comfortable fortune, because one Joh. Alex. Brassicanus, in a poem of that year, laments his premature death and bewails the loss of a Maecenas.[4]

His letter is undeniably a valuable source of information about the Magellan voyage; for a while, in fact, it was the only printed account of the expedition. Furthermore it is a good index to the state of geographical learning at the time. Maximilian commits mistakes, such as calling Magellan an admiral in the service of Portugal before coming to Spain and implying that he arrived in 1518 instead of 1517, but these are easily rectified.

The following translation of the letter is by James Baynes of the Printed Book Department of the British Museum. The translation includes the preliminary discourse of Giovanni Battista Ramusio (1485–57), who published the letter in his collection entitled *Delle navigationi et viaggi*. The work appeared in three volumes, and the Maximilian letter is from the first, which was published in 1550.

Ramusio, a native of Treviso, studied at Padua and became a friend of the famous Piedmontese geographer and map-maker, Giacomo Gastaldi. Though he published works in other fields, the collecting of narratives of voyages became his principal interest, and he is said to have spent thirty years on the first volume of his *Navigationi*. He served as a model for such later students of exploration as Théodore de Bry in France and Richard Hakluyt and Samuel Purchas in England.

[4] *Ibid.*

Discourse of
M. Giovanni Battista Ramusio
upon the
Voyage Made by the Spaniards
Round the World

The voyage made by the Spaniards round the world in the space of three years is one of the greatest and most marvelous things which have been heard of in our times; and, although in many things we surpass the ancients, yet this expedition far excels every other that has been made up till now. The voyage was described very minutely by Peter Martyr, who belonged to the Council of the Indies of His Majesty the Emperor, and to whom was entrusted the duty of writing this history; and by him were examined all those who remained alive of that expedition, and who reached Seville in the year 1522. But, as it was sent to be printed in Rome, it was lost in the miserable sacking of that city; and nothing is known even now as to where it is. And he who saw it, and read it, bears testimony to the same; and, amongst other things worthy of recollection

271

that the aforesaid Peter noted concerning the voyage, was this, that the Spaniards, having sailed about three years and one month, and the greater part of them, as is usual amongst seafaring men, having noted down the days of the months one by one, found, when they arrived in Spain, that they had lost a day, for the day on which they arrived at Seville, which was the 7th of September, was, by their reckoning, the 6th. And the aforesaid Peter having mentioned this peculiarity to a certain excellent and extraordinary man, who was at that time ambassador for his Republic to His Majesty; and, having asked him how it could be, he, who was a great philosopher and learned in Greek and Latin literature, so that for his singular learning and rare excellence, he was afterwards promoted to much higher rank, gave this explanation: That it could not have fallen out otherwise, as they had travelled for three years continuously and always accompanied the sun, which was going westward. And he told him besides, that those who sailed due westwards towards the sun, lengthen their day very much, as the ancients also had noticed. Now, the book of the aforesaid Peter having disappeared, Fortune has not allowed the memory of so marvellous an enterprise to be entirely lost, inasmuch as a certain noble gentlemen of Vicenza called Messer Antonio Pigafetta (who, having gone on the voyage and returned in the ship "Vittoria," was made a Knight of Rhodes), wrote a very exact and full account of it in a book, one copy of which he pre-

272

sented to His Majesty the Emperor, and another he
sent to the most Serene Mother of the most Christian King, the Lady Regent. She entrusted to an
excellent Parisian philosopher called Jacomo Fabre,
who had studied in Italy, the work of translating it
into French. This worthy person, I suppose to save
himself trouble, made only a summary of it, leaving
out what seemed fit to him; and this was printed,
very incorrectly, in France, and has now come into
our hands; and along with it a letter from one called
Maximilianus of Transylvania, a secretary of His
Majesty the Emperor, to the most Reverend Cardinal of Salzburg. And this we have wished to add to
this volume of travels, as one of the greatest and
most remarkable that there has ever been, and one
at which those great philosophers of old, hearing of
it, would have been stupefied and beside themselves.
And the city of Vicenza may well boast, among the
other cities of Italy, that in addition to its nobility
and high qualities; in addition to its many rare and
excellent geniuses, both in letters and arms, there
has been a gentleman of such courage as the aforesaid Messer Antonio Pigafetta, who has circumnavigated the whole globe, and has described it so
exactly. There is no doubt that the ancients would
have erected a statue of marble to him, and would
have placed it in an honourable position, as a
memorial and example to posterity of his great
worth, and in acknowledgment of so stupendous an
enterprise. But if, in this letter or in the summary,
there be seen any discrepancy of names or things, let

no one be astonished; for the bent of men's minds is various, and one notices one thing and one another, just as the things appear most deserving of attention. Let it suffice if, in the principal things they agree, and many parts which are left out in one can be read at length in the other. Fabulous stories, too, are noted for what they are. This may be safely affirmed by anyone, that the ancients never had such a knowledge of the world, which the sun goes round and examines every twenty-four hours, as we have at present, through the industry of the men of these our times.

Most Reverend and Illustrious Lord, my only Lord, to you I most humbly commend myself.

One of those five ships has lately returned which Caesar sent in former years,[5] when he was living at Saragossa, to a strange, and for so many ages, an unknown world, in order to search for the islands where spices grow. For though the Portuguese bring a great quantity of them from the Golden Chersonesus, which we now suppose to be Malacca, yet their own Indies produce nothing but pepper. Other spices, such as cinnamon, cloves, and the nutmeg, which we call muscat, and its covering, which we call muscat flower, are brought to their own Indies from distant islands till now only known by name, and in ships which are fastened together not by iron but by palm leaves. The sails of these

[5] Charles V, who was His Caesarian Majesty of the Holy Roman Empire.

ships are round and woven, too, of the palm-fibre. This sort of ships they call junks, and they only use them with a wind directly fore and aft.

It is no wonder that these islands should be unknown to any human beings almost up to our time.[6] For whatever we read concerning the native soil of the spices has been told us by ancient authors, and is partly, certainly, fabulous; and, partly, so far from the truth, that even the very countries in which they said that they grew naturally, are but little less distant from those where it is now known that they grow, than we are. For to omit others, Herodotus, in other respects a most famed author, has said that cinnamon is found in birds' nests, to which the birds have brought it from most distant regions, and specially the Phoenix, and I know not who has seen his nest. But Pliny, who thought himself able to give more certain information, because, before his time, many things had been made clear by the voyages of the fleets of Alexander the Great and of others, relates that cinnamon grows in Aethiopia on the borders of the land of the Troglodytae, whilst now it is known that cinnamon is produced very far from any part of Aethiopia, and specially from the Troglodytae (that is, the dwellers in subterranean caverns). But our men, who have now returned, and who were perfectly acquainted with Aethiopia, have been obliged to make a complete circuit of the world, and that a very wide one, before they could find the islands and return. As this voyage may be

[6] Maximilian means to say occidental human beings.

considered marvellous, and not only unaccomplished, but even unattempted either in our age or in any previous one, I have resolved to write as truly as possible to your Reverence the course [of the expedition] and the sequence of the whole matter. I have taken care to have everything related to me most exactly by the captain and by the individual sailors who have returned with him. They have also related each separate event to Caesar and to others with such good faith and sincerity, that they seemed not only to tell nothing fabulous themselves, but by their relation to disprove and refute all the fabulous stories which had been told by old authors. For who can believe that these were Monosceli, Scyopodae, Syritae, Spitamei, Pygmies, and many others, rather monsters than men.[7] And as so many places beyond the Tropic of Capricorn have been sought, found, and carefully examined, both by the Spaniards in the south-west and by the Portuguese sailing eastwards, and as the remainder of the whole world has now been sailed over by our countrymen, and yet nothing trustworthy has been heard concerning these man-monsters, it must be believed that the accounts of them are fabulous, lying, and old women's tales, handed down to us in some way by no credible author. But lest I, who have to travel over the whole world, should seem too diffuse in my introduction, I return to my story.

[7] Monosceli and scyopodae were one-legged men; syritae and spitamei, persons a span high. (A span is the distance from the thumb to the little finger when extended.)

When, nearly thirty years ago, the Spaniards in the west, and the Portuguese in the east, began to search for new and unknown lands, their two kings, lest one should be a hindrance to the other, divided the whole globe between them by the authority, most likely, of Pope Alexander the Sixth, in this manner: that a straight line should be drawn 360 miles, which they call *leucae*,[8] west of the islands of the Hesperides, which are now called the islands of Cape Verd; towards the north, and another towards the south Pole, till they should meet again, and so divide the world into two equal parts. And whatever strange land should be discovered eastwards [of this line] should be ceded to the Portuguese, and whatever west of it to the Spaniards. In this manner it happened that the Spaniards always sailed southwest, and there they discovered a very large continent and very great and innumerable islands, rich in gold and pearls and in other wealth, and now, quite lately, have they discovered the vast Mediterranean city, Tenostica, situated in a lake, like Venice.[9] About this city Peter Martyr, an author more careful about his facts than the elegance of his style, has written many wonderful, and yet true, things. But the Portuguese, passing southwards by the shores of the Hesperides, and of the ichthyophagous Aethiopians, and crossing the equinoctial line and the Tropic of Capricorn, sailed

[8] Maximilian is a little off here. The line was drawn 370 leagues west.

[9] The Aztec city of Tenochtitlán (Mexico City), recently captured by Cortés.

eastward, and discovered many great and unknown islands, and afterwards the sources of the Nile and the land of the Troglodytae. Thence they sailed past the Arabian and Persian Gulfs to the shores of India, within the Ganges, where there is now the mighty emporium and kingdom of Calicut. Thence they sailed to Taprobanes, which they now call Zamatara. For there is now no island which either can be, or can be supposed to be, Taprobanes, in the position in which Ptolemy, Pliny, and the other cosmographers placed it.[10] Going thence, they arrived at the Golden Chersonesus, where now is situated that most famous city of Malacca, the greatest emporium of the East. After this they entered the Great Gulf, which reaches as far as the country of the Sinae, which they now call Schinae, where they found a white and tolerably civilized people, like our Germans.[11] They believe that the Seres and the Asiatic Scythians extend as far as there. And though there was a certain rumour afloat that the Portuguese had progressed so far to the East as to cross their own limits and enter the territory of the Spaniards, and that Malacca and the Great Bay were within our limits, still all these things were said rather than believed, until four years ago Ferdinand Magellan, a distinguished Portuguese, who, for many years had explored the coasts of the whole of the East as Admiral, took a great hatred to his king,

[10] By Taprobanes Ptolemy and the ancients meant Ceylon.

[11] Maximilian here forgetfully insults the paternal recipient of the letter, himself a German, by referring to the Germans as "tolerably civilized."

whom he complained of as being most ungrateful
to him, and came to Caesar. Christopher Haro, too,
my own father-in-law's brother, who had traded for
many years in the East by means of his agents, he
himself staying in Ulyssipone, commonly called
Lisbon, and who had lastly traded with the Chinese,
so that he has great practice in such things, having
also been unjustly treated by the King of Portugal,
came also home to Spain. And they both showed
Caesar that though it was not yet quite sure whether
Malacca was within the confines of the Spaniards or
the Portuguese, because, as yet, nothing of the longitude had been clearly proved, yet that it was quite
plain that the Great Gulf and the people of Sinae
lay within the Spanish boundary. This, too, was held
to be most certain, that the islands which they call
the Moluccas, in which all the spices are produced,
and are thence exported to Malacca, lay within the
Spanish western division, and that it was possible to
sail there; and that spices could be brought thence to
Spain more easily, and at less expense and cheaper,
as they came direct from their native place.

Their course would be this, to sail westward,
coasting the southern hemisphere [till they came]
to the East. The thing seemed almost impossible
and useless, not because it was thought a difficult
thing to go from the west right to the east under the
hemisphere, but because it was uncertain whether
ingenious nature, which has done nothing without
the greatest foresight, had not so dissevered the east
from the west, partly by sea and partly by land, as to

make it impossible to arrive there by either land or sea travelling. For it had not then been discovered whether that great region which is called Terra Firma did separate the western sea from the eastern; it was clear enough that that continent, in its southern part, trended southwards and afterwards westwards. It was clear, also, that two regions had been discovered in the North, one of which they called Regio Bacalearum (Cod-fish Land),[12] from a new kind of fish; and the other Terra Florida. And if these two were united to that Terra Firma, it was impossible to get to the east by going from the west, as nothing had ever been discovered of any channel through this land, though it had been sought for most diligently and with great labour. And they considered it a very doubtful and most dangerous enterprise to go through the limits of the Portuguese, and so to the east. For which reason it seemed to Caesar and to his counsellors that these men were promising a thing from which much was to be hoped, but still of great difficulty. When they were both brought to an audience on a certain day, Magellan offered to go himself, but Christopher offered to fit out a fleet at his own expense and that of his friends, but only if it were allowed to sail under the authority and protection of Caesar. Whilst they both persisted rather obstinately in their offers, Caesar himself equipped a fleet of five ships, and appointed Magellan its admiral. Their orders were, to sail southwards along the coast of Terra Firma till

[12] Newfoundland.

280

they found either its termination or some channel through which they might reach the spice-bearing Moluccas. So Magellan set sail on the 10th of August, 1519, with five ships from Seville. A few days after he reached the Fortunate Islands, which are now sometimes called the Canaries. Thence they arrived at the Islands of the Hesperides, from which they took a south-western course towards that continent which we mentioned before; and after some days' fair sailing they sighted a promontory, to which the name of Santa Maria has been given. Here Juan Ruy Diaz Solis had been eaten, with some of his companions, by the anthropophagi, whom the Indians call cannibals, whilst, by order of Ferdinand the Catholic, he was exploring the coast of this continent with a fleet. Sailing thence, our men coasted in an unbroken course along the coasts of this continent, which extend a very long way south, and tend a little west, so that they crossed the Tropic of Capricorn by many degrees. I think that this continent should be called that of the Southern Pole. But it was not so easy as I have said; for not till the last day of March of the following year did they reach a bay, to which they gave the name of Saint Julian. Here they found the Antarctic Pole star 49⅓ degrees above their horizon, both by the altitude and declination of the sun from the Equinoctial, and also by the altitude of the Antarctic (Pole star) itself. This star our sailors generally make use of more than of any other. They state also that the longitude was 56 deg. west of the Fortunate Isles.

For, as the ancient cosmographers, and specially Ptolemy, reckoned the longitude from the Fortunate Islands eastward to Catigara at 180 deg., so our men, sailing as far as they could westward also, began to reckon another 180 deg. westward to Catigara, as was right. Yet our sailors seem to me rather to be mistaken in the calculation of the longitudes than to have fixed them with any certainty, because in so long a voyage, and being so distant from the land, they cannot fix and determine any marks or signs for the longitude. Still I think that these accounts, whatever they be, should not be cast aside, but rather accepted till more certain information be discovered.

This Gulf of Saint Julian seemed very great, and had the appearance of a channel. Wherefore Admiral Magellan ordered two ships to explore the Gulf and anchored the rest outside. After two days, information was brought to him that the Gulf was full of shoals, and did not extend far inland. Our men, on their way back, saw some Indians picking up shell-fish on the shore; for they call the natives of all unknown lands Indians. They were of extraordinary height, that is to say, about ten spans, were clothed in the skins of wild beasts, and seemed darker than would be expected from the situation of the country. When some of our men went on shore to them and showed them bells and pictures painted on paper, they began a hoarse chant and an unintelligible song, dancing round our men, and, in order to astonish them, they passed arrows a cubit and a half long down their throats to the bottom of their stomachs, and without being sick. And forthwith drawing them out again, they seemed to rejoice greatly, as having shown their bravery by this exploit.

At last three came as ambassadors, and prayed our men, by certain signs, to go further inland with them, as if they would receive them with all hospitality. Magellan sent seven men, well armed, with them, to investigate as carefully as possible both country and people. When they had gone with them about seven miles inland, they came to a thick and pathless wood.

Here was a rather low hut, covered with skins of wild beasts. There were two apartments in it; in one lived the women with their children, in the other the men. There were thirteen women and children, and five men. These received their guests with a [ferali apparatu] barbarous pomp, which seemed to them a royal one. An animal was slaughtered, which seemed to differ little from the onager, and they served it up half roasted to our men, without any other food or drink.[18] Our men were obliged, contrary to their custom, to sleep under skins, on account of the severity of the snow and wind. Wherefore, before they slept, they set watch. The Indians did the same, and lay down near our men, snoring horribly.

When the day had broken, our men asked them

[18] An onager is a wild donkey. The Patagonian animal in question was the guanaco, a relative of the llama.

to return with them to the ships, with the whole family. When the Indians had refused for a considerable time, and our men had insisted upon it rather imperiously, the men entered the den-like women's apartment. The Spaniards thought that they were consulting with their wives concerning this expedition; but they returned covered, from the sole of their feet to the crown of their heads, with different horrible skins, and with their faces painted in different colours, and equipped in this terrible and horrible garb with bows and arrows for battle, and [seemingly] of much greater stature than before. The Spaniards, who thought that it would come to a fight, ordered [a shot] to be fired. Though this shot was harmless, still the giants, who looked just before fit to contend with Jove, were so frightened by this sound, that they began forthwith to speak of peace. The upshot was, that three men returned with our fellows to the ships, having sent away the rest of the family. So they started for the ships. But, as our men could not only not keep up with these almost giants when the latter were running, but could not, even by running, keep up with them walking, two of them escaped upon the march, on the pretext of pursuing an onager, which they saw feeding at a distance upon a mountain. The third was brought to the ship, but died, within a few days, of fasting, which he had imposed upon himself, according to the habit of the Indians, through homesickness. And though the admiral sent again to that hut, in order to catch some one of these giants to take to Caesar on account of their novelty, yet no one was found there, but all had gone elsewhere with the hut. Whence it seems clear that that race is a wandering one, nor did our men ever see another Indian on that coast, though they remained in that bay for many days, as we shall mention farther on. They did not think that there was anything in that region of sufficient importance to justify their exploring it and the interior any farther. Though Magellan perceived that any longer stay there was useless, yet, as the sea for several days was stormy and the sky threatening, and the land stretched continuously southwards, so that the farther they went the colder they would find that region, his departure was necessarily put off from day to day, till the month of May was close upon them, from which time the winter there begins to be most severe, so that it became necessary to winter at the very time when we have our summer. Magellan foreseeing that the voyage would be a long one, ordered provisions to be served out more sparingly among his crews, so that the stock might last longer. When the Spaniards had borne this patiently for some days, fearing the severity of the winter and the barrenness of the country, they at last petitioned their admiral, Magellan, that, as he saw that the land stretched uninterruptedly to the south, and that no hope remained of its terminating or of the discovery of a strait through it, and that a severe winter was imminent, and that many of them were dead of starvation and hardships; and declared that they could no longer bear the rule which he had made about the allowance of provisions [*lex sumptuaria*], and begged that he would increase the allowance of provisions, and think about going home; that Caesar never intended that they should too obstinately attempt what nature itself and other obstacles opposed; that their exertions were already sufficiently known and approved of—for they had gone farther than either the boldness or rashness of mortals had ever dared to go as yet; and that they could easily reach some milder shore, if they were to sail south [north?] for a few days, a south wind being then blowing. But in reply, Magellan, who had already made up his mind either to die or to complete his enterprise, said that his course had been laid down for him by Caesar himself, and that he neither could nor would depart from it in any degree, and that he would in consequence sail till he found either the end of the land or some strait [through it].

That though they could not at present succeed whilst winter was against them, yet that it would be easy in the summer of that region. But that, if they would continue towards the Antarctic portion of this country, the whole of its summer would be one perpetual day. That there were means if they would only try them, by which they might avoid famine and the rigour of the winter, inasmuch as there was abundance of wood, and the sea provided shellfish and many sorts of the very best fish. The springs there were wholesome, and birdfowling and hunting would supply many wants; and neither bread nor wine had as yet been lacking, nor would they lack in future if they would only bear that they should be served out when needed, or for health's sake, and not for pleasure or for luxury. They had done nothing as yet worthy of admiration, or which could serve as an excuse for their return, inasmuch as the Portuguese crossed the tropic of Capricorn by as much as 12 deg. not only every year, but almost every day, when they were sailing eastwards. They would be thought worthy of very little praise who had gone only 4 deg. southwards.[14] He had certainly made up his mind to endure the worst rather than return ignominiously to Spain, and he trusted that all his comrades, or at least those in whom the noble Spanish spirit was not yet dead, would be of the same mind.

He advised them to bear at least the remainder of the winter patiently, and said that their rewards would be the more abundant the more difficulties and dangers they had endured in opening to Caesar a new unknown world, rich in spices and gold. Magellan thought that the minds of his crews were soothed and cheered by this harangue, but within a few days was harassed by a shameful and foul conspiracy.[15] For talking began amongst the crews about the old eternal hatred between the Portuguese and

[14] There must be some slip or error here. Magellan could not possibly have expected these skilled seamen to believe that they had gone only four degrees south of Capricorn.

[15] Maximilian here shows the Pigafetta influence. He would never have gained the impression of a "foul and shameful conspiracy" from El Cano and his friends at Valladolid.

the Spaniards, and about Magellan's being a Portuguese. He, they said, could do nothing more glorious for his own country than to cast away this fleet, with so many men. Nor was it credible that he should wish to discover the Moluccas, even if he were able; but he would think it sufficient if he could lure Caesar on for some years with a vain hope, and meanwhile something new would turn up, by which the Spaniards would for the future be diverted from the search for spices. Nor even had their course begun to turn towards those happy Moluccas, but rather to distant snows and ice, and to perpetual storms.

Magellan, very much enraged by these sayings, punished the men, but rather more harshly than was proper for a foreigner, especially when commanding in a distant country. So, having planned a conspiracy, they seize upon a ship, and make ready to return to Spain. But he, with the rest whom he had still obedient to his commands, attacked that ship, and put to death the head man and the other ringleaders, those even who could not lawfully be so treated sharing the same fate. For these were certain servants of the king, upon whom no one but Caesar and his Council could lawfully pronounce a sentence of death. Nevertheless, no one from that time dared to disparage the power of the commander. Still, there were not wanting some who whispered that Magellan would, in the same manner, murder all the Spaniards to the last man, until he, having got rid of them all, might return with

the few Portuguese with the fleet to his own country. And so this hatred settled more deeply in the
hearts of the Spaniards.

As soon as ever Magellan saw the storminess of
the sea and the rigour of the winter mitigated, he
set sail from the gulf of St. Julian on the 24th of
August. And, as before, he followed the course of
the coast southwards for many days. A promontory
was at last sighted, which they called Santa Cruz,
when a severe storm, springing from the east, suddenly caught them, and one of the five ships was
cast on shore,[16] the men being all saved, with the
merchandise and equipment, except one Ethiopian
slave, who was caught and drowned by the waves.
After this the land seemed to bear a little east and
south, and this they began to coast along as usual,
and on the 26th of November certain inlets of the
sea were discovered, which had the appearance of a
strait. Magellan entered them forthwith with the
whole fleet, and when he saw other and again other
bays, he gave orders that they should be all carefully
examined from the ships, to see if anywhere a
passage might be discovered; and said that he would
himself wait at the mouth of the strait till the fifth
day, to hear what might happen.

One of the ships, which Alvarus Meschito, his
nephew, commanded, was carried back by the tide to
the sea, to the very place where they entered the
gulf. But when the Spaniards perceived that they
were far away from the other ships, they made a plot

[16] The "Santiago."

to return home, put Alvarus, their captain, in irons, bent their course northwards, and were at last carried to the coast of Aethiopia [Guinea], and, having victualled there, they reached Spain eight months after they had deserted the rest. There they compel Alvarus to stand his trial in chains, for having, by his counsel and advice, induced his uncle Magellan to practise such harshness on the Spaniards.

But when Magellan had waited for this ship some days longer than the time fixed, another returned, which had discovered nothing but a bay full of shoals and shingle, and very lofty cliffs. The third ship, however, reported that the largest bay had the appearance of a strait, as in three days' sail they had found no way out; but the farther they had gone the narrower the sea was, and they had not been able to sound the depth of it in many places by any length of line, and that they had also noticed that the tide was rather stronger than the ebb, and that so they were persuaded that a passage was open in that direction to some other sea. He made up his mind to sail through it. This channel, which they did not then know to be a channel, was at one place three Italian miles wide, at another two, sometimes ten, and sometimes five, and pointed a little westward. The altitude of the southern pole was found to be 52 deg.,[17] and the longitude to be the same, as at St. Julian's Bay. The month of November was upon them, the night was rather more than five hours

[17] Meaning that they estimated the entrance to the strait as 52° S., which is substantially correct.

long, and they had never seen any human beings on the shore.

But one night a great number of fires were seen, mostly on their left hand, from which they guessed that they had been seen by the natives of the region. But Magellan, seeing that the country was rocky, and also stark with eternal cold, thought it useless to waste many days in examining it; and so, with only three ships, he continued on his course along the channel, until, on the twenty-second day after he had entered it, he sailed out upon another wide and vast sea. The length of the channel they attest to be nearly a hundred Spanish miles.

There is no doubt that the land which they had upon their right was the continent of which we have spoken, but they think that the land on the left was not a mainland, but islands, because sometimes on that side they heard on a still farther coast the beating and roaring of the sea.

Magellan saw that the continent stretched northwards again in a straight line; wherefore, leaving that huge continent on the right hand, he ordered them to sail through that vast and mighty sea (which I do not think had ever seen either our or any one else's ships) in the direction whence the wind called Corus generally blows—that is, 'twixt north and west—so that he might, by going through west to east, again arrive at the torrid zone; for he thought that it was proved sufficiently clearly that the Moluccas were in the most remote east, and could not be far from the equator. They kept this course uninterruptedly, nor did they ever depart from it, except when rough weather or violent winds compelled them to diverge; and when they had in this manner been carried for forty days by a strong and generally favourable wind, and had seen nothing but sea, and everywhere sea—when they had almost reached the tropic of Capricorn once more, two islands were sighted, but small and barren.[18] These they found uninhabited when they tried to land; still, they stopped there two days for their health's sake, and general recruiting of their bodies, for there was very fair fishing there. They named these the Unfortunate Islands by common consent. Then they again set sail thence, following their original course and direction of sailing. And when, for three months and twenty days, they had been sailing over this ocean with great good fortune, and had traversed an immense part of the sea— more vast than mind of man can conceive, for they had been driven almost continuously by a very strong wind—they were now at last arrived on this side of the equinoctial line, and at last they saw an island, called, as they learnt afterwards, Inuagana by the natives. When they had approached nearer, they discovered the altitude of the Arctic pole to be 11 deg. The longitude they thought to be 158 deg. west of Gades. Then they saw other and still more islands, so that they knew they had arrived at some vast archipelago. When they reached Inuagana, the island was discovered to be uninhabited. They then

[18] Probably Clipperton and Clarion.

approached a rather small island, where they saw two Indian canoes—for that is the name by which this strange kind of boat is called by the Indians. The canoes are cut and hollowed out of a single trunk of a tree, and hold one, or, at most, two men; and they usually speak by gestures and signs, as if the dumb were talking with the dumb.

They asked the Indians the names of the islands, and where they could get provisions, of which they were in great want. They understood that the island in which they had been was called Inuagana, and that the one where they now were was Acaca, but both of them uninhabited. They said that there was an island not far off, which was called Selani, and which they almost showed with their finger, and that it was inhabited, and that an abundance of everything necessary for life was to be found there.

Our men, having taken in water in Acaca, sailed towards Selani; here a storm took them, so that they could not bring the ships to that island, but were driven to another island called Massaua, where lives a king of [the?] three islands, after that they arrived at Subuth.[19] This is an excellent and large island, and, having made a treaty with its chieftain, they landed immediately to perform divine service, according to the manner of Christians, for it was the feast of the resurrection of Him who was our salvation. Wherefore they built a small chapel of the sails of the ships, and of boughs, and in that they

[19] Maximilian appears to make no distinction between the Marianas and the Philippines. Subuth is Cebu.

built an altar according to the Christian rites, and performed service after their home fashion. The chieftain came up with a great number of Indians, who seemed in every way delighted by this worship of the gods. They led the admiral and some of the officers to the chief's hut, and put before them whatever food they had. Their bread, which they call sago, was made of the trunk or wood of a tree, rather like a palm. This, when cut in pieces, and fried in oil in a pan, supplies them with bread, a small piece of which I send to your reverence. Their drink was a liquor which flows and trickles from the boughs of the palm-trees when cut. Fowling, too, supplied the feast, and the rest was the fruit of that region.

Magellan beheld, in the chief's hut, one sick, and almost at the last gasp. He asked who he was, and what illness he was suffering from. He learnt that he was the chief's grandson, and had now suffered for two years from a raging fever. But he told him to be of good cheer, and that he would immediately recover his health and former strength, if he would only become a Christian. The Indian accepted the condition, and, having adored the Cross, he received baptism, and the next day declared that he was well, rose from his bed, walked, and took food like the rest. He told I know not what visions to the Indians. What need I say more? The chief himself, with two thousand two hundred Indians, was baptized, and professed the name and religion of Christ. But Magellan, judging this island to abound in gold and ginger, and, besides, to be convenient from its position with respect to the neighbouring islands, for exploring with ease their wealth and produce of the earth, goes to the Chief of Subuth, and persuades him that as he had abandoned that vain and impious worship of the gods, and had turned to the religion of Christ, it was only fair that the kings of the neighbouring isles should be subject to his rule and command; and he said that he had resolved to send ambassadors concerning this, and compel by arms those who did not listen to his command.

This proposition pleased the savage, and the ambassadors were sent. The chiefs came in one by one, and did homage. The nearest island was called Mauthan,[20] the king of which excelled the others in number of soldiers and in arms, and he refused to do homage to one whom he had been accustomed for so long to command.

Magellan, who desired to finish what he had once begun, gave orders that forty of his men, whose bravery and prowess he had proved, should arm, and he crossed over to Mauthan in boats, for the island was very near. The Chief of Subuth added some of his own men to show him the situation of the island, and to fight, if matters came to that. The King of Mauthan, seeing our men coming, draws up about three thousand of his subjects in the field, and Magellan draws up his on the shore, with their guns and warlike engines, though only a few; and though he saw that he was far inferior to the enemy in num-

[20] Mactan.

ber, yet he thought it better to fight this warlike race, which made use of lances and other long weapons, than either to return or to use the soldiers from Subuth. So he orders his men to be of good cheer and brave hearts, and not to be alarmed at the number of the enemy, for they had often seen, as formerly, so in quite recent times, two hundred Spaniards in the island of Yucatan put sometimes two or three hundred thousand men to flight.[21] But he pointed out to the Subuth islanders that he had brought them, not to fight, but to watch their bravery and fighting power. So, having charged the enemy, both sides fought valiantly: but, as the enemy were more numerous, and used longer weapons, with which they did our men much damage, Magellan himself was at last thrust through and slain. But the rest of our men, though they did not seem quite conquered, yet retreated, having lost their leader. And the enemy dared not follow them, as they were retreating in good order.

So the Spaniards, having lost their admiral, Magellan, and seven of their comrades, returned to Subuth, where they chose another commander, John Serrano, a man not to be despised. He immediately renewed with fresh gifts the alliance that had been made with the King of Subuth, and promised to subdue the King of Mauthan.

Magellan had a slave, born in the Moluccas,

---

[21] By Yucatan Maximilian appears to mean roughly Aztec Mexico. Of course Magellan could not have reminded his men of any such battles, as they had not occurred when he left Spain.

whom he had bought in Malacca some time back; this man was a perfect master of the Spanish language, and, with the assistance of one of the islanders of Subuth as interpreter, who knew the language of the Moluccas, our men managed all their communications. This slave had been present at the battle of Mauthan, and had received some slight wounds in it. For which reason he lay all day long nursing himself. Serrano, who could manage nothing without him, spoke to him very harshly, and told him that he had not ceased to be a slave and bondsman because Magellan was dead, but that the yoke of slavery would be heavier, and that he would be severely flogged unless he did the services required of him more zealously.

This slave conceived an intense hatred of us from these words; but, concealing his anger, he went a few days after to the Chief of Subuth, and told him that the greed of the Spaniards was insatiable, that they had resolved and determined, after they had conquered the King of Mauthan, to make a quarrel with him and take him away prisoner, and there was no other remedy possible than to anticipate their treachery by treachery. The savage believed it all. He made peace secretly with the King of Mauthan and the others, and they plotted our destruction. Serrano, the commander, with all the rest of his officers, who were about twenty-seven in number, were invited to a solemn banquet. They, suspecting no evil—for the savages had cunningly dissimulated in everything—land, careless and unsuspecting, as men who were going to dine with the chief would do. Whilst they were feasting they were set upon by those who had been placed in ambush. Shouts were raised on all sides, and news flew to the ships that our men were murdered, and that everything on the island was hostile to us. Our men see from the ships that the beautiful cross which they had hoisted on a tree was hurled to the ground, and kicked to pieces by the savages with great fury. But the remaining Spaniards, who had stopped on board, when they knew of their comrades' murder, feared some still greater treachery. Wherefore, when they had weighed anchor, they begin to set sail quickly. Shortly after, Serrano was brought down to the shore bound most cruelly, and he begged them to redeem him from so harsh a captivity. He said he had prevailed upon them to permit his being ransomed, if our men would only do it.

Though our men thought it shameful to leave their commander in this way, yet, fearing fraud and treachery, they put out to sea, leaving Serrano on the shore, weeping bitterly, and imploring the help and assistance of his fellow countrymen with great and grievous lamentation. The Spaniards sailed along, sad and anxious, having lost their commander and their shipmates, not only alarmed by their loss and by the slaughter of their mates, but because their number was reduced so low that it was quite insufficient for the management of three ships. Wherefore they hold a council, and, having taken the votes, they agree that there was nothing better to do than to burn some one of the three ships, and keep only two.

So they go to an island near, Cohol [Bohol] by name, and transfer the equipment to the other two ships, and burn the third. Then they sailed to the island called Gibeth. Though they found that it was rich in gold and ginger and many other things, yet they thought it better not to stay there long, because they could not, by any kindness, attract the Indians to them. And their scantiness of number prevented their fighting. Thence they went to the island Porne [Borneo]. There are two great and rich islands in this archipelago, one of which was called Siloli [Gilolo], the king of which had six hundred children; and the other Porne.

Siloli was greater than the one called Porne. For it takes nearly six months to sail round it, but Porne only three. But just so much as the former is larger, so much is the latter better situated as regards fertility of soil, and more famed also for the size of a city of the same name as itself. And, as Porne must be considered of more importance than any of the other islands which they had examined, and seemed to be the source whence the others received their good customs and civilization, I have resolved to touch, in a few words, upon the customs and laws of these peoples. All these islanders are *Caphrae,* that is, heathen, and worship the sun and moon. They ascribe the rule of the day to the sun, but that of the night to the moon; the former they call male, and the latter female; and them, too, they call the parents of the stars, which they deem to be all gods, though small ones. They salute the rising sun with certain hymns before they worship it. This they do also to the moon, when it shines at night, to whom they pray for children, and fruitful increase of cattle, and abundant fruits of the earth, and other things of that sort.

But they practise justice and piety, and specially do they love peace and quiet, but war they greatly detest, and they honour their king as a god whilst he is bent upon peace. But if he be too desirous of war, they rest not till he has fallen by the hand of the enemy in battle. Whenever he has determined to wage war, which is rarely done, he is placed by his subjects in the vanguard, where he is compelled to bear the whole onslaught of the enemy. Nor do they fight against the enemy with any spirit until they know that their king is dead; then, first do they begin to fight for their liberty and for their future king, nor has there ever been seen among them a king who began a war who has not died in battle. Wherefore they rarely wage war, and think it unjust to extend their territories; but the special care of all is not wantonly to attack either the neighbouring or the distant peoples. But if at any time they are attacked, they meet force by force [*par pari referunt*]. But lest the mischief should spread farther they look immediately to making peace. There can be nothing more honourable among them than to be the first to ask for peace, nor more disgraceful than to be anticipated in asking for it, and they think it shameful and hateful to refuse it to anyone, even if he had attacked them without provocation. And all the neighbouring people unite against the one [who refuses peace] for his destruction, as against a cruel and impious man. Whence it happens that they almost always enjoy quiet and repose. There is no robbery among them, and no murder. No one but his wives and children may speak to the king, except by means of canes, which they place to his ear from a distance, and whisper what they wish through them. They say that man, after his death, has no feeling, as he had none before his birth. They have small houses, built of logs and of earth, partly roofed with rubble, and partly with palm leaves. It is, though, quite certain that in Porne there are twenty thousand houses. They marry as many wives as they can afford, and live on food, which bird-fowling or fishing supplies them with. They make bread of rice, and a drink which drops from the severed branches of the palm, as we said before.

Some carry on traffic in the neighbouring islands, to which they go in junks; some devote themselves to hunting; some to fishing; and others to agriculture. They have dresses of cotton, and almost all the animals that we have, except the sheep, the ox, and the ass; but their horses are very small and feeble. The produce of camphor, of ginger, and of cinnamon, is great among them. Thence our men, having saluted this king, and heaped him with presents, directed their course to the Moluccas, which had been pointed out to them by the same king. They came to the shores of the island of Solo, where they heard that there were pearls as big as dove's eggs, and sometimes as hen's eggs, but which can only be fished up from the very deepest sea. Our men brought no large pearl, because the season of the year did not allow of the fishery. But they testify that they had taken an oyster in that region, the flesh of which weighed forty-seven pounds. For which reason I could easily believe that pearls of that great size are found there; for it is clearly proved that pearls are the product of shell-fish. And to omit nothing, our men constantly affirm that the islanders of Porne told them that the king wore in his crown two pearls of the size of a goose's egg. Hence they went to the island of Gilo, where they saw men with ears so long and pendulous, that they reached to their shoulders. When our men were mightily astonished at this, they learnt from the natives that there was another island not far off where the men had ears not only pendulous, but so long and broad, that one of them would cover the whole head, if they wanted it. But our men, who sought not monsters but spices, neglecting this nonsense, went straight to the Moluccas, and they discovered them eight months after their admiral, Magellan, had fallen in Mauthan. The islands are five in number, and are called Tarante, Muthil, Thidore, Mare, and Matthien: some on this side, some on the other, and some upon the equinoctial line.

One produces cloves, another nutmegs, and another cinnamon. All are near to each other, but small and rather narrow.

The kings [of] Marmin began to believe that souls were immortal a few years ago, induced by no other argument than that they saw that a certain most beautiful small bird never rested upon the ground nor upon anything that grew upon it; but they sometimes saw it fall dead upon the ground from the sky. And as the Mahometans, who travelled to those parts for commercial purposes, told them that this bird was born in Paradise, and that Paradise was the abode of the souls of those who had died, these kings embraced the sect of Mahomet, because it promised wonderful things concerning this abode of souls. But they call the bird *Mamuco Diata,* and they hold it in such reverence and religious esteem, that they believe that by it their kings are safe in war, even though they, according to custom, are placed in the fore front of battle. The common folk are *Caphrae,* and of almost the same manners and laws as the islanders of Porne; they are rather poor, as would be likely with people in whose land nothing grows except spices. These they willingly barter for poisons, namely, arsenic and what is commonly called sublimate of mercury, and for linens, in which they generally are dressed; but for what purpose they use these poisons, we have not yet found out. They live on sago bread and fish, and sometimes on parrots, and they shelter in low huts. What need of many words. Everything there is humble, and of no value, but peace, quiet, and spices. The best and noblest of which, and the greatest good possible, namely peace, seems to have been driven by men's wickedness from our world to theirs. But avarice and the insatiable greed of the belly, have driven us to seek for spices in their unknown world. But, our men having carefully inspected the position of the Moluccas and of each separate island, and also having inquired about the habits of the kings, went to Thedori, because they learnt that in that island the supply of cloves was far above that of the others, and that its king also surpassed the other kings in wisdom and humanity. So, having prepared their gifts, they land, and salute the king, and they offer the presents as if they had been sent by Caesar. He, having received the presents kindly, looks up to heaven, and says: "I have known now for two years from the course of the stars, that you were coming to seek these lands, sent by the most mighty King of Kings. Wherefore your coming is the more pleasant and grateful to me, as I had been forewarned of it by the signification of the stars."

And, as I know that nothing ever happens to any man which has not been fixed long before by the decree of fate and the stars, I will not be the one to attempt to withstand either the fates or the signification of the stars, but willingly and of good cheer, will henceforth lay aside the royal pomp and will consider myself as managing the administration of this island only in the name of your king. Wherefore draw your ships into port, and order the rest of your comrades to land; so that now at last, after such a long tossing upon the seas, and so many dangers, you may enjoy the pleasures of the land and refresh your bodies. And think not but that you have arrived at your king's kingdom. Having said this, the king, laying aside his crown, embraced them one by one, and ordered whatever food that land afforded to be brought. Our men being overjoyed at this, returned to their comrades, and told them what had happened. They, pleased above measure with the friendly behaviour and kindness of the king, take possession of the island. And when their health was completely restored, in a few days, by the king's munificence, they send envoys to the other kings, to examine the wealth of the islands, and to conciliate the other kings. Tarante was the nearest, and also the smallest, of the islands; for it has a circumference of a little more than six Italian miles. Mathien is next to it, and it, too, is small. These three produce a great quantity of cloves, but more every fourth year than the other three. These trees only grow on steep rocks, and that so thickly as frequently to form a grove. This tree is very like a laurel (or bay tree) in leaf, closeness of growth, and height; and the gariophile which they call clove from its likeness [to a nail, *clavus*] grows on the tip of each separate twig. First a bud, and then a flower, just like the orange flower is produced.

The pointed part of the clove is fixed at the extreme end of the branch, and then growing slightly longer, it forms a spike. It is at first red, but soon gets black by the heat of the sun. The natives keep the plantations of these trees separate, as we do our vines. They bury the cloves in pits till they are taken away by the traders.

Muthil, the fourth island, is not larger than the rest, and it produces cinnamon. The tree is full of shoots, and in other respects barren; it delights in dryness, and is very like the tree which bears pomegranates. The bark of this splits under the influence of the sun's heat, and is stripped off the wood; and, after drying a little in the sun, it is cinnamon. Near to this is another island, called Bada, larger and more ample than the Moluccas. In this grows the nutmeg, the tree of which is tall and spreading, and is rather like the walnut tree, and its nut, too, grows like the walnut; for it is protected by a double husk, at first like a furry calix, and under this a thin membrane, which embraces the nut like network. This is called the Muscat flower with us, but by the Spaniards mace, and is a noble and wholesome spice. The other covering is a woody shell, like that of hazelnut, and in that, as we have already said, is the nutmeg. Ginger grows here and there in each of the islands of the archipelago. It sometimes grows by sowing, and sometimes spontaneously; but that which is sown is the more valuable. Its grass is like that of the saffron, and its root is almost the same too, and that is ginger. Our men were kindly treated by the chiefs in turn, and they, too, submitted freely to the rule of Caesar, like the King of Thidori. But the Spaniards, who had but two ships, resolved to

bring some of each [spice] home, but to load the
ships with cloves, because the crop of that was most
abundant that year, and our ships could contain a
greater quantity of this kind of spice. Having, therefore, loaded the ships with cloves, and having received letters and presents for Caesar from the
kings, they make ready for their departure. The letters were full of submission and respect. The gifts
were Indian swords, and things of that sort. But,
best of all, the *Mamuco Diata;* that is, the Bird of
God, by which they believe themselves to be safe
and invincible in battle. Of which five were sent,
and one I obtained from the captain, which I send
to your reverence, not that your reverence may
think yourself safe from treachery and the sword by
means of it, as they profess to do, but that you may
be pleased by its rareness and beauty. I send also
some cinnamon and nutmeg and cloves, to show that
our spices are not only not worse, but more valuable than those which the Venetians and Portuguese bring, because they are fresher. When our
men had set sail from Thedori, one of the ships, and
that the larger one, having sprung a leak, began to
make water, so that it became necessary to put back
to Thedori. When the Spaniards saw that this mischief could not be remedied without great labour
and much time, they agreed that the other ship
should sail to the Cape of Cattigara, and afterwards
through the deep as far as possible from the coast
of India, lest it should be seen by the Portuguese,
and until they saw the Promontory of Africa, which

projects beyond the Tropic of Capricorn, and to which the Portuguese have given the name of Good Hope; and from that point the passage to Spain would be easy. But as soon as the other ship was refitted, it should direct its course through the archipelago, and that vast ocean towards the shores of the continent which we mentioned before, till it found that coast which was in the neighbourhood of Darien, and where the southern sea was separated from the western, in which are the Spanish Islands, by a very narrow space of land. So the ship sailed again from Thedori, and, having gone twelve degrees on the other side of the equinoctial line, they did not find the Cape of Cattigara, which Ptolemy supposed to extend even beyond the equinoctial line; but when they had traversed an immense space of sea, they came to the Cape of Good Hope and afterwards to the Islands of the Hesperides. And, as this ship let in water, being much knocked about by this long voyage, the sailors, many of whom had died by hardships by land and by sea, could not clear the ship of the water. Wherefore they landed upon one of the islands, which is named after Saint James, to buy slaves. But as our men had no money, they offered, sailor fashion, cloves for the slaves. This matter having come to the ears of the Portuguese who were in command of the island, thirteen of our men were thrown into prison. The rest were eighteen in number. Frightened by the strangeness of this behaviour, they started straight for Spain, leaving their shipmates behind them.

And so, in the sixteenth month after leaving Thedori, they arrived safe and sound on the sixth of
September, at the port near Hispalis [Seville].
Worthier, indeed, are our sailors of eternal fame
than the Argonauts who sailed with Jason to Col-
chis. And much more worthy was their ship of being
placed among the stars than that old Argo; for that
only sailed from Greece through Pontus, but ours
from Hispalis to the south; and after that, through
the whole west and the southern hemisphere, pene-
trating into the east, and again returned to the
west.

I commend myself most humbly to your Reverence.
Given at Vallisoleti, [Valladolid], on the 23rd of
October, 1522.
Your most Reverend and Illustrious Lordship's
Most humble and constant servant,
MAXIMILIANUS TRANSYLVANUS.

Cervicornus, in the year of the Virgin's Child, 1523,
in the month of January.

Gaspar Corrêa

Corrêa, the least literary and polished of the major sixteenth-century Portuguese historians, compensated for his lack of style by being the most widely traveled and possessing the most intimate knowledge of the places and scenes figuring in his writings. Born probably in 1496, he became a page in the household of King Manuel at the age of about ten, and in 1512 embarked for India in the fleet of Jorge de Melo Pereira. Almost upon his arrival there, Corrêa became secretary to Afonso de Albuquerque and in this way gained an inside knowledge of what went on in the Portuguese East. He also acquired much of Albuquerque's factual, unadorned, and yet impressive, literary style.[1]

As long as the great governor lived, Corrêa accompanied him from place to place, and after his death continued to hold important posts in India. He was probably at Goa when the Spaniards under El Cano and Espinosa arrived in the Moluccas and was either there or at Cochin when Brito captured the "Trinidad," with so many valuable Spanish papers aboard.[2] As Corrêa already had in mind writing the history of Portuguese Asia, these events must have interested him exceedingly. He returned to Portugal about 1526, but we find him in India again by 1530; it is doubtful whether he ever saw Portugal again. He spent the rest of his life holding various government posts in the East and writing and revising his history, called *Lendas da India*.[3] He was alive in 1563, though it might have been late

[1] Aubrey F. G. Bell, *Gaspar Corrêa*, Oxford, 1924, pp. 3–4.
[2] *Ibid.*, p. 9.
[3] *Ibid.*, pp. 17–18.

in that year that an assassin struck him down in the streets of Malacca. Corrêa's widow, Anna Vaz, petitioned for the punishment of her husband's murderer and identified him as Henrique Mendes, a retainer of Estevão da Gama, great-grandson of the discoverer of India.[4] Mendes is otherwise unknown to us, and we can only say that if he received punishment it would have been an unusual event for the Portuguese Orient at that time, in view of the name and influence of his powerful protector.

Corrêa began writing the *Lendas* early in the sixteenth century and completed them, if he ever regarded the work as finished, shortly before his death.[5] Sixteenth-century readers liked a display of culture and frequent classical allusions, and Corrêa had almost none to offer. His more learned contemporaries, Castanheda and Barros, had meanwhile published their histories, and he must have realized that these seriously lessened the market demand for his own. After he died, his manuscript—of some 3,500 pages containing more than a million words—was taken to Portugal by Miguel da Gama. It remained unpublished until the nineteenth century, when the Portuguese Academy of Sciences decided to present it to the public. The publication, in four volumes of two parts each, took place from 1858 to 1866 under the direction of Rodrigo José de Lima Felner with the assistance of the paleographer José de Gomes Góis. Except for the part now offered dealing with Magellan and another portion concerning Vasco da Gama, the *Lendas* have not been translated into English.

[4] The widow says, "They killed him with many wounds, and the murders were seen and known and nothing was done about it, rather without fear of God or the law they went about publicly and were always in the company of D. Estevam, the captain." *Ibid.,* p. 24.

[5] The Portuguese word *lendas* commonly means "legends," and this has discredited Corrêa's work in some eyes. But the author really meant "record" or "log"—"disto nom tinham lenda, somente assi lembranças dos antigos." *Ibid.,* p. 78.

Magellan's Voyage as Described in Lendas Da India

Ferdinand Magellan went to Castile to the port of Seville, where he married the daughter of a man of importance, with the design of navigating on the sea, because he was very learned in the art of pilots, which is that of the sphere. The emperor kept the House of Commerce in Seville, with the overseers of the treasury, with great powers, and much seafaring traffic, and fleets for abroad. Magellan, bold with his knowledge, and with the readiness which he had to annoy the King of Portugal, spoke to the overseers of this House of Commerce, and told them that Malacca, and Maluco, the islands in which cloves grew, belonged to the emperor on account of the demarcation drawn between them both [the Kings of Spain and Portugal]: for which reason the King of Portugal wrongfully possessed these lands: and that he would make this certain before all the doctors who might contradict him, and would pledge his head for it. The overseers replied to him, that they well knew that he was speaking truth, and that the emperor also knew it, but that the emperor had no navigation to that part, because he could not navigate through the sea within the demarcation of the King of Portugal. Magellan said to them: "If you would give me ships and men, I would show you navigation to those parts, without touching any sea or land of the King of Portugal; and if not, they might cut off his head." The overseers, much pleased at this, wrote it to the emperor, who answered them that he had pleasure in the speech, and would have much more with the deed; and that they were to do everything to carry out his service, and the affairs of the King of Portugal, which were not to be meddled with; rather than that everything should be lost. With this answer from the emperor, they spoke with Magellan, and became much more convinced by what he said, that he would navigate and show a course outside of the seas of the King of Portugal; and that if they gave him the ships he asked for, and men and artillery, he would fulfil what he had said, and would discover new lands which were in the demarcation of the emperor, from which he would bring gold, cloves, cinnamon, and other riches. The overseers hearing this, with a great desire to render so great a service to the emperor as the discovery of this navigation, and to make this matter more certain, brought together pilots and men learned in the sphere, to dispute upon the matter with Magellan, who gave such reasons to all, that they agreed with what he said, and affirmed that he was a very learned man.[6] So the overseers at once made agreements with him, and arrangements, and powers, and regulations, which they sent to the emperor, who confirmed everything, reserving specially the navigation of the King of Portugal; thus he commanded and prohibited, and ordered that everything which Magellan asked for should be given him. On this account, Magellan went to Burgos,[7] where the emperor was, and kissed his hand, and the emperor gave him a thousand cruzados alimony for the expenses of his wife whilst he was on his voyage, set down in the rolls of Seville, and he gave him power of life and death over all persons who went in the fleet, of which he should be captain-major, with regard to which he assigned him large powers. So, on his return to Seville, they equipped for him five small ships, such as he asked for, equipped and armed as he chose, with four hundred men-at-arms,[8] and they were laden with the merchandise which he asked for. The overseers told him to give the captaincies, with regard to which he excused himself, saying that he was new in the country and did not know the men; and that they should seek out men who would be good and faithful in the emperor's service, and who would rejoice to endure hardships in his service, and the bad life which they would have to

[6] There is no record of such discussions in the Spanish documents relating to Magellan.

[7] Magellan visited Charles at Valladolid and Barcelona, but apparently never at Burgos.

[8] Probably 241. See Introduction, page 67.

go through in the voyage.[9] The overseers were
obliged to him for this, and held it to be good advice, and decided to inform the captains they might
make, and the crews they might take, of the powers
which he had received from the emperor. This they
did, and they sought in Seville for trustworthy men
for captains, who were Juan de Cartagena, Luis de
Mendoça, Juan Serrano, Pero de Quesada. This
fleet having been fitted out, and the crews paid for
six months, he sailed from San Lucar de Barrameda
in August of the year 1519.[10] So he navigated to the
Canary Islands, and took in water; whilst he was
there a vessel arrived with letters from his father-in-
law, in which he warned him to keep a good watch
for his personal safety, because he had learned that
the captains whom he took with him had said to
their friends and relations, that if he annoyed them
they would kill him, and would rise up against him.[11]
To this he replied, that he would do them no in-
juries so that they should have reason to act thus;
and on that account he had not appointed them, but
the overseers, who knew them, had given them; and
whether they were good or bad, he would labour to
do the service of the emperor, and for that they had
offered their lives. The father-in-law showed this
answer to the overseers, who greatly praised the
good heart of Magellan.

[9] If anything is certain, it is that Magellan preferred to enlist
his own captains and crews.

[10] The correct date, of course, is September 20.

[11] Corrêa's report of a warning from Diogo Barbosa, though
not verified elsewhere, may well be correct.

He sailed from the Canaries of Tanarife, and made the Cape Verde, whence he crossed over to the coast of Brazil, and there entered a river which is named Janeiro. There went, as chief pilot, a Portuguese named Joan Lopes Carvalhinho, who had already been in this river, and took with him a son whom he had gotten there of a woman of the country. From this place they went on sailing until they reached the Cape of Santa Maria, which Joan of Lisbon had discovered in the year 1514; [12] thence they went to the river San Julian. While they were there taking in water and wood, Juan de Cartagena, who was sub-captain-major, agreed with the other captains to rise up, saying that Magellan had got them betrayed and entrapped. As they understood that Gasper de Quesada was a friend of Magellan's, Juan de Cartagena got into his boat at night, with twenty men, and went to the ship of Gaspar Quesada, and went in to speak to him, and took him prisoner,[13] and made a relation of his captain of the ship, in order that all three might go at once to board Magellan and kill him, and after that they would reduce the other ship of Joan Serrano, and would take the money and goods, which they would hide, and would return to the emperor, and would tell him that Magellan had got them entrapped and

[12] This evidently refers to the Portuguese expedition sent by Cristóbal de Haro, which may have been piloted by João de Lisboa. See Introduction, page 24.

[13] Corrêa is badly off here. Quesada was the ringleader of the mutineers and the only one later executed by Magellan's order. Corrêa has Quesada confused with Alvaro de Mesquita.

deceived, having broken faith with his instructions, since he was navigating in seas and countries of the King of Portugal: for which deed they would get first a safe conduct from the emperor. So they arranged matters for their treason, which turned out ill for them.

Magellan had some suspicion of this matter, and before this should happen, he sent his skiff to the ships to tell the captains that the masters were to arrange their ships for beaching them to careen them; and with this pretext he warned a servant of his to notice what the captains answered. When this skiff came to the revolted ships they did not let it come alongside, saying that they would not execute any orders except those of Juan de Cartagena, who was their captain-major. The skiff having returned with this answer, Magellan spoke to Ambrosio Fernandes,[14] his chief constable, a valiant man, and gave him orders what he was to do, and to go secretly armed; and he sent a letter to Luis de Mendoça by him, with six men in the skiff, whom the chief constable selected. And the current set towards the ships, and Magellan ordered his master to bend a long hawser, with which he might drop down to the ships if it suited him. All being thus arranged, the skiff went, and coming alongside of Luiz de Mendoça, they would not let him come on board. So the chief constable said to the captain that it was weakness not to bid him enter, as he was one man alone who was bringing a letter. Upon which the captain

[14] Really Gonzalo Gómez de Espinosa.

bade him enter. He came on board, and giving him the letter, took him in his arms, shouting: "On behalf of the emperor, you are arrested!" At this the men of the skiff came on board with their swords drawn; then the chief constable cut the throat of Luis de Mendoça with a dagger, for he held him thrown down under him, for so Magellan had given him orders. Upon this a tumult arose, and Magellan hearing it, ordered the hawser to be paid out, and with his ship dropped down upon the other ships, with his men under arms, and the artillery in readiness. On reaching the ship of Mendoça, he ordered six men to be hung at the yard-arms,[15] who had risen up against the chief constable, and these were seized upon by the sailors of the ship, of which he at once made captain, Duarte Barbosa, a Portuguese, and a friend of his: and he ordered the corpse of Mendoça to be hung up by the feet, that they might see him from the other ships. He then ordered Barbosa to prepare the men for going and boarding one of the other ships; and to avoid doing the harm which it was in its power to have done, and since he was a Portuguese, and the crews belonged to the emperor, he used a stratagem, and spoke secretly to a sailor, whom he trusted, who fled to the ship of Cartagena, where, at night when the current set for Magellan's ship, which was astern, the sailor seeing his opportunity, cut the cable or loosed the ship of Cartagena, so that it drifted upon that of Magellan, who came up, shouting: "Treason! treason!"

[15] There is no record of this in the Spanish documents.

Upon which he entered the ship of Cartagena, and took him and his men prisoners, and made captain of the ship one Alvaro de Mesquita, whom Cartagena had arrested and put in irons, because he found fault with him for the mutiny which he was making. Seeing this, the other ship at once surrendered. He ordered Cartagena to be quartered,[16] having him publicly cried as a traitor; and the body of Luis de Mendoça also was quartered; and he ordered the quarters and the executed men to be set on shore, spitted on poles. So the Castilians had great fear of him, for he kept the mutineers prisoners in irons, and set to the pumps, during three months that he remained in this river, in which he careened and refitted his ships very well.

When he was about to set sail, he ordered the prisoners to be set at liberty, and pardoned them, and he sent them to go along the shore, following the bank of the river until they found the headland from which they could see the sea on the other side; and whoever returned to him with this news he would give him a hundred ducats as a reward for good news. These men went for more than forty leagues, and returned without news; and they brought back two men, fifteen spans high, from a village which they found. He then sent Serrano, because his vessel was the smallest, to go along the river to discover its extremity; and he went with a strong current, which carried him without wind. And, going along thus, his ship grounded on some

[16] Needless to repeat, Cartagena was marooned.

rocks, on which it was lost, and the boat returned laden with the crew. Magellan sent the boats thither, and they saved everything, so that only the hull was lost. Then he ordered two priests, who had taken part in the mutiny, to be set on shore,[17] and a brother of Cartagena, whom he pardoned at the petition of Mesquita, and he left them thus banished.

Then he sailed from the river and ran along the coast until he reached a river, to which they gave the name of Victoria, and which had high land on either side. From this river Mesquita's ship ran away, and it was not known whether they had killed him, or if he had gone of his own accord; but an astrologer and diviner told him that the captain was a prisoner, and that they were returning to Castile, but that the emperor would do them an injury.[18]

Then Magellan, with the three ships which he had, entered the river, through which he ran for more than a hundred leagues, and came out on the other side into the open sea, where he had a stern wind from the east, with which they ran for more than five months without lowering their sails, and they fetched some uninhabited islands, in one of which they found some savages, who lived in huts underground.[19] They went to another island where

[17] One priest, Calmette, underwent this fate.

[18] Needless to say, this touch about the astrologer is entirely gratuitous. Pigafetta makes it clear that Magellan did not know the "San Antonio" had deserted but feared, rather, some accident.

[19] Corrêa evidently means the Marianas. He is careless when he speaks of uninhabited islands and in the next breath mentions their inhabitants, but his work is full of similar slips.

they gave them gold for its weight of iron, by which means they collected much gold: the people also were of a good disposition, and had a king. They were well governed people, who were at war with other neighbours who were more powerful than themselves; for which reason the king became Christian, with all his people, in order that Magellan might assist him against his enemies. This Magellan offered to do, and with his armed men, and the people of the country, he went against the enemy, of whom he killed many, and burned a village. The enemy got assistance from others, and many came to fight with Magellan, who defeated them, and the struggle was a severe one. They acted with cunning, for they had placed ambuscades of men hidden in the bush, who, seeing the Castilians wearied, came out against them and killed many, and another ambuscade came out of the bush to seize the boats, which were on the beach without men: then the king came out, and fought with them, and defended the boats, and brought off the men.

The king who had fled, seeing himself defeated, plotted treachery with the Christian king, and made an agreement with him to give him his daughter in marriage, and plighted his troth to him, that when he died, for he was already old, all would remain to him, and they would always live as friends; because the Castilians would depart, and if he did not act thus he would always make war on him: and this was with the condition that he was to find him means for killing the Castilians. And the

Christian king, like a brutal man, consented to the treachery, and prepared a great feast and banquet for carrying it out, to which he invited Magellan, who went to the banquet with thirty men, of the most honourable and well dressed: while they were enjoying themselves at the banquet, the armed enemies entered, and killed Magellan,[20] and all the Castilians, and none of them escaped, and they stripped Serrano, and dragging him along, brought him to the beach, where they executed him, and killed him thrown down on the ground.

Those who were in the ships, seeing the misfortune on shore, which the sailors who had gone in the boats related to them, raised up from among them as captain, Carvalhinho, the pilot of the flagship, whom all obeyed. He ordered one of the ships, which was very leaky, to be stripped, and set fire to it in the midst of the sea, so that the people on shore should not profit by the iron, and he made captain of the ship of Serrano one Gonzalo Gomez d'Espinosa, who was a relation of the astrologer, who also died with Magellan, and did not divine the evil which befell him.

The two ships departed thence, running between many islands, and they went to one which had much very fine cinnamon. From this place they went running through many islands to the island of Borneo, where they found in the port many mer-

---

[20] Magellan, of course, died in the battle on Mactan. His successors Barbosa and Serrano were massacred at the king of Cebu's banquet.

chant junks from all the parts of Malacca, which
made frequent visits to Borneo. Here Carvalhinho
sent a present to the king of scarlet cloth, and col-
oured silks, and other things, with which the king
was much pleased, and he did him great honour,
and gave him leave and safe conduct to remain on
shore for twenty days, for such was their custom to
give to new people, the first time that they came to
their port, in which they could buy and sell freely
as much as they pleased. But the king, knowing how
much goods the ships contained, got up a plot to kill
them, and take the ships. This treachery was con-
certed by the king with the Javanese who were in
the port in large junks; and for this object the king
showed great honour to those who went on shore,
and sent refreshments to the ships, and leave to remain in the port as long as they pleased. Carvalhinho became suspicious at this, and ordered good
watch to be kept day and night, and did not allow
more than one or two men to go ashore. The king
perceiving this sent to beg Carvalhinho to send him
his son who had brought the present, because his
little children who had seen him, were crying to see
him. He sent him, very well dressed, with four men,
who, on arriving where the king was, were ordered
by him to be arrested. When Carvalhinho knew this
he raised his moorings, and with armed men went
to board a junk which was filled with many people
and ready to sail. They entered this junk and plun-
dered much gold and rich stuffs, and captured a son
of the King of Luzon, who was captain of the junk

and of three others which were in the port, and who had come in them to marry a daughter of this King of Borneo. They found in this junk valuable things of gold and jewellery which he had brought for his wedding; and they found there three girls of extreme beauty, whom Carvalhinho took care of, saying that he would take them to the emperor: at which all rejoiced. But he did not act thus, but slept with them, so that the Castilians were near killing him; but he divided with the Castilians so liberally that they became friends; for he agreed with the bridegroom, that he and his people should escape by night, and for that should give him much wealth of precious stones, and by night they got away by swimming; and Carvalhinho pretended to have been asleep, and woke up complaining of the watch. But the Castilians understood the deceit, and took Carvalhinho and put him in irons, and took from him all he had, and raised up as captain one Juan Bautista, master of the ship, because he understood pilot's work.

Thence they sailed and went to Maluco, Ternate, and Tidore, where they took to the kings the presents which Magellan had set apart for them. They paid them great honour, and received them hospitably, for they also gave to their ministers; and to the kings they gave an embassage on the part of the emperor, relating to them his magnificence, so that both soon obeyed him, and did homage as vassals for ever; and they established trade and prices for buying and selling, and established factories on shore, and began to collect cloves, and very much was brought to them, because the Castilians gave what they asked, for they had a superfluity of merchandise; thus they became lords of the land. As the ships were much injured, they patched them up a little, the best they could, and hastened to fill both ships with cargo, which they did in one month. When they were about to sail there came to the Castilians a Portuguese, named Juan de la Rosa, who had come to Ternate, saying he was a pilot, and would take them to Castile, upon which they agreed with him to give him fifty quintals of cloves in each ship, because he said he would take them to the island of Banda, which had more riches than Maluco. So the Castilians rejoiced greatly at taking this man back to the emperor, for the greater certainty as to their discovery. This Juan de la Rosa warned the Castilians that they would come from India and seek for them, and kill them all, for this was spoken of in India. To this the Castilians gave much credit, and on that account did him great honour. They settled with the King of Tidore to leave with him a factor with the merchandise, which they had, because many ships would soon come, sent by the emperor; for which reason they should have much cloves collected together. They then set sail, making de la Rosa captain of the ship of Carvalhinho.

When they were at sea they freed him from his irons, from the need they felt for his navigation, and they went to the island of Banda, where they restored to Carvalhinho his captaincy,[21] and they went to Banda, where they took samples of nutmeg and mace, as they had nowhere to take in cargo of it. All having been consulted, they set sail to make for the Cape of Good Hope, and navigate thence to Castile, for they did not dare take any other course. Setting sail with this design, they met with hard weather, with which the ship of Carvalhinho put into port, and that of la Rosa continued her course. Carvalhinho put into Maluco, where he discharged half the ship's cargo, and heeled her over, and repaired her as well as possible; this he did in twenty days, and again set to taking in cargo and departing; but he fell ill with the labour, and died on setting sail. They made Gonzalo Gomez d'Espinosa captain of the ship again, and he, by the instructions of Carvalhinho, took a course to search for the river [strait] through which they had come; but when at sea, the ship again took in so much water, that they ran before the wind to beach her on the first land they made, which was in Batochina, where they beached the ship, and saved from her no great quantity of goods. Whilst they were at this juncture D. Gracia Anriques arrived at Maluco, with a ship to take in cloves, which came from Malaca, and learning how these Castilians were there he sent to call them under his safe conduct, that they should all come, because if they did not he

[21] An error. The deposed Carvalho remained at Tidore when the "Victoria" departed, and died soon after.

326

would hold them as enemies, and would go at once and fetch them. The Castilians therefore, constrained by fortune, went to where D. Gracia was, like as men who were lost, so that D. Gracia had compassion upon them, and gave them a good reception, and supplied them with necessaries, and having laden his ship, he embarked them all with him, and they were more than thirty, and he took them to Malaca, where Jorge d'Albuquerque was captain, who ordered the factor to give them provisions for their maintenance, and in the monsoon to send them to India, where D. Duarte [de Meneses] was governor. He commanded those who chose to be written down in the rolls for pay, and he forbade the ships of the kingdom to take them, that they might not return to Castile; and in fact all died, only Gonzalo Gomes d'Espinosa passed to Portugal in the year 1525, and he was made a prisoner in Lisbon, and set at liberty by a letter which the empress sent to the king.

The other ship followed its course, so that la Rosa [22] made the Cape of Good Hope, and while she was going near the land Pero Coresma, who was going to India in a small ship, met her, and spoke her; [23] and he was told she belonged to the emperor, and came from Maluco, and it did not come into his understanding to send her to the bottom, that

[22] Putting Lorosa in command of *"Victoria"* is Corrêa's crowning error. This Portuguese trader sailed under Espinosa in the "Trinidad" when the latter tried in vain to reach Panama.

[23] The brief interview with Cuaresma is generally accepted as authentic.

she might not return to Castile, and the ship entered the watering place of Saldanha, and thence fetched Cape Verde, where they went ashore to get wood and water; there some Portuguese, learning that the ship came from Maluco, took the boat when it came ashore, with twenty Castilians; and as there was no ship in the port they got into a boat to go and capture the ship; but the ship seeing the boat come with armed men, for the arms glittered, weighed and set sail for Cape St. Vincent, and thence entered San Lucar with thirteen men, for now there were no more, and it arrived in the year 1521. From Cape Verde they wrote to the king about the Castilians, who remained there; the king ordered that they should let them go till they died, but never to allow them to embark for any port; and so it was done.

Aftermath

Aftermath

EL CANO AND ANOTHER EXPEDITION

Upon landing, El Cano's first thought was to send a letter to the emperor giving him an account of the voyage, and he evidently did so before the "Victoria" left Sanlúcar to ascend the Guadalquivir to Seville. The letter is short, having been written or dictated in haste, and it adds little or nothing to what we know from other sources.[1] Not everything in it was new to the Spanish government, because the crew of the deserting "San Antonio" had returned more than a year earlier bringing news, however garbled, of the voyage as far as the strait. On the same day he wrote to Charles, El Cano procured a large ship's boat to replace the one he had lost at the Cape Verdes, because he needed it for his ascent of the river. With the aid of fresh seamen supplied him for the purpose, he was largely towed to Seville while he and his men wondered whether the "Victoria's" rickety hull would stand even the gentle river trip. The ship proved once more equal to the occasion and on September 8 was tied up to a Sevillan wharf.[2]

Shortly after El Cano's letter reached Emperor Charles there came a reply instructing the com-

mander to come to Valladolid and bring with him
the two most discreet and intelligent men of his
crew. El Cano selected the pilot Albo and the bar-
ber (surgeon) Hernando de Bustamante, conspicuously omitting Pigafetta, of whom he obviously had
no high opinion. (The Italian chronicler, who had
a sufficiently good opinion of himself, soon repaid
this slight by conspicuously omitting El Cano from
his narrative.) The three voyagers received good
clothes and money from the *Casa de Contratación*
in order that they might show off to good advantage
before the throne. When they reached Valladolid,
the emperor gave them a gracious reception,
showed pleasure at their discovery of the Moluccas,
and accepted their erroneous calculation that the islands lay in the Spanish sphere as marked at Tordesillas.[3] For the benefit of the returning seamen, as
well as those left in the Cape Verdes, he renounced
a quarter of his own share of the goods brought
home in the "Victoria." El Cano received the right
to sell his own private stock of spice in Spain without payment of the *alcabala,* or sales tax. The suc-
cessful commander also gained permission to bear a
coat of arms consisting of a gilded castle in the middle of a red field on a shield additionally decorated
with two cinnamon sticks, three nutmegs, and
twelve cloves. The shield would be held up by two
kings, evidently those of Ternate and Tidore,
dressed in green from the waist up and in white below, one bearing a clove branch in his hand and
the other a nutmeg branch. At the top of the coat of

arms would be a globe with the inscription *Primus circumdedisti me.*[4]

A few days later El Cano underwent his examination at the hands of Alcalde Santiago Leguizamo. Several of the questions he had to answer had no bearing on personal feelings, but there were also such thorny ones as the cause of enmity between Magellan and Cartagena, the facts concerning the San Julián mutiny, and the circumstances of Magellan's death. The court later put the same questions to Albo and Bustamante and took precautions to prevent exchanges of impressions among the three men. El Cano, who made no pretense of friendship for Magellan, gave harsh answers. He expressed the opinion that the late captain-general had largely precipitated the mutiny and had severely punished the leaders because he wished to put Portuguese friends and relations in command of the ships. El Cano showed that he regarded Cartagena as legally equal in authority to Magellan and that he himself had been acting to carry out royal instructions when he took part in the mutiny. About the death of Magellan he had little to say, as he had not been present at the battle of Mactan, but from his words we can infer that he considered the cause of the battle a trivial one and the captain-general's conduct unnecessarily reckless.[5] Albo and Bustamante, when their turns came, underwent briefer interrogations, but their answers agreed substantially with El Cano's.[6] The emperor appeared satisfied with the statements. If he had reservations regarding their judgments of Magellan, the captain-general was dead, and these men who expressed their dislike of him had at least performed good service.

Juan Sebastián del Cano's life was not to be a long one. The king-emperor added to the emoluments bestowed on the Gipúzcoan mariner early in the following year, when he granted him a life pension of 500 gold ducats a year, to be paid from the funds of the *Casa de Contratación de la Especiería*.[7] This new organization, which is not to be confused with the older *Casa* at Seville, was being set up at La Coruña as an immediate result of the Magellan–El Cano voyage. The Seville *Casa* dealt with the trade of the Spanish New World and had enough to do without assuming charge of the voluminous commerce expected shortly with the Moluccas. As these islands now seemingly belonged to Castile, the Coruña body came into existence to handle their traffic, which presumably would soon flourish.

El Cano now received a full pardon for an offense committed by him years earlier in the Mediterranean. To obtain money to pay his crew, he had sold a ship he commanded in government service to some Savoyard merchants.[8] This was an old and virtually forgotten matter that perhaps need not have been raked up, but El Cano wanted it definitely disposed of now that he had become fortune's favorite. The ruler obligingly granted the pardon, though not without reminding the captain that his offense had been a serious one. Juan Sebastián next overplayed his hand when he petitioned the emperor for four favors: leadership of the next expedition to the Moluccas; [9] command of the fortress expected to be constructed in the same islands; permission to wear the habit of the Order of Santiago, such as had been conferred on Magellan and Faleiro; and financial remuneration for several poor relatives who had supposedly aided the recent expedition.[10]

Charles found these requests a little more than he was able to grant in full, but gave them consideration and a courteous reply.[11] Leadership of the next expedition to the Moluccas had already been assigned to Garcia Jofré de Loaisa, but El Cano ultimately did go as second in command. As for the Moluccan fortress, the monarch promised to bear the petitioner in mind when it was built. The habit of the Order of Santiago, explained Charles, was not quite his to bestow and could only be awarded by the order itself. (He conveniently forgot having granted it to Magellan, presumably without consulting anyone.) The fourth request, for aid to impecunious relatives, the ruler declared he had already taken under consideration, though he appears to have forgotten the matter later. It might also be added that El Cano never received a ducat of the income promised him from the funds of the new *Casa* at Coruña, because that body at the time existed only on hopes and did not possess even one maravedí.

Juan Sebastián was meanwhile attending to his

love life. In Valladolid he had an affair with a Maria de Vidauretta, who bore him a daughter.[12] This amour must have enraged either Maria's relatives or her other admirers, for El Cano considered his life in danger and petitioned the sovereign in May 1524 for permission to employ a bodyguard of two armed men. He did not say just why or by whom he felt threatened, but when he swore to employ these protectors for defensive purposes only, the king obligingly granted him permission to take whatever measure he considered necessary.[13] El Cano evidently did not behave in a thoroughly gentlemanly fashion to Maria de Vidauretta, because he was soon on intimate terms with a Maria Hernández Dernialde, who obliged by producing a son, Domingo del Cano.[14] No wedding bells rang this time either, and in his final will and testament El Cano left 40 ducats to his first love and 100 to his second, either because he cared more for the latter or because he considered the production of a son a higher achievement than that of a daughter.

El Cano's last public service before sailing for the final time was his participation in the conference of Badajoz-Elvas. Meeting alternately in these two towns on the Castilian-Portuguese frontier in 1524, pilots and cosmographers of the two kingdoms attempted to settle the question of the ownership of the Moluccas.[15] Neither side wanted an accurate decision for its own sake. Each desired the islands and was willing to resort to any falsification or misrepresentation to obtain them. The negotiations

broke up without result, and El Cano is not recorded as having said much at the conference. All
indications are that he was a laconic man of meager
formal education, and he seems to have left most of
the talking to his more cultured colleagues.

Meanwhile the Loaisa expedition, consisting of
seven ships including two much larger than any of
Magellan's and a complement of 450 men, was preparing at La Coruña. El Cano, put in command of
the "Sancti Spiritus," a ship of 250 *toneles,* was second only to Loaisa as well as pilot major and guide
of the fleet. This expedition, which sailed May 24,
1525, had worse luck than Magellan's, but we can
follow it only as far as El Cano went.[16] Loaisa, like
his predecessor, crossed the Atlantic, coasted Brazil,
and passed the Río de la Plata. Though scattered
in transit, the ships assembled at the mouth of the
strait, but an injury to Loaisa's flagship "Santa Maria" forced them all back to Santa Cruz on the Patagonian coast. After repairs, they attempted the
strait again, and now El Cano's "Sancti Spiritus"
was wrecked off the Cape of Eleven Thousand Virgins, though the lives of the commander and most
of the crew were saved. Two more ships deserted
in the strait, and Loaisa had but four left when he
entered the Pacific. Magellan had so named this
new ocean because of the calm weather it afforded
him, but it did not behave so well this time. Within
a few days a storm had scattered the ships and the
"Santa Maria," in which Loaisa and El Cano now
both sailed, went on alone. Sickness aboard took a

toll of lives comparable to that in Magellan's crossing, and surviving descriptions indicate that the disease must have been scurvy. On July 30, 1526, Loaisa died. Emperor Charles had prepared a sealed envelope, to be opened only in the event of the commander's death, designating a successor. When the officers broke the seal they read, as they probably expected, the name Juan Sebastián del Cano. This may be called the supreme irony, for the man who had so much wanted to command the fleet achieved command only when it had ceased to be a fleet and when he himself lay so near death that he had already dictated his final will and testament.

He exercised what command he could from his sickbed for exactly five days, and during that time his only recorded activity was the appointment of several officers to replace those who had died. His own death came on August 4. His successor Torribio Alonso de Salazar, who died in less than a month, superintended the simple funeral and drew a cross in the air as the body splashed into the water. We do not know where El Cano was committed to the Pacific, beyond the fact that the ship lay between 6° and 8° N. and a month's sail from the Marianas.[17]

El Cano's first crossing of the great ocean had led to a rendezvous with glory; his second, to a rendezvous with death. In Spain and the rest of Europe his fate was not known for years. Meanwhile Europeans learned the Magellan story from Antonio

338

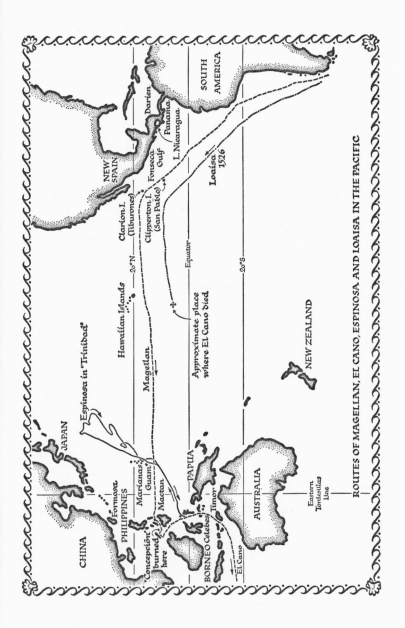

ROUTES OF MAGELLAN, EL CANO, ESPINOSA, AND LOAISA IN THE PACIFIC

Pigafetta—a story that without Juan Sebastián del Cano would have been dramatically incomplete.

NEW KNOWLEDGE AND OLD PRECONCEPTIONS

The Moluccas, as it turned out and as a glance at the map will show, belonged to Portugal on the basis of the Treaty of Tordesillas. However, it was not the treaty but expediency that finally decided the question of ownership. The Spanish crown, in pardonable ignorance, claimed the islands but had no way of taking effective possession. The Magellan voyage had resulted in the loss of four ships, and the Loaisa expedition had failed, although some of its members reached Tidore and held out there for a time until overpowered by the Portuguese.[18] Alvaro de Saavedra Cerón, whom Hernán Cortés sent to the Moluccas from Mexico in 1527, reached the islands, but adverse winds thwarted his two attempts to return to the New World.[19] Not until 1565, following the Spanish invasion of the Philippines, did Alonso de Arellano and Andrés de Urdaneta find a feasible sailing route eastward across the Pacific.[20] Without such a route Spain could not hope, in the early years, to grasp and hold the Moluccas, for possession of the islands depended upon regular communication with the Spanish-American empire.

By 1529 Emperor Charles V, with all his European commitments and the numerous heavy drains on his treasury, had decided to give up the Moluccas on the best terms he could obtain. His

341

neighbor John III of Portugal had cash and was willing to buy a settlement. At Zaragoza on April 23, 1529, representatives of the two rulers signed an agreement whereby John paid Charles the sum of 350,000 ducats and the Spanish monarch relinquished his claim to the islands.[21] They remained in Portuguese possession until the seventeenth century, when they fell before the forces of the Dutch East India Company.

The Magellan voyage and the expeditions that followed did not change conceptions of world geography so suddenly and drastically as might be supposed. To be sure, they removed whatever lingering doubts may have existed about the roundness of the earth, but geographers still made an attempt to reconcile the new knowledge with old preconceptions. For many of them America remained an appendage of Asia, although the venerable *Magnus Sinus* now had to be enormously expanded to become what Magellan had called the Pacific Ocean. An example of how the scientific mind worked can be seen in the world map of Giacomo Gastaldi, made in oval projection about 1550 (see sketch, p. 343). It has Asia and North America united by a great stretch of imaginary land forming a northern shore of the Pacific. Of course those who, like Gastaldi, joined the Old and New Worlds were not far from the truth. It remained for Vitus Bering and James Cook in the eighteenth century to show how narrow a strait separated the two giant land masses.

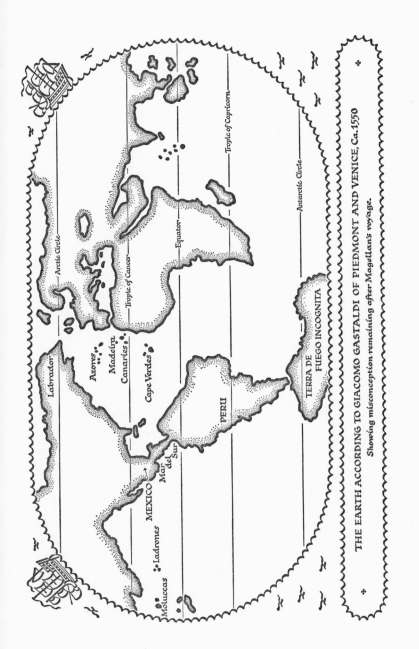

THE EARTH ACCORDING TO GIACOMO GASTALDI OF PIEDMONT AND VENICE, Ca.1550

Showing misconception remaining after Magellan's voyage.

Labrador

Arctic Circle

Azores
Madeira
Canaries
Cape Verdes

Tropic of Cancer

Equator

Tropic of Capricorn

Antarctic Circle

MEXICO

Mar del Sur

PERU

TERRA DE FUEGO INCOGNITA

Moluccas
Ladrones

Notes

1. *Raccolta Colombiana,* III, I, 103–4. The letter is in Italian translation, and evidently the original no longer exists. A Spanish version published by Medina (IV, 291–94) is a translation from this Italian version.

2. This did not end the "Victoria's" career, however worthy she was of retirement. She later made two voyages to Hispaniola and, when returning from the second, went down with all her crew. Medina, III, cccxxiv. An unknown annotator placed the following statement in the margin of the manuscript of Gonzalo de Oviedo's *Historia general y natural de las Indias:* "The ship 'Victoria' was run aground on the beach of the king's ship-building yards at Sevilla, and there I saw her in the year 1580. There she was being made into barks for the Portuguese run; some pieces of her remained." The quotation is in II, 102, of the 1944 Asunción edition of Oviedo. (First published 1535.) The informant, needless to say, was mistaken.

3. Melón, p. 716.

4. Medina, III, ccclxix–lxx.

5. Navarrete, *Colección,* IV, 263. His words are ". . . the said Ferdinand Magellan went to fight and burn the houses of the town of Mactan to make the king of Mactan kiss the hands of the king of Cebu, and because he did not send him a bushel of rice and a goat as tribute."

6. *Ibid.,* 264–68.

7. Arteche, *Elcano,* p. 172.

8. Eustaquio Fernández de Navarrete, *Historia de Juan Sebastián del Cano,* Vitoria, 1874, pp. 290–91.

9. It will be remembered that this command had first been promised to Ruy Faleiro, who was now, however, incapacitated.

10. Arteche, *Elcano,* pp. 173–74.

11. *Ibid.*

12. *Ibid.*, p. 179.

13. Eustaquio F. de Navarrete, *Juan S. del Cano*, pp. 292–93.

14. Arteche, *Elcano*, p. 179.

15. The principal discussions of the Badajoz-Elvas controversy from the Spanish side are published by Navarrete, *Colección,* IV, 296–337.

16. The entire fifth volume of Navarrete's *Colección* is devoted to the Loaisa expedition. It consists of a considerable narrative by Navarrete and all the major documents. Of great value is Pablo Pastells, S. J., *El descubrimiento del estrecho de Magallanes*, 2 vols., Madrid, 1920, I, 139–61. See also Nowell, "The Loaisa Expedition and the Ownership of the Moluccas," *Pacific Historical Review,* X, 1936, 325–36.

17. Navarrete, *Colección,* V, 249, 252. Hernando de la Torre, who kept a log of this voyage similar to Albo's for the Magellan expedition, did not take the latitude on August 4 but had taken it on August 2 and found it to be 6° 35′ N. On the sixth he found it to be 8° 40′ N. On September 4 he reports the sighting of the Ladrones, or Marianas. For August 21 and 22 he reports the discovery of an island called San Bartolomé at 14° 02′ N. There was evidently some delay to investigate, which may have slowed progress toward the Marianas a little.

18. Nowell, *Pacific Historical Review,* X, 334–45.

19. Ione Stuessy Wright, *Voyages of Alvaro de Saavedra Cerón,* Coral Gables, 1951; see especially pp. 43–52.

20. Henry Raup Wagner, *Spanish Voyages to the Northwest Coast of America in the Sixteenth Century,* San Francisco, 1929, pp. 110–20.

21. Navarrete, *Colección,* IV, 351–67; *Alguns documentos,* pp. 495–512; Frances G. Davenport, *European Treaties Bearing on the History of the United States and Its Dependencies to 1648,* Washington, 1917, 169–98, with English translation.

Index

347

348

Index